The Phenomenon of Globalization

Philipp Strobl / Manfred Kohler (eds.)

The Phenomenon of Globalization

A Collection of Interdisciplinary
Globalization Research Essays

Bibliographic Information published by the Deutsche Nationalbibliothek
The Deutsche Nationalbibliothek lists this publication in the Deutsche Nationalbibliografie; detailed bibliographic data is available in the internet at http://dnb.d-nb.de.

This publication was sponsored
by the Austrian National Union of Students (ÖH)
and by the office of the Vice-Rector for Research
at the University of Innsbruck.

www.oeh.ac.at

Cover Design:
© Olaf Gloeckler, Atelier Platen, Friedberg

Cover Illustration and Typesetting: Daniel Holzer

ISBN 978-3-631-63684-8
© Peter Lang GmbH
Internationaler Verlag der Wissenschaften
Frankfurt am Main 2013
All rights reserved.
PL Academic Research is an imprint of Peter Lang GmbH

This book is especially dedicated to Dr. Günter Bischof of the University of New Orleans, Center Austria, tho whom we want to express our utmost graditude for having so strongly supported us over the last years.

Preface

The term globalization arouses different feelings. Some people regard it with fear; others consider it the incarnation of a new time – a time when the relations between different cultures and parts of the world intensify increasingly. Consequently, the term is not only used to explain highly diverse phenomena but also to shed light on the alleged darkness of a world in change. The term per se originated from the United States and became popular during the 1980s and 1990s. Since then, it has become increasingly widespread and fashionable, and is frequently used as an explanation for "just everything", but despite its frequent use, no uniform definition has yet been found. In view of the large quantity of different uses, one could very easily lose track of the subject.

The scientific world is not only affected by the evolution of globalization, but, quite the contrary, different academic disciplines even played a pioneering role in introducing the term. Already in 1994, John Cavanagh and Richard Barnet stated that "globalization is so portentous and wonderfully patient as to puzzle "Alice in Wonderland" and thrill the Red Queen because it means precisely whatever the user says it means." Since then, no significant changes with respect to a narrower conceptualization have taken place. Depending on the academic discipline, there are still many different explanations of how to understand globalization. When studying the term, it seems necessary to go beyond the borders of one's own scientific field. Much more than usual, interdisciplinarity seems absolutely inevitable. As the name already suggests, globalization is a global phenomenon that affects different regions of the world in a quite different way. That also means that the term is reflected very differently, not only in various academic research fields, but also in different parts of the world. The consideration of the ideas of researchers from various parts of the world thus seems to be a natural consequence.

In this collective volume, scientists from different academic disciplines and regions of the world wanted to make available their perceptions of this ample term to a broader audience. Twenty contributions comprising nine academic disciplines depict the process of the growing together of the world via different approaches. However, we should like to propose here that finding a uniform definition of the term globalization has never been the overall aim of this volume. It rather seeks to depict the concept from as many angles as possible. This is to offer the reader a small insight into the variety of research about globalization. This may contribute to a better understanding of this phenomenon that is treated differently in diverse academic disciplines and different parts of the world. Apart from the contributions from historians, the reader will find articles from the fields of philosophy, architecture, economics, sociology, political science, journalism, anthropology, and law.

A special feature of the volume is that all contributions were written by scientists who worked on their dissertation projects at the time of the publication of this book. Every single article hence reflects state of the art of scientific globalization research. The insights of the contributions are highly up-to-date and most of them have not yet been published and will only be published when the dissertation theses of the individual contributors are finalized. This volume thus provides an insight into future research results.

In order to enable a better overview of the variety of different topics, we divided the volume into three sections. The first part ("Definitions and Measurements") deals with theoretical questions on the phenomenon of globalization and discusses different possibilities of defining and measuring the term. The second part gives an insight into the functioning and understanding of the phenomenon ("Functioning and Understanding"). The main part of the book contains case studies of the phenomenon's impact in different parts of the world. Here again, special emphasis is put on a preferably global approach.

The realization of this comprehensive project would not have been possible without the support of many individuals and institutions. We owe thanks to the Austrian National Union of Students (ÖH) and the office of the Vice Rector for Research of the University of Innsbruck. Both institutions provided the financial means for the project. We particularly want to thank our team of volunteers who did a tremendous job and eventually were responsible for the success of this volume. Manfred Kohler and Natalia Marczewska spent many hours proofreading the articles of this volume. Daniel Holzer was responsible for the graphic design and the layout, and Doris Stauder took care of organizational issues. Furthermore, we want to thank Andreas Exenberger for his friendly support and his introductory words.

Last but not least we want to thank you, the reader, for being interested in the topic of globalization and for buying this collective volume. We hope you will enjoy reading it.

Philipp Strobl

Bratislava, November 2012

Table of Contents

Introduction

The Phenomenon of Globalization: A First Orientation

Andreas Exenberger

Globalization is a catch-word, albeit a much used one.[1] This becomes clearer and clearer, the deeper one digs into the abundance of texts about globalization and different aspects of this phenomenon. As Jürgen Osterhammel and Niels Peterson phrased it in the introduction to their small book about the history of globalization, one already needs "pathfinder literature" to master this intellectual cornucopia.[2] Those who talk or write about globalization often do not talk or write about what it is – and consequently do not really enter communication about this phenomenon. Consequently, whenever the term globalization is used, categories become confused, concepts are mixed, a general meaning is presumed or a very specific applied more or less uncommented (particularly the last point is rather conspicuous in the economic debate about globalization). Sometimes the usage of the term is similar to the re-labelling of perishables, when "globalization" – maybe for marketing reasons – is simply affixed to something already known and differently named. The most prominent example of this strategy is the mix-up of "globalization" with free trade, liberalization or even progress. But the contrary is also true, of course, and some critiques of globalization equate it with the increasing destructive power of trans-national co-operations or with nothing less than all the evil in the world.

Given all these caveats, is the term "globalization" at all suitable as a scientific category? I propose a clear "Yes" as an answer to that question, for a simple reason: it is a "macro concept" (and as such comparable to concepts like "industrialization" or "modernization"). This refers to Osterhammel and Peterson and is consistent – for example – with the concepts of David Held (and others), editors of the *Global Transformations Reader*, one of the seminal publications in

---

1   The word as such originated in the mid-20th-century (it first appeared in English dictionaries in the early 1960s), but did not become academically popular before the 1980s, when it was applied in business research (its first use there is ascribed to an article by Theodore Levitt in 1984), and generally in the 1990s, when it became the catch-word it has been until today.

2   This book – interestingly enough – is one of the rare examples of a text originally published in German as Geschichte der Globalisierung (2003) and later translated into English as Globalization (2005).

the field (although mainly a collection of already published works). They strongly emphasize the multi-dimensional character of the phenomenon, which they view from different angles, most notably "concept", "power", "culture", "economy", "inequality" and "order". When one refers to these views it is crucial for a proper understanding of globalization to preserve analytical sensibility for its political, cultural, institutional, ethical and economic dimension. Even though the social (or societal) dimension is as underscored here as the technological one, the overall picture is clearly more valuable analytically, particularly compared to concepts of globalization, which remain restricted to something like cross-border chains of production, finance and/or consumption.

Further, globalization is procedural by nature (hence there is no such thing as a "globalization process") and hence obviously interesting when analysing social or economic change. Sociologist Ulrich Beck, one of the founding fathers of German globalization research, has described it – in unnecessary stringency – as a process by which trans-national actors connected nation states by their actions, at the same time undermining the sovereignty of these states. By doing so, he mainly distinguished it from his concepts of "globality" and "globalism". While it is important to stress the concept of agency as done by Beck, this understanding is too narrow, because a process can also consist in "occurance", hence not controllable or intended by the actors, even if it owes its very existence to their actions (or omissions). This strange contradiction is to be resolved by the remark that globalization is also connected to humans and human action by necessity (the concept does not make sense without human involvement), but the result of these actions is of course not necessarily consistent with the intentions, the patterns of legitimacy, or the actions as such of certain actors. Unintended consequences exist, and globalization is a likely candidate at least from the perspective of some of the actors involved.

The historical concepts of trend and cycle, both actually results of collective human action, can further clarify this. Both go back to the French *Annales* school (Fernand Braudel and others) and the world system approach (Immanuel Wallerstein and others). They are useful tools for globalization research, especially when globalization is understood as a trend – maybe a very basic one – in the sense of a "macro concept" (Jürgen Osterhammel and others) or a *dispositif* (Michel Foucault and others), shaping humankind's history, while at the same time acknowledging the disruptions and breaks in this meta-narrative. These contribute to a "thickening" of the understanding of globalization as a process much more cyclical than linear, in which it starts and enfolds, often in an asynchronous manner in time and space, collapses and restarts again. This becomes even more interesting, when historical processes are seen – like Wallerstein does in *Unthinking Social Sciences* – as shaped by the conflict between different trajectories related to trend(s) and cycle(s) leading to growing imbalances in the "system". These imbalances enable (or at least facilitate) change, particularly in a temporal-spatial setting, which Wallerstein refers to as "transitional Time-Space".

However, these models also guide thinking about globalization without direct reference, while the picture of a "wave" or "waves" of globalization is much used in academia. In that respect, economic research still focuses on the most recent wave, often dazzled by the astonishing speed of a process also personally witnessed and the scientific establishment of the term only in the 1980s. But historical research, prominently including economic historical research as for example by Michael Bordo, Kevin O'Rourke or Jeffrey Williamson, has rapidly shown that comparable processes had already existed long before. These analyses of course referred to and were connected with earlier research on the world economy, colonialism and imperialism and particularly stressed the parallels between globalization waves at the end of the 20th and at the end of the 19th century. This first wave was interrupted catastrophically by the two world wars and the Great Depression, as already shown by Karl Polanyi in *The Great Transformation* – again without any reference to the concept of "globalization" of course. Only a bit later new parallels were drawn to early colonialism in the aftermath of the so called voyages of discovery, and a new, even earlier "first" wave was born (Robert Robertson and others). Finally, scholars with even more courage for generalization and thinking in long terms departed from the concept of Kondratieff's business cycles to inscribe the idea of globalization in even longer time periods (most pronounced Andre G. Frank und Frank Gills in *The World System: Five Hundred Years of Five Thousand?*, but analytically even more valuable by George Modelski and others).

The lively and sometimes fierce debates about the question, when "globalization" began,[3] indeed are often essentially influenced by different answers to the question, what globalization actually is. While opinions diverge in that field, often widely, it is generally accepted that the process is not restricted to the contemporary world and is non-linear in unfolding (including discontinuities and asynchronies). However, in the light of the tremendous and multifaceted literature about the issue, coming from different disciplines, it seems – beside the aforementioned points and strictly restricted contexts – to be impossible to achieve something like a general meaning or at least understanding of globaliza-

---

3   An interesting debate about that unfolded in the European Review of Economic History in 2004 between Kevin O'Rourke und Jeffrey Williamson on the one side and Dennis Flynn und Arturo Giraldez on the other. While the former see globalization (as measurable price convergence) not present before the mid-19th century, the latter see it (as a real potential actually influencing human behaviour) already in place in the 16th.

tion today (if it ever was possible). Aside from discipline-specific discourses focussing on partial (often very partial) phenomena and processes, only a few operationalizable inter-disciplinary approaches to the concept exist. When, for example in economic history, globalization is defined as something like the progressive global connection of goods, capital and labour markets (like Michael Bordo et al. do already at the beginning of their collection of essays about *Globalization*), the term remains very general and abstract, certainly with answers remaining open to the questions what "progressive", "global" and "connection" mean – not to speak about measurement. But whoever strives for measuring, is rapidly to be found in environments like the world of price convergence (the decreasing difference between the prices of the same good at varied places), which is common in economics, or the question, how many languages are spoken worldwide (David Northrup), or recent ranking exercises of countries or cities with respect to their "degree" of globalization or interconnectedness (Axel Dreher and others).

A real and intellectually fruitful debate about questions related to globalization is thus in need of either a convention about what it is or a critical acclaim of the approaches in the discourse, including one's own. What it definitely does not need is an obfuscation of a specific approach, hidden behind a seemingly objective and actually inexistent general understanding of globalization. It is thus necessary to explicate the specific concept and to adjust it to the relevant context (i.e. also to allow for different views) to be able to proceed, particularly in empirical research. At the same time, efforts to clear the terminological thicket must be pursued, omitting it would lead to a tattering of the debate into manifold increasingly unconnected branches and hence to complete intellectual confusion. Thus, next to a case-specific understanding of globalization, which is indispensable for any meaningful analysis, a general concept is to be developed. What could that general concept be? David Held and his collaborators have proposed to view globalization as a combination of the extensity of global networks, the intensity of global connections, the velocity of global flows and the impact propensity of global interconnectedness. Further, it is multi-dimensional and spatial as well as – with regard to contents – expanding and intensifying at the same time, comparable to a net with many interwoven layers, which is knotted more and more densely (or to be even more exact: not the net as such, but the process of knotting the net).

This idea is presented graphically in figure 1.

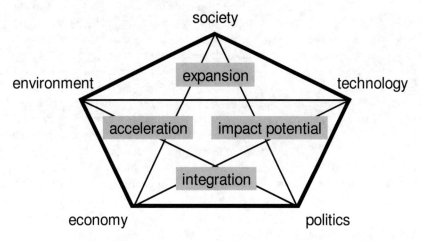

Figure 1: A Proposed General Understanding of Globalization

Globalization in that sense has its place in global history as well as in economics or other social sciences as an independent concept. Its analysis is generally focussed on the process of synchronous integration, expansion, acceleration and the growing impact potential in a multi-dimensional field and against the background of a world regarded as global from a contemporary viewpoint (in the sense of a "whole world"). It is trans-epochal and trans-regional and at the same time – as "global" from the beginning – essentially different,[4] particularly from usual national historiographies. The idea behind this is the acknowledgement of a very crucial dichotomy resulting in a real challenge for the scholar preoccupied with it: For an understanding of historical processes, phenomena and structures it is necessary to think about the basics of human existence in a very general way on the one hand and on the other hand to place these thoughts (in the sense of both application and evaluation) in the correct and at least potentially completely unique context without ignoring the in the same way fully developed interdependence – in content, time and/or space – of the local and specific with the global and general. It should be remembered that this interdependence is necessarily double-edged. Even if the influence looks rather hierarchical, there is

---

4   It is not about some kind of global synthesis of regional or national historiographies, but
     it departs from "the global" to tell the world's history or – against the background of the
     global and while acknowledging the indispensable mutual influences to and from the
     global – to tell a contextionally different kind of regional, national or local history.

always agency on both sides and hence mutual interference. Further, not only does the past influence the present (and future) in the sense of – for example – path-dependence, but also the future the present and the past, by transmitting motivations, targeted on future developments, back in time to rewrite history, for example to legitimize a territorial claim. Hence the interpretation of history is not stable and always strongly dependent on today's interests and expectations about tomorrow.

Hence, globalization research is especially in need of inter- and transdisciplinary research. This publication is thus very welcome, not only for being fully up to date in assembling the state of the art works of promising young scholars from all over the world and different disciplinary angles, but also for addressing a wide array of highly relevant questions, historically as well as contemporarily. Issues like migration, minorities, inequality or global exchange, places like a global city, challenges for international law, human rights, and identity formation, as well as representations of new global perceptions in the media, museums, architecture and historical research, are all pointing to important problems associated with globalizations, which need new kinds of solutions. Here, experiences and different answers from all over the world are particularly helpful, as well as historical perspectives revealing that some of these challenges may only be seemingly new, while the past may provide some lessons already learned. If the volume does not work well, it will provide all this. But if is does work well, it may be one example for the "pathfinder literature" suggested by Jürgen Osterhammel and Niels Petersson, and it may provide a compass (or a GPS, if you prefer a more modern means of path-finding) to find a way across at least parts of the field only vaguely confined by the phenomenon of globalization. This field of human activity is large, indeed, and it will neither disappear nor be sufficiently tilled in the near future, but it is likely to spread further. Hence, all kind of orientation knowledge about it will help us to master the associated challenges ahead.

Part One

Definitions and Measurements

Globalizations, Globalities, Global Histories
Some theoretical corner stones

Christoph Mertl

Globalization is a worldwide longterm process, hence a topic of global history. If this simple statement would make sense, there would not be any need for this article. But, unfortunately – the meaning of „globalization" is everything else than clear, and so is the meaning of „global history".

This article will try to find a specific terminology for the various concepts of globalization and global history. Furthermore, we will try to match adequate methods of global historical research to appropriate concepts of globalization.

1. Globalizations

The more frequently we use a term, the less we are clear what we are talking about. What is culture? What is democracy? What is a process? None of these very common words is based on a solid scientific definition. So: what is globalization?

There *are* definitions, yes – the problem is, there are *too many*. I tried to subsume different definitions of „globalization" as presented in the more recent works. My conclusion is that you can differ between three basic understandings of globalization: the phenomenon of increasing worldwide interactivities[1]; the

---

1 „Globalization is a transplanetary process or set of processes involving increasing liquidity and the growing multi-directional flows of people, objects, places, and information as well as the structures they encounter and create that are barriers to, or expedite, those flows". See George Ritzer, Globalization. The Essentials (Chichester: Wiley-Blackwell 2011), 2 – „It is also possible to read globalization ... as the terrain for conflicting discourses, which both unites and divides in unprecedented ways. Arif Dirlik, Global Modernity. Modernity in the Age of Global Capitalism (Boulder-London: Paradigm Publishers, 2007), 153 – Definition: Glob. "is widely agreed to be a process that transforms economic, political, social and cultural relationships across countries, regions and continents by spreading them more broadly, making them more intense and increasing their velocity." Hopkins, in A[nthony] G. Hopkins, ed., Globalization in World History (London: Pimlico, 2002), 16. – Osterhammel sees globalization „als Sammelbegriff für konkret beschreibbare Strukturen und Interaktionen mit planetarischer Reichweite". Jürgen Osterhammel and Niels Petersson, Geschichte der Globalisierung (München: Piper, 4th ed. 2007), 110.

phenomena of increasing worldwide interconnections and interdependencies[2];
and the phenomenon of increasing worldwide economic, political, and social
integration[3]. Interestingly, divergent contents come up if we do without definitions and look for *descriptions* of what is understood by „globalization". The
main points refer to:

2   „'Globalization' refers to the processes by which more people across large distances be-
     come connected in more and different ways." Frank J. Lechner and John Boli eds., The
     globalization reader (Chichester: Wiley-Blackwell, 4th ed. 2012) – Influenced by Roland
     Robertson und Robbie Robertson, O'Byrne and Hensby state: „globalization involves
     twin processes: the physical process of interconnectedness, or ‚compression', which im-
     plies that the world is getting smaller; and the awareness that we as individuals have of
     our relationship to the world as a single place." Darren J. O'Byrne and Alexander
     Hensby, Theorizing Global Studies (Basingstoke: Palgrave Macmillan, 2011), 11. –
     „Globalization means that any major international event can affect us, in varying ways,
     and likewise every major national issue is, in varying ways, an international issue." Wil-
     liam R. Nester, Globalization. A Short History of the Modern World (New York: Pal-
     grave MacMillan, 2010), 2. – "The process of increasing interconnectedness between so-
     cieties such that events in one part of the world more and more have effects on peoples
     and societies far away". John Baylis and Steve Smith, eds. The Globalization of World
     Politics. An Introduction to international relations (Oxford: Oxford University Press,
     2006), 8. – Globalization interconnects the planet's different ‚worlds' (as socual con-
     cepts) and develops general interdependency of all on all. Charles Lemert et al., Globali-
     zation. A reader (London-New York: Routledge, 2010), xviii – „weltweite Vernetzung
     von Wirtschaft, Politik und Kultur durch die grenzüberschreitenden Handels-, Finanz-,
     Tourismus- und Migrationsströme". Markus Völkel, Geschichtsschreibung. Eine Einfüh-
     rung in globaler Pespektive (Köln-Weimar-Wien: Böhlau, 2006), 341
3   „the ‚process of transformation of local phenomena into global ones … a process by
     which the people of the world are unified into a single society and function together". Pe-
     ter N. Stearns, Globalization in World History (London-New York: Routledge 2010), 1.
     – Globalization consists of expansion, networking, reciprocity, transformation. Peter E.
     Fäßler, Globalisierung. Ein historisches Kompendium (Köln-Weimar-Wien: Böhlau
     2007), 30. – First in the history of the world system, all older forms of economy get ab-
     sorbed by capitalism (William I. Robinson, in Lechner and Boli, Globalization, 23). – „If
     globalization means anything, it is the incorporation of societies globally into a capitalist
     modernity, with all the implications of the latter" (Dirlik, Global Modernity, 49) – How-
     ever the spread of capitalism is also supported: "What capitalism has uncovered is what
     many people really want. The value systems of the past grew out of scarcity and restraint.
     Traditions prioritized ways to behave and ennobled values compatible with the scarcity
     of food and other goods." Joyce Appleby, The Relentless Revolution. A History of Capi-
     talism (New York-London: Norton, 2010), 361.

- IT and Media revolutions
   - Massive global *flows* of capital and informations, affecting most of mankind[4]
   - Possible abandonment of territorial and hierarchical structures in favour of less formal networks[5]
- Easier access to travels
   - increasing global consciousness[6]
   - powerful *imaginations*, motivating migrations[7]
- Global institutions coping with global challenges[8]
   - decreasing decision-making power of national states

These definitions and descriptions represent most of the debate which relates mostly to the economy or the economy and society, rather seldom to politics[9].

At first glance, we would associate these developments with the global changes which occurred since the late 1980s: political liberalization in Latin America, Eastern Europe and Africa; the emergence of „turbo capitalism"; the introduction of PCs, cellphones and internet in most of middle class households; the UN world conferences, the rise of NGOs and social movements; international head hunting and trafficking. In fact, the changes around 1990 gave reason for big hopes[10], and it has a reason that „globalization" established itself as a common word in those years. The initial expectation that the free maket, democracy and cultural universalism would now prevail worldwide[11] turned around by the late

4   David Held and Anthony McGrew, Global Transformations. Politics, Economics and Culture (Cambridge-Oxford: Polity, 1999), 431

5   A central thesis of Manuel Castells, here quoted from Osterhammel and Petersson, Globalisierung, 13.

6   Roland Robertson, Globalization. Social Theory and Global Culture (London-Newbury Park-New Delhi: Sage, 1992), 184.

7   Arjun Appadurai, Modernity at Large. Cultural Dimensions of Globalization (Minneapolis-London: University of Minnesota Press, 1996), 4.

8   Held and McGrew, Transformations, 431.

9   On globalization in the political sense, see Baylis and Smith, World Politics, and Nester, Globalization

10   see for example, Club of Rome, Die erste globale Revolution. Bericht zur Lage der Welt (Frankfurt: Horizonte Verlag, 1992). The end of communism turned the then dominant (and frustrating) endism-debate into a mere positive expectation. Ulrich Menzel, Globalisierung versus Fragmentierung (Frankfurt: Suhrkamp 1998), 11-12

11   Malcolm Waters, Globalization (London-New York: Routledge, 1995), 159.

1990s, due to criticisms on „turbo capitalism", unresolved social problems and growing political conflicts[12].

But globalization is not only a historical frame concept specifically for our times. In fact, all the phenomena we listed up are consequences of 19th century developments: the telegraph (1833) was as revolutionary then as internet is today; railways (1825) and fast steamers (1889) „shrinked the world"; there was a British-dominated world market; inter-governmental organizations and international NGOs came up, both playing crucial roles in transnational standard setting[13]; social movements like the Socialist emerged; and there was a huge wave of migrations from Eurasia to America and elsewhere. Most global historians agree that globalization started in the 19th century[14]. The processes continued but with many ups and downs[15]: a deterministic view is still inappropriate[16].

---

12 On the history of the term "globalization" see Olaf Bach, Die Erfindung der Globalisierung. Untersuchungen zu Entstehung und Wandel eines zeitgeschichtlichen Grundbegriffs (Ph. Diss., University of St. Gallen, 2007)

13 John Boli and George M. Thomas. Constructing World Culture. International nongovernmental organizations since 1875 (Stanford: Stanford University Press, 1999)

14 Robbie Robertson, The Three Waves of Globalization. A history of a global consciousness (Nova Scotia: Fernwood Publications/London-New York: Zed Books, 2003) declares 1800; Hopkins, Globalization: after 1800; Fäßler, Globalisierung: 1840; Held and McGrew, Transformations: 1850; O'Byrne and Hensby, Global Studies: 1870, following an „Incipient Phase" c. 1750-1870.

15 the period until the outbreak of World War I (1914) is often called the „First globalization"; a „Second globalization" started only by the end of World War II (1945). In between, world economy disintegrated due to ultra-nationalist politics; however, not all agree that this represents an interruption of globalization. Then again, the acceleration of worldwide flows since the late 1980 is named „Third globalization" . The latter is doubtful, since world economy seems to have been more integrated in the year 1913 than in the year 2000. – See Hartmut Elsenhans, „Globalisierung I und Globalisierung II zwischen Konvoimodell und unterkonsumtionistischer Krise". In Vom Welthandel des 18. Jahrunderts zur Globalisierung des 21. Jahrhunderts. Leipziger Überseetagung 2005, ed. by Markus A. Denzel, 75-128. (Stuttgart: Franz Steiner, 2007), 75-128; Fäßler, Globalisierung; Kumon, Shumpei and Yasuhide Yamanouchi, "Three globalizing phases of the world system". In Globalization as Evolutionary Process, ed. George Modelski, Tessaleno Devezas, and William R. Thompson (London-New York: Routledge, 2008) 269-283; indirectly also Samir Amin, Die Zukunft des Weltsystems. Herausforderungen der Globalisierung (Hamburg: VSA-Verlag, 1997); Held and McGrew, Transformations; Hopkins, Globalization; Robertson, Three Waves; Andrea Komlosy, Globalgeschichte. Methoden und Theorien (Wien-Köln-Weimar: Böhlau, 2011)

16 See Peter Feldbauer, Gerald Hödl and Jean-Paul Lehners, eds., Rhythmen der Globalisierung. Expansion und Kontraktion zwischen dem 13. und 20. Jahrhundert (Wien: Mandelbaum, 2009), 8-9. Their point is that there is a determinism in the globalization debate

Yet this is not the whole story. The 19th century revolutions did not come out of the blue. Their roots lie in the early modern age which started along with the European expansion around 1500. From then onwards, European merchants looted, conquered, de-populated, transformed, populated countries and achieved control over older trade networks, backed by well-armed navies and massive government support. This lead to the emergence of extremely powerful companies with an abundance of capital, which tended to concentrate in economic *centers* such as Amsterdam and London, thus producing vast *peripheries* of have-nots out of Europe. Wallerstein called this phase, c. 1500-1800, *modern world system*[17], recent historians call it *proto-globalization*[18]. Some see the beginning of *world systems* even earlier[19], but most agree on the mark of 1500. During the times of proto-globalization, Europe conquered the Americas; during the first globalization, Europe took possession of most parts of Asia, Africa and Australia. By then, most of the world was interconnected.

As we can see, there is a disappointing *master narrative* about globalization: the whole timeframe goes along with the *modern age*, proto-globalization is more or less *proto-industrialization*, the beginning of globalization represents the *industrial revolution*; all these terms refer intrinsicly to European[20] history.

---

because historical research is said to be too less concerned with stagnations and downturns; this gives the wrong picture of a general, even if interrupted, upturn.

17 Wallerstein, Immanuel M. Capitalist agriculture and the origins of the European world-economy in the sixteenth century (New York: Academic Press, 1994); similarly Fernand Braudel, Aufbruch zur Weltwirtschaft. Sozialgeschichte des 15.-18. Jahrhunderts Bd.3 (München: Kindler, 1986), calling it „world economy".

18 A.G. Hopkins, in Hopkins, Globalization, 4-8; Dietmar Rothermund, in Margarete Grandner, Dietmar Rothermund and Wolfgang Schwentker, eds., Globalisierung und Globalgeschichte (Vienna: Mandelbaum, 2005), 12, quoting Schäfer; alternative denominations are „early modern globalization" (Held and McGrew, Transformations) or „germinal g." (O'Byrne and Hensby, Global Studies, 12, quoting Robinson]

19 In the „middle ages": Janet L. Abu Lughod, Before European Hegemony. The World System A.D. 1250-1350 (New York-Oxford: Oxford University Press, 1989). At the beginning of agro-urban cultures: Andre Gunder Frank, and Barry K. Gills, The world system. Five hundred years or five thousand? (London: Routledge, 1996). Both works belong to the well-established canon of world history. Less serious taken are proposals to start globalization with the spreading of Homo Sapiens himself [see Paul Mellars and Chris Stringer, eds. The human Revolution. Behavioural and biological perspectives on the origins of modern humans. (Edinburgh : Edinburgh Univ. Press, 1989)] – because the term would lose any specific meaning.

20 From here onwards, I understand by "Europe" the western Eurasian subcontinent plus its settlement areas as soon as the population majority is of European descendence, that is large parts of America, Australia and New Zealand.

The whole story tells us again about the *„rise of the West"*[21] and is basically eurocentric[22], although there are now serious efforts to incorporate the role of non-European agents during the early phases of world-wide interconnection[23]. And very subtly, the current „rise of the East" becomes noticeable in the debate[24]. But this is more a hidden content in the extremely polemic debate on the pros and cons about globlization[25] - a debate which is sometimes a bit frustrating because, as we showed in the beginning, people discuss about different things.

The point is that globalization is not *one* process: it is a verbal container for *very many*, which we are used to associate with the experience of more and more influences from „the rest of the world". Hence it is even not clear if globalization objectively exists at all![26] However *what* exists empirically are the many

21 so the title of one of the most influential works in world history, by William H. McNeill
22 A quite unexpected interpretation of history gives Richard Pomfret, The Age of Equality. The Twentieth Century in Economic Perspective (Cambridge, Ma. – London: The Belknap Press of Harvard University Press, 2011), describing the 19th century as age of liberty, the 20th as age of equality, and the 21st is predicted to become the age of fraternity!
23 See the fundamental global historical work Hopkins, Globalization; in German-speaking literature, e.g. Reinhard Wendt, Vom Kolonialismus zur Globalisierung. Europa und die Welt seit 1500 (Paderborn-Wien-München-Zürich: Ferdinand Schönigh, 2007)
24 Some suspect Europe to have lost its interest in globalization since it became clear that the very comfortable vision of a „europeanized world" becomes rather incredible. A.G. Hopkins, ed., Global History. Interactions Between the Universal and the Local (Basingstoke-New York: Palgrave Macmillan 2006), 6. On the other hand, especially scientists from Asia defend globalization. See Jagdish Bhagwati: In Defense of Globalization (New York: Oxford University Press, 2004); Nayan Chanda, Bound Together. How Traders, Preachers, Adventurers, and Warriors shaped Globalization (New Haven-London: Yale University Press, 2007)
25 Good overviews and summaries on the various positions are found in Held and McGrew, Transformations, 10; Baylis and Smith, World Politics, 7-8 and Franz Kolland et al., Soziologie der globalen Gesellschaft. Eine Einführung (Wien: Mandelbaum, 2010). As reader of anti-globalistist movements see Lechner and Boli, Globalization.
26 The sociologist Ammann describes globalization as a constructive-cognitive phenomenon which is mixed together of various single phenomena (quoted in Kolland et al., Soziologie, 28) – A historical argument against the true existence of globalization is found in Osterhammel and Petersson, Globalisierung, 109. They point out that global openness which is associated with globalization, emerges as innovation only in contrast to the national state which is a phenomenon specific for 19th century European history; for the rest of world history, open borders are rather the normality. – The formerly influential points of Hirst/Thompson against the existence of globalization which are based on the view that most of the flows circulate in the capitalist „triad" Europe / North America / Japan, are mostly outdated by the developments in the early 21st century. See Paul Hirst

partial processes of which globalization consists. In the following, I will propose seven categories in order to sort these processes systematically, and I will try to find out if there is anything like an „essence" of globalization.

1.1. Global spreads

It might be helpful to start with the common understanding of globalization effects: the spreading of innovations and ideas[27]. „The globalization of cardriving" could be such an example, or „the globalization of using guns". Even political régimes like the Khmer Rouge (Cambodia, 1975-79) or the Taliban (Afghanistan, 1996-2001) followed rigidly their policies of isolation, but they would not have done without motorized vehicles and of course not without all kinds of modern weapons to defend their isolation. This shows us two perspectives: one is that you cannot completely dissociate from globalization. The other is that globalization is not a consistant historical process; its partial processes follow their own dynamics.

It seems analytically of advantage to name these „globalizations" *„global spreads"*, forming partial processes of globalization. Is that all? Can we say: *Globalization consists in global spreads of different phenomena with varying acceptances?* We hardly suppose that the whole is more than the sum of its parts, meaning the addition of all global spreads alone does not yet explain globalization. What else is there?

1.2. Partial globalizations

We cannot apply „global spreads" on the globalization of systems, as there is an economic, political, or societal globalization. Of course, every culture has its own economy etc., with or without globalization. What we mean by „economic globalization" etc. refers to global spreads, a worldwide diffusion of ideas and methods how to run, for example, the economy. The difference to "regular" spreads is that whole systems – complex sets of ideas and methods – are spread[28].

If one considers a culture to be only composed of, say, the economy, politics and society: what is the relation of *partial processes* like economic, political, societal globalization to globalization as a whole? The interplay between these

---

and Grahame Thompson, Globalization in Question. The International Economy and the Possibilities of Governance (Cambridge-Oxford-Malden: Polity Press, 2nd ed. 1999), 2.

27 Resulting from a literal understanding of „globalization": „the process of becoming global" (O'Byrne and Hensby, Global Studies, 10.)

28 which you can also say about car driving – no car wihout gas station and roads; but these „sets" are comparably limited

partial processes integrates the spheres of a culture, leads to various changes; it is definitely „something more" than the sum of the partial processes and belongs surely to the "essence" of globalization. However, is there still anything more?

1.3. „Cognitive" globalization

There is something fundamental, interconnecting all globalization processes. Literally, „globalization" points to something (the earth) which takes the shape of a ball. This „process of becoming a ball" can be concretely understood as the worldwide spread of knowledge about the global shape of the earth. This is an imaginary form of global spread which is of „genetic" relevance.

It is known when it started: on the 6th of September A.D. 1522. On this day, the „Victoria", Magellan's last ship in being, reached the Spanish harbour of Sanlúcar near Seville. The core of its crew were the first people in history who managed to travel around the whole earth. The global shape of the earth, contested for a long time, was proved. This was not an event which rocked mankind's world view at once: it took generations to spread within Europe, and centuries to spread over the whole world. And yet – people could only believe it, they could not see it until NASA released the first satellite photograph of the whole earth in January 1968[29].

The phase 1522-1968 can be called *cognitive proto-globalization*[30]. This development is extremely important, since it created awareness of a limited planet with a limited set of resources[31]. Whatever we think about globalization, we cannot deny this basic fact; and whoever acts as „globaliser" is guided by this very basic knowledge.

1.4. „Mundialization"

As a consequence of „turbo capitalism" and according social conflicts, globalization debates focus on the *cui bono* question. I consider this a fatal misunderstanding.

Whatever we think of transnational capitalism or, to be more precise, economic exploitation: all these phenomena are not related to the global shape of

---

29   Jochen Schilk, Raumschiff Erde. Wie der Anblick der Erde aus dem All die Welt veränderte. Accessed April 24, 2012,
     http://www.kurskontakte.de/media/article_pdfs/KK122RaumschiffErde.pdf

30   Right: here is a determinism included, and the story sounds again eurocentric. But in this case, the role of Europe is a matter of fact, and the knowledge about the global shape will not be challenged or forgotten so soon.

31   The first satellite photograph of the earth is said to have inspired the global environmental movement (Ritzer, Globalization, 19)

the earth and therefore, not connected to *globalization* as such. Areas with intensive exchanges, with tendencies to accumulate resources and ideas in „centres", thus depriving „peripheries", have been called *world systems* (Wallerstein) or *world economies* (Braudel) – but the saying is about *world*, not *globe*. I propose to call such an entity with the Latin word *„mundus"* (world).

It is not very clear when the first *mundi* emerged – probably more than 5000 years ago, building the foundations for later empires in Egypt, Mesopotamia, the Indus valley, and China. The emergences of the great empires of antiquity – such as the Neo-Assyrian, Persian, Alexandrine, Maurya-Indian, Roman, Qin/Han-Chinese – appear as political integrations of older *mundi*, founded on solid traditions of inter-exchanges with compatible standards, means of payments, rules etc. And when the great antique empires disintegrated (as all of them did), exchanges still continued.

One outstanding *mundus* we can call the great revolution of the middle ages[32]: the „house of Islam", *Dar al-Islam*. This faith-based *mundus* goes the opposite way from the older ones: it starts in the 7th century as a huge empire which disintegrates after a few centuries, but the *mundus* grows on – forming a *multi-polar community* which finally reaches from Senegal to the Philippines, bound together by a common religion, *lingua franca* and law, inter-city relations, the annual pilgrimage and especially the continuously growing activities of traders who are often scholars[33]. Among many other elements of the modern „international community" which *Dar al Islam* anticipates is the concept of a worldwide community of equals, no matter which culture they belong to.

This powerful *mundus* became the main development engine of Eurasia before 1500. For this reason it is associated with the true initial phase of „globalization"[34]. I cannot agree with this – because the „genetic structure", cognitive globalization, is not yet in existence –, but what needs to be supported is that *Dar al-Islam* paved the way.

---

32   And in fact, it gives this almost abandoned concept a new world historical meaning – as a transition period between the antique, imperial mundi, and the modern global one

33   See, for example, Amira K. Bennison, in Hopkins, Globalization, 76ff

34   Stearns, Globalization, 32. Similarly, Kirti N. Chaudhuri, Trade and civilization in the Indian ocean. An economic history from the rise of Islam to 1750 (Cambridge etc.: Cambridge Univ. Press, 1985). Also Abu-Lughod, Before European Hegemony.

I propose to name these phenomena of *mundus*-building and expansion, *mundialization*[35]. Globalization then appears as a special phase of mundialization: that is, when all the mundi melt together to a single one.

1.5. Regionalization

We observe in the world's history an on-going rhythm of integrations and refragmentations. *Mundi* as well as today's „global mundus"create *regions*. Regions are usually deeply rooted exchange areas and transform after their integration into a bigger *mundus*. They become more „compatible" with other members of the same *mundus*, but they would not easily give up their sense of belonging. In cases of mundial disintegration, regions will most likely persist[36].

This leads us to a crucial point. European rule in the proto-global period was not a common imperial adventure; it is, simply speaking, the sum of Spanish and Portuguese, later also Dutch, British and French thalassocracies. Europe expanded as a *mundus*, not as an empire. In fact, Europe represents another multipolar *mundus* besides the *Dar al Islam*[37] with which it started merging latest by now. Merging means that the agents of older networks – not only Islamic; also South Indian, Malay, Chinese – contributed actively to the processes of "European expansion". Similar developments went on in America, though European control was tighter here. This is why we should use the term *proto-globalization* instead of *European expansion* – it leaves more options for the role of non-European agents[38].

The result is the emergence of a single, global *mundus* which was accomplished around 1900. The world knows only six nations which had never known direct or indirect European rule: Turkey and Persia; Thailand; China, Korea and Japan. Even these few nations survived European imperialism only under the condition of political reforms, adapting European models. The whole world be-

---

35 This word is similar with the Spanish mundialisación (synonymous for globalisación) and to the French word for globalization, which is mondialization; we propose this specific meaning for English and German.

36 Maybe a good example is what I call the „Mediterranean cross": four regions („Latin" and „Greek" Europe, Maghreb and Mashriq) have been participating in various mundi constellations, sometimes connected with, sometimes separated from some of the others; but as regions or sub-regions, they still exist today.

37 The Dar al Islam and Europe were not the only "multipolar" mundi: the same can be said about India, areas in Africa and America during the "middle ages". Dar al Islam was just the most attractive and expansive one.

38 See Michael Geyer and Charles Bright, "World History in a Global Age" in, The Global History Reader, eds. Bruce Mazlish and Akira Iriye, (London-New York: Routledge, 2005), 27f

came politically and economically "compatible". But again, the global *mundus* produced "world regions" as we know them today, based on earlier *mundi* (even if deformed). Regionalization is a partial globalization process, and the opposite of mundialization.

1.6. Localization

Local contexts became more important during the last 20 years, often enough connected to animosities against external influences. This *localization* cannot be interpreted as an anti-globalization movement: it is a part of globalization. A general lack of orientation in post-modern societies could be one reason for the desire to belong to a community (*integrisme*). This includes parochial entities as well as religious and ideologic movements[39], sometimes fanatic and violent[40].

Another role surely plays the weakening of nation-states under the combined pressures of "turbo capitalism" and "integrisme", the latter becoming thus a self-strenghtening system. Popular hope rests on smaller units – this can lead to independence movements of territories[41] or efforts to reach more autonomy and autarchy on the very local level.

Robbie Robertson introduced the term *glocalization*[42] to establish a research line on how global and local levels influence and shape each other. This had a strong impact not only on science; it inspired also social movements who made the word *glocalization* their own. *Glocalization* became one of the most influencing concepts of the globalization debate.

1.7. Global cooperation

Since the late 19th century, it is a political reality that global projects are planned and global challenges are seen. This produces broader global con-

---

39 Ralf Dahrendorf in Ulrich Beck, ed., Perspektiven der Weltgesellschaft (Frankfurt/Main: Suhrkamp 1998), 50ff – connected with a clear warning about the development perspectives of democracy

40 Benjamin R. Barber, Jihad vs McWorld. Terrorism's Challenge to Democracy (New York: Ballantine Books, 2001)

41 Niels Lange, Globalisierung und regionaler Nationalismus. Schottland und Québec im Zeitalter der Denationalisierung (Baden-Baden: Nomos, 2000), showing such effects for Scotland and Quebec

42 Roland Robertson "Glokalisierung: Homogenität und Heterogenität in Raum und Zeit" in Perspektiven der Weltgesellschaft, ed. Ulrich Beck (Frankfurt/Main: Suhrkamp 1998), 192-220.
in Beck, Weltgesellschaft, 192-220 (orig. 1994), further developed by Appadurai, Modernity.

sciousness and, maybe, even solidarity[43]. Besides governments, international NGO's and social movements play important roles here, and some of them are already organized on a trans-national base. One of the most successful examples of cooperative globalization is the anti-globalization movement.

Global consciousness also results from migrations. These are not expected to create a *world society*; immigrants and majority population do not automatically intermix, they can also form separate communities[44]. Intra-societal segregation seems to be another aspect of globalization. However, larger cities which face a high degree of immigration appear as stages on which inter-cultural cooperation is practised on a daily base.

2. Globalities

Let's do an interim result. We said that globalization consists of different forms of spreads, of which "cognitive globalization" is a kind of core; partial processes influence each other and create new phenomena; globalization is based on mundialization and creates regionalization; there is a tension between global and local levels, and likewise there is cooperation on addressing global challenges. Globalization splits and unites likewise. But where is the connection between all these qualities?

On the search, we stumble across the term *globality*. Is this the final stage of globalization? The English version of Wikipedia supports this[45], also science uses the term similarly[46]. But it is not clear if *globality* refers only to the abstract concept of *globalization*; it could also describe a cosmopolitan lifestyle[47]. A third meaning relates to global cooperation[48].

Do these approaches have anything in common which could lead us to a synthesis? Every case – regarding the understandings of *globalization* as well as of *globality* – implies one basic thing: *the possibility of exchange*. Having realized this, I propose as definition:

---

43 Zygmunt Bauman claims the responsibility of all humans for each other, due to global inter-connection (Lemert et al., Globalization, 208)
44 Beck, Weltgesellschaft, 9; Tomlinson in Lemert et al., Globalization, 303.
45 http://en.wikipedia.org/wiki/Globality, accessed on March 31, 2012
46 „Globality is the omnipresence of globalization" (Ritzer, Globalization, 318 and 3, referring to Jan Aart Scholte)
47 According to Roland Robertson, this is the central aspect of globalization: the cultural capital of a global middle class (O'Byrne and Hensby, Global Studies, 16-17.)
48 Osterhammel and Petersson, Globalisierung, 13.

Globality is a status which allows all cultures unlimited exchange with each other.[49]

This understanding of *globality* guides us now on the way to a definition of globalization. My proposal is:

Globalization is the sum of all phenomena which lead or refer to a status of permanent and unlimited possibilities of interaction between all cultures.

Consciously we speak of "possibilities of interaction", not of actual "interdependence". The latter can be an effect of the first but it does not need to be. Thus, our definition is not dependent on the findings of the world system and other theories, and isolationistic regimes like the above mentioned Khmer Rouge and Taliban do not stop globalization[50].

This definition makes mundialization a part of globalization as well as regionalization and localization, like global spreads as well. Partial processes can analogously be defined ("economic globalization" related to "economic interaction" etc.). Again, *cognitive globalization* plays a key role here, since it limitates the "all".

3. Global Histories

After a phase of frowning faces[51] globalization has eventually arrived in historical sciences. On one hand, this is welcome: historians receive new possibilities of interpretation from a global context, and in exchange, they can contribute to global sciences through descriptions, causal analyses, revisions, theory building and impact assessments[52].

On the other hand, the relationship "history/globalization" is tricky. First of all: since the end is not known (and actually, the origins neither), there is no *story* to tell. Therefore, eurocentrism, determinism and stage theories have a

---

49 Almost identical is the concept of „world society" by Armin Nassehi (1998): it is determined not by any social equality, but by the possibility to interact (see Kolland et al., Soziologie, 37)

50 A positive side effect of this understanding of globalization is that it liberates the globalization term from all kinds of polemics which shape the debate so much and which not at all helpful: we talk about possibilities. How they will be implemented is a question of management!

51 Because global history is said not to work with historical sources: Dietmar Rothermund in Grandner, Rothermund and Schwentker, Globalgeschichte, 23. See also Sebastian Conrad, Andreas Eckert, and Ulrike Freitag, eds., Globalgeschichte. Theorien, Ansätze, Themen (Frankfurt-New York: Campus, 2007)

52 Fäßler, Globalisierung, 24-26.

walk-over. [53] The good old "big theory" could be a way out, but it seems to remain dead[54] . . . a certain contradiction, especially if we recognize that writing world history is always a highly constructivist, sometimes a purely theoretical enterprise[55]. Constructivism (as well as theory) means methodic selection and is unavoidable, since the amount of available information makes encyclopedic completeness of modern historiography impossible[56]. But even less ambitioned projects require teamwork; compact narrations become seldom[57]. But how shall we explain the world to people, or rather since we cannot do it, at least tell them about it? [58]

3.1. The big outlines

The need for a big historical "master narrative" is deeply rooted. Its written traditions go back to the ages of epics and holy scripts. Simultaneously with globalization, historical science has come up. Since then, we enjoy a few "big" outlines (following the German-speaking tradition):

- *Universal history*: an innovation of the 18th century, it searches for meaning in human development and allows also the imagination of a *Weltgeist*. Today, the concept is abandoned[59]: there is no *Weltgeist*, so the post-modern view, as any search for a deeper sense of history is senseless itself.

- *History of world systems*: a development of the 1970s, it can be seen as a secret successor of universal history: it delivers patterns of explanations

53   Völkel, Geschichtsschreibung, 343.
54   Lothar Kolmer: Geschichtstheorien (Paderborn: Wilhelm Fink, 2008), 94.
55   Jürgen Osterhammel, ed., Weltgeschichte (Stuttgart: Franz Steiner, 2008), 14.
56   Osterhammel, Weltgeschichte, 18.
57   Völkel, Geschichtsschreibung, 342.
58   We are obliged to respect this demand. Braudel claimed a "histoire globale" as borderless science; according to him, only „a science of mankind" can satisfy nowadays. Hodgson wrote straightly, "The inadequacy of our knowledge becomes increasingly painful year by year in our present world where peoples of traditionally different historical backgrounds – Europeans and Indians, Muslims and Chinese – must live together and forge a sense of common humanity." Marshall G.S.Hodgson, Rethinking world history. Essays on Europe, Islam, and World History. Edited by Edmund Burke, III. (Cambridge-New York-Melbourne: Cambridge University Press, 1993), 248. In 1995, Michael Geyer and Charles Bright said in a programmatic article that the central challenge is now, to elaborate the world's past for an age of globality. See Noel Cowen, Global History. A Short Overview (Cambridge: Polity Press, 2001), 5.
59   Osterhammel sees a continuity in theories of social evolution. Osterhammel, Weltgeschichte, 14.

for the history of "worlds" and potentially the world as a whole. Developments are not lead by a *Weltgeist*, but they follow common principles[60].
- *World history*: This well-established direction shows the histories of nations or regions in parallel, often comparatively[61].
- *History of mankind*: This one is ill-defined; according to my own use, it looks for common grounds in history. The main ambition is to make them out; finding explanations is a minor aim.
- *Historical anthropology* looks for the being of man as a physical, social, psychological creature; the leading question is how humans have behaved and what a view they had on themselves in different ages and cultures. Research is done preferably in micro-historical contexts.[62].
- Big History: This very young movement[63] tries to include the complete past since the big bang. Human history is embedded in a bigger history of nature.

Big outlines are quite popular, looking for answers on top mankind questions about itself. But we find also traps: pressures of thematic selections bear the danger to neglect happenings which could be of great relevance; moreover, meaningful selections can be done only with the help of background theories which are not always very durable.

3.2. Global history as alternative draft

With seemingly less ambitions[64] and explicitly team-oriented approaches, global history is forming now[65] - a historiography with a strong consciousness for

---

60 The world system theory is strongly connected to Immanuel Wallerstein; its basements stem inter alia from Fernand Braudel, further developments are done by André Gunder Frank. The latter drafted the narrative of the „Chinese world system" in order to identify a long-term center of global history, which is supported by many [for example, Pamela Kyle Crossley, What is Global History? (Cambridge-Malden: Polity Press, 2008), 108-109]

61 There are different, partly contradictory definitions of World History in the German-speaking tradition; I follow Osterhammel [Jürgen Osterhammel, „'Weltgeschichte': Ein Propädeutikum". Geschichte in Wissenschaft und Unterricht 56(2005)9, 452-479] – who changed his opinion later and turned "World history" into an umbrella term for all globally oriented historical disciplines (Osterhammel, Weltgeschichte, 15-22).

62 On this, see Aloys Winterling, ed., Historische Anthropologie (Stuttgart: Franz Steiner, 2006)

63 Constitutive: David Christian, Maps of Time. An Introduction to Big History (Berkeley-Los Angeles-London: University of California Press, 2011), orig. 2004

64 Not really: almost every research question can imply aspects of global history (Komlosy, Globalgeschichte, 8.)

global contexts[66]. In a way, global history is more "tender" than the big outlines are. Global history is closely connected to the concept of *glocalization*[67] which is likewise relevant for earlier times. From place to place, global history spins its net of relations, mostly on the basis of one certain topic – for example trade goods like salt, spices, clothes. Global history works on details and depends upon specialized skills; hence it needs inter-disciplinary cooperation.

The main difference between world history and global history is that the latter is in first instance a "history of relationships instead of historical comparisons [that] allows us to focus on the interplay between involved research objects, which eventually changes their characters", as Andrea Komlosy points out[68]. For a better processual understanding of history, this is most significant. As specific "phenomena of global history", four types of relationship developments can be analyzed[69]:

- Divergence – things become more different
- Convergence – things become more similar
- Contagion – things change after crossing a border
- Systemic changes – structural interactions lead to mutual changes

Notwithstanding its short existence, global history has already formed a couple of branches. The most important are:[70]

- *Entangled History*: a common history of at least two objects, the history of each could not be told without including the other;
- *Connected History*: the history of steady relations between cultures[71]
- *Histoire croisée*: research on the multi-dimensionality of relationships between subjects

---

65   It was founded in 1991 on a conference in Bellagio, Italy; the results were published two years later: Bruce Mazlish and Ralph Buultjens, eds., Conceptualizing Global History (Boulder-San Francisco-London: Westview Press, 1993). Almost a decade later, the first global history reader was issued which was written exclusively by historians: Hopkins, Globalization. Since then, the sub-discipline develops extraordinarily dynamic. – A different tradition sees the beginning of global history in the establishment of the „Journal of World History", 1990 (Conrad, Eckert and Freitag, Globalgeschichte, 8.)

66   Conrad, Eckert and Freitag, Globalgeschichte, 27.

67   Globalization itself is multi-centric; historians are invited to interconnect the local with the universal (Hopkins, Global History, 5)

68   Komlosy, Globalgeschichte, 62. [translation C.M.]

69   Crossley 2008, Global History, 9

70   Komlosy, Globalgeschichte, 63, mentioning in this context also the world system history

71   Founded in the 1990s by Sanjay Subrahmanyam, researching on deep rooted relations between the cultures of the Old world

- *Transfer history*: history of the diffusion of objects, ideas and phenomena, and of their receptions (which often lead to adaptations and new changes).

Success seems to endorse the new concept. Histories of single items like trade goods are not only appreciated by the world of science: they also *sell*! This is no disadvantage. Obviously, this is a straight way to answer some of the questions people raise to historians.

3.3. Globalization history

One party votes for focussing global history on the periods of globalization[72]. Another sees global history as a sub-discipline independent from historical periods[73]. One might intuitively say thatglobal history as a method is not connected to globalization as such. On the other hand, we should be aware that the "founders" of global history understood it as a history of globalization[74].

I think it is anyways helpful to separate content from method. Therefore I propose to use the term *globalization history* for the research *on all phenomena which lead or refer to a status of permanent and unlimited possibilities of interaction between all cultures*, no matter which method will be applied.

3.4. Neighbouring areas of global history

Global history did not appear out of the blue. There are methodic predecessors which have also been accompanying global history since it emerged.

This relates especially to *Area Studies*. They aim for a holistic understanding of world regions, thus forming a counter-model to the on-going split-up of sciences. Critics claimed that Area Studies limit their areas according to nowa-

---

72 "global history – that is, the study of globalization". Mazlish and Iriye, Global History, 19; Osterhammel, „Propädeutikum", 460, later reconsidered (Osterhammel, Weltgeschichte, 19); Conrad, Eckert and Freitag, Globalgeschichte, 25; implicitely also Lemert et al., Globalization; Komlosy states clearly: „Globalgeschichte im heutigen Sinn bezieht sich in Abgrenzung von der älteren Universalgeschichte nicht auf Menschheitsgeschichte schlechthin, sondern auf die Geschichte der Globalisierung" (Komlosy, Globalgeschichte, 49.)

73 Dietmar Rothermund in Grandner, Rothermund and Schwentker, Globalgeschichte, 13 – According to Sachsenmaier, the majority of German-speaking global historians follows this point of view. See Dominic Sachsenmaier, Global Perspectives on Global History. Theories and Approaches in a Connected World (Cambridge et al.: Cambridge University Press, 2011), 160.

74 Bruce Mazlish in Mazlish and Buultjens, Conceptualizing, 2-6; but even in the beginnings there was no clear consent on this, see the much more generous concept of Neva R. Goodwin in Mazlish and Buultjens, Conceptualizing, 29-30)

day's world and also neglect inter-regional relations[75]. Later delimitations of Area Studies eventually lead to global history[76]. Some declare Area Studies already "dead"[77]; albeit, there is now again a discourse on „civilizations" coming up[78]. Its critical observation could be another task for global historians.

Closely interrelated with global history is the branch of *transnational studies*. They deal with typologies of all kinds of transnational structures and research on their interactivities[79]. Transnational studies research rather on *structures*, global history on *processes*; but the border line is not always sharply drawn.

Finally, classic *diplomatic history* needs to be mentioned; this is surely the oldest of all exchange-oriented histories and researches on the histories of intergovernmental relations.

3.5. Historical research on globalization

We have analyzed seven categories of globalization processes and thirteen branches of research. Now the question remains, how we can apply the thirteen to the seven. It becomes evident that each of the thirteen – even those which are supposed to be "dead" – can play a role here.

- *Global spreads* are surely "the" research area of Connected History, Histoire Croisée, history of transfers and transnational studies.

- *Partial globalizations* can be researched by the same, but also comparisons coming from classic world history and history of mankind can help us to understand how societal spheres adapt to changing environments;

- „*Cognitive globalization*" seems to be a research area of central relevance. The nucleus is the question how far human imaginations shape later developments. Here, universal history could resurrect: if imaginations are shared by many and influence their behaviours, then we have found the *Weltgeist* – turning out as common human aspirations[80]. His-

---

75 Conrad, Eckert and Freitag, Globalgeschichte, 13; Birgit Schäbler in Schäbler, Area Studies, 32 und Angelika Epple in Schäbler, Area Studies, 103
76 Birgit Schäbler in Schäbler, Area Studies, 11-44
77 Conrad, Eckert and Freitag, Globalgeschichte, 13
78 Conrad, Eckert and Freitag, Globalgeschichte, 46
79 Sanjeev Khagram and Peggy Levitt (eds.), The Transnational Studies Reader. Intersections and Innovations (New York-London: Routledge, 2008)
80 A modern topic of the Weltgeist could be "proto-galactization", starting with the first human in space, in 1957. An older one could be imaginations of early neolithic villagers who create visions of a city. Again another one would be the old human dream to be able to fly.

torical anthropology could also find interests to research on cognitive processes, and a new (upgraded) status of "the idea" would be a topic for Big History.

- *Mundialization and regionalization* are clearly fields of Area Studies and classic world history, as well as all fields of global history and transnational studies.
- *Localization* would be again a typical area of global history, accompanied by historical anthropology.
- *Global cooperation*: Here, good old diplomatic history will be extremely helpful for researching on the governmental part, as well as transnational studies on the non-governmental. Historical anthropology may contribute with observations on human ways of cooperation, as Big history can do – if cooperation is understood as a evolutionary "survival principle".

3.6. Epilogue on the purpose of globally oriented histories

A general purpose of history is denied by historians[81]. On the other hand, social sciences which follow evolutionary models imply a concept of purpose, and likewise, historical sciences are invited to understand historical examples as tools for (political) decision-making[82]. So there is a purpose of *our knowledge about* history. For example, reflections on globalization processes can influence their developments.

Also the opposite is relevant: we need to show it clearly if there are no examples available which support (political) decisions. For example, it was said that the view of human behaviour economic neo-classicism implies would be ahistoric[83]. If this statement is true, then historians are obliged to unveil this and give notice of it; strategies based on *ahistoric* premises will hardly ever work. But we can only do so if we have a truly global knowledge of mankind's history.

The „big outlines" are still in fashion – as the youngest branch, „Big history", proves. The "big picture" has its own relevance. We know: *the more exactly we look into something, the more it disintegrates right in front of our eyes.*

---

81 Kolmer, Geschichtstheorien, 95
82 „Am Ende der Geschichte stellt sich die Frage nach ihrem Sinn und damit nach der Kompetenz der Geschichtswissenschaft als Institution, Kontingenz in der Lebenswelt zu mindern." Andreas Leutzsch, Geschichte der Globalisierung als globalisierte Geschichte. Die historische Konstruktion der Weltgesellschaft bei Rosenstock-Huessy und Braudel (Frankfurt-New York: Campus, 2009) – But even a simpler view is possible: knowledge of history improves societal orientation in general. See Gerhard Schulz, Geschichte im Zeitalter der Globalisierung (Berlin-New York: Walter de Gruyter 2004), 376-377
83 Dietmar Rothermund in Grandner, Rothermund and Schwentker, Globalgeschichte, 33

This happens whenever you look at an object through a microscope, or when you think about deeper meanings of an idea. The object or the idea will not be seen anymore; we see other objects, and other ideas will come up instead. But still, the "original" object or idea has an impact on them. If you turn it around, then we see these "other things" in our daily life, but the greater "original" thing, influencing us daily and directly, is not easily visible for us. In order to find it, we need to research more on the "big pictures" – which can be equally *constructed* and *true* [84].

Global history gains its inputs from micro contexts; macro history, the big outlines, painting on the "big picture", is a common output of micro historical research and subjected to micro-historical checks. Often enough, there will be conflicts, micro history will falsify results of macro history and inspire further research. But wherever we come to a point of coherence, we are learning more about all of us – about mankind belonging together.

---

84 Whereupon Hodgson's warning has to be taken very seriously: "Large scale history" includes comparisons which are lead by culturally influenced world views; "They are, in a sense, impossible questions; yet they are the most important sorts of questions to which a sense of history is commonly applied." [Hodgson, World History, 255]

Defining the "Indefinable"
World Cities as Indicators for the Process of Globalization[1]

Philipp Strobl

1. Introduction

Globalization is a widespread, ample and universal term. It is very difficult to define its role and function - not to mention the undertaking of measuring the process. A person interested in the topic faces numerous different models of explanation frequently depending on their inventors' main field of interest. According to Richard Barnet and John Cavanagh,

"Globalization" is the most fashionable word of the 1990's, so portentous and wonderfully patient as to puzzle Alice in Wonderland and thrill the Red Queen because it means precisely whatever the user says it means. Just as poets and songwriters celebrated the rise of modern nationalism, so in our days corporate managers, environmental prophets, business philosophers, rock stars, and writers of advertising copy offer themselves as poet laureates of the global village."[2]

This was said in 1994 at the very beginning of the public globalization discourse, and it still shows impressively the manifoldness of the term and its various possible uses. As Peer Fiss and Paul Hirsch state, globalization has become "a grand contest of social constructions and an umbrella construct that enables conflicting claims to coexist and to coevolve".[3] For most of the observers, the term is very vague and often poorly defined. Fiss and Hirsch further stated, "There is little consensus on what it does or what it should encompass, or even on the term's definition."[4]

One of the future tasks of globalization research hence must be the search for descriptive measuring points to define the process, or at least to make it more

---

1   I want to thank Andreas Exenberger for his tremendous support in finding ideas for the conceptualization of that paper.
2   Richard J. Barnet and John Cavanagh, Global Dreams. Imperial Cooperations and the New World Order (New York: Simon and Schuster, 1994), p.13f.
3   Peer C. Fiss, C and Paul M. Hirsch, "The Discourse of Globalization: Framing and Sensemaking of Emerging Concept," in: American Sociological Review 70 (2), 29-52.
4   Fiss/Hirsch, Discourse, 32.

tangible. While looking for definitions, we always have to consider the universal dimension of processes. According to the sociologist Roland Robertson, one should understand it as a multifaceted procedure that "refers both to the compression of the world and the intensification of consciousness of the world as a whole".[5] The term hence stands for two developments. Firstly, it represents the material integration process of different parts of the world. Secondly it describes a mental procedure. The main difficulty in finding measuring points is to include different aspects (economic, political, cultural, social, environmental, etc.) in a conclusive investigation grid.

In this essay, we want to delve deeper into the field of academic globalization research in order to get an idea of the measurability of globalization. This can help capturing the phenomenon in its whole dimension as well as finding answers on its questions, challenges and chances. We want to show some methods and approaches that can be useful to analyze the phenomenon. The research field today heads into several different directions. But there is no overall agreement on the questions of what globalization actually is, or when it has begun. Two approaches could provide answers.

The historical world system approach offers a very conclusive explanation for global developments. It is characterized by comprehensive theoretical concepts that try to define some ground rules for an analysis of world systems, such as the "human web concept" by John and William McNeill[6], the "world economy theory" by Fernand Braudel[7], or the "world system analysis" by Immanuel Wallerstein[8]. These theories are extensive in time and space and give a rather generalized overview about a long period of humankind's development and the growing together of our world. The current non-historic globalization research work, on the other hand, is very much focused on globalization as a recent development. Many scholars have a sociological or economic-scientific background, and they respect mainly the latest developments in the growing together process of our world. They trace the origins of globalization back to the 1970's,

---

5   Roland Robertson, Globalization: Social Theory and Global Culture (London: Sage, 1992), p. 8.
6   John R. McNeill and William H. McNeill, The Human Web. A Bird's-Eye View of World History. (New York: WW Norton and Company, 2003).
7   Fernand Braudel, Sozialgeschichte des 15.-18. Jahrhunderts: Aufbruch zur Weltwirtschaft 3. (München: Kindler, 1986).
8   ImmanuelWallerstein, World System Analysis. An Introduction (Durham/NC: Duke University Press, 2004).

when formerly industrialized cities adopted themselves to the "new postindustrial mode" and hence became interconnected "global cities".[9]

To get a more universal background for a historical globalization study, we want to link concepts of both fields, namely Fernand Braudel's world city-theory, and the global city analysis by Saskia Sassen[10], Mark Abrahamson[11], and Peter Taylor[12]. We intend to show that a historical globalization study focused on cities as the main nodes of the phenomenon is a good means to capture the phenomenon in its whole dimension. Such a modernized concept can serve as a point of departure for a kind of globalization research that not only theoretically describes spacious processes, and not only offers an explanation for a very limited spectrum of the process, but also delivers comparable data about the history of the phenomenon. That will help making the term better definable. Practical case studies of city regions, give us the opportunity of breathe life into the history of the process without a focus on national perspectives and finally allow placing events into a broader context as well as avoiding the "notorious methodological nationalism of the historical sciences", criticized by Conrad and Eckert.[13]

For globalization "refers both to the compression of the world as well as the intensification of consciousness of the world as a whole,"[14] logical points of departure for an examination of the world's growing together could be spaces of compression of interpersonal relations on different levels. Such fields could be the economic integration, the changing relationship between state and market, the cultural homogenization process, as well as changes in the conception of time and space initiated by technological change.[15] Both research strings described above locate urban core areas in the heart of globalization processes. So-called world cities or global cities have always played an essential role for the spread of the phenomenon and are thus the most tangible spaces of compression available for an analysis. Because of their dominant role as interfaces of the

9   Mark Abrahamson, Global Cities (Oxford: University Press, 2004), p.4.
10   Saskia Sassen, The Global City: New York, London, Tokyo, (Princeton: University Press, 2001).
11   Abrahamson, global city.
12   Peter Taylor, World City Network: A Global Urban Analysis. London: Routledge, 2004).
13   Sebastian Conrad, and Andreas Eckert, "Globalgeschichte, Globalisierung, multiple Modernen: Zur Geschichtsschreibung der modernen Welt," in: Sebastian Conrad and Andreas Eckert, Eds., Globalgeschichte: Theorien, Ansätze, Themen. (Frankfurt/New York: Campus Verlag, 2007): 7-52, 20.
14   Robertson, Globalization, p. 8.
15   Conrad and Eckert, Globalgeschichte 20.

whole world, they predetermine the economic and cultural direction the world pursues. Hence, it makes sense to stress the characteristics of both concepts to portray a global or world city.

The first section of this paper wants to offer an overview about Fernand Braudel's theory of world economies and world cities. We seek to emphasize the most important characteristics of his theory with respect to the integration of broad parts of the world in to an emerging city dominated world economy. We further want to show what Braudel regarded as a world city. The second section focuses on current global city research work. It describes the most important theories about the role of so-called global cities as nodes in a worldwide network of exchange and tries to summarize the main characteristics of a global city. The third section connects both research fields in order to get an idea of a more current spatial base for globalization research. It aims at describing the important role of cities as useful spatial criteria for an examination of the phenomenon. The fourth section tries to shed light on the difficult question when globalization has begun. In the last part we summarize our results and propose a temporal and spatial basic skeleton in order to get the basis for a more current city dominated basis for a globalization analysis that captures the long history of the phenomenon as well as the latest developments.

2. Fernand Braudel and World Cities

During the postwar years and particularly until the 1980's, a significant movement in history, as an academic discipline, emerged around the journal "Les Annales" with Fernand Braudel as its mental leader.[16] The so-called *Annales* School was groundbreaking in the field of historical sciences. It played an important role in moving the historical sciences away from historicism, positivism, as well as its former restriction to political and national history towards a depiction of all aspects of humankind's history. It was among the first to talk about the necessity of the creation of a *histoire globale*, a global history. The members of the *Annales* School found out some trends, cycles, and structures that surfaced again and again. As a result of those cognitions, Fernand Braudel developed an analysis tool that should help to understand the complex processes within world history.

In this section, we want to discuss his theoretical thoughts with regard to a classification of a shrinking world. Finally, we want to emphasize Braudel's characteristics of a world city.

---

16 Michael Wieviorka, Michael, "From Marx and Braudel to Wallerstein," in: Contemporary Sociology 34 (2005): 1-7, 1.

Braudel divided the world in to several independent core areas, so-called world economies.[17] According to him, those spaces are "economically autonomous sections of the planet able to provide for most of its own needs."[18] He decided to see the growing together of the world from an economical perspective. According to him, "of all the ways of apprehending space, the economic is the easiest to locate and the widest-ranging."[19]

Besides the first depiction of the term of world economy, he further stated that it is a concept that applies to the whole world. It corresponds to the market of the universe, to the human race, or that part of the human race which is engaged in trade, and which today in a sense makes up a single market.[20] He specified some general rules for world economies. At first, he depicted the overall trend that they tend to develop a conjoint culture in order to distance themselves from other world economies. He further described that border regions of world economies are less animated, inert zones or borderlands that are difficult to traverse. A transgression of such a border economically happens only in exceptional cases because the financial losses of the trans-border trade activities would exceed the gains.[21] He, secondly, stated that a world economy consists of a hierarchy of several interlaminated areas of different importance. He locates at least three zones. The least developed is the periphery. It is characterized by old-fashioned and underdeveloped structures. Those regions are sparsely populated and subject to exploitation by other zones.[22] The next category is a higher developed middle region. At the center of each world economy, he located a well-developed urban core area, a so-called world city, that serves as epicenter for the whole world economy - as a place where information, goods, capital, credits, people, orders, and business letters of the whole system coalesce.

According to him, there are some attributes characterizing a world city. There must be only one dominant world city in a world economy. It serves as an urban center of gravity, as the logistic heart of the system. Every other city within the system only functions as a so-called "subordinate."[23] Those towns are located "at varying and respectful distances around the center playing the role of

---

17 Braudel, Sozialgeschichte, p. 8.
18 Fernand, Braudel, "Economies in Space: The World-Economies," in: Ross E. Dunn, Ross, ed.: The New World History: A Teacher's Companion, (Boston: Bedford/St.Martin. 2000): 246-253, 246.
19 Braudel, Economies, p. 246.
20 Braudel, Sozialgeschichte, p. 18.
21 Braudel, Sozialgeschichte, p. 23.
22 Braudel, Sozialgeschichte, p. 38.
23 Braudel, Economies, p. 250.

associate or accomplice, but more usually resigned to their second-class role. Their activities are governed by those of the metropolis: They stand guard around it, direct the flow of business toward it, redistribute or pass on the goods it sends them, live off its credit or suffer its rule."[24] The core area and its subordinates are in a constant competitive battle. But no world city has its leading role evermore. Sometimes a subordinate outstrips its world city and will become the new core area of the world economy. As another central characteristic, Braudel describes that the core area attracts people, ideas, and investment from the whole system. Hence a world city is something like a melting pot incorporating people of nearly all cultures of the world economy. In this context, he named the Amsterdam stock exchange of the 17th century that looked like a "miniature version of the whole world economy."[25] As a logical result of that diversity, the population of the core area becomes open-minded and tolerant in order to guarantee the peaceful growing together of different people within its limited boundaries. Diversity led to the creation of a new cosmopolitan culture and because of the world city's important position within the world system, the new culture acts as role model for all other areas of the system. Based from the core, it spreads to subordinated cities and from there to the periphery. The distinctive social segmentation that already can be detected very early is a further important characteristic of a world city.[26] Braudel recognizes mainly three social layers: the proletariat, the bourgeoisie, and a very self-conscious aristocracy. According to him, the differences between the proletariat and the aristocracy diverge increasingly, finally leading to the fact that the poor get poorer and a few rich get richer. Simply spoken, he blamed the phenomenon of price increases for that development.[27] Because of the city's overall importance, it attracts people, investors, and companies from all around the world system. Hence price levels increase constantly what led to high costs of living. That finally boosts inflation. As a result, the divide between the rich and poor increases.

To conclude, Braudel, detected several economically and culturally independent units alias world systems. There is either none or at least less exchange of goods, information, or thoughts between those spaces. Every world economy develops its own conjoint culture to differentiate itself from other areas. Inventions such as advances in the field of transport, discoveries or conquest led to the extension of world economies. That results in the fact that more dominant areas devoured less dominant regions. As a consequence, former independent world

---

24 Braudel, Economies, p. 250.
25 Braudel, Sozialgeschichte, p. 25.
26 Braudel, Sozialgeschichte, p. 28.
27 Braudel, Sozialgeschichte, p. 28.

economies were incorporated into expanding economic areas. That development is still proceeding. Today, the world has increasingly become a single world economy. Braudel spatially divided a world economy into three parts. According to him, a central world city is the interface where everything runs together. It administers the whole system and hence mainly participates in the process of shaping a conjoint culture for the whole world economy.

3. Present Global City Research Theories – Saskia Sassen and Mark Abrahamson

Contrary to Braudel, global city analysts want to depict the growing together of the world either as a new development or as a phenomenon that had changed its structure entirely during the last two to three decades. Saskia Sassen, who was among the first to coin the term global city, stated that she intentionally had not used one of the existing descriptions of major cities (world city, *supervilles*, etc.) because she attempted to show the difference between those types of cities, namely "the specificity of the global as it get structured in the contemporary period."[28] Most of the authors of global city studies have an economic or sociologic background. Consequently economic factors are the dominant element in their studies.

As the name global city research already indicates, scholars of that field are focused on cities as the major designers of the course of our planet. Sassen, for example, predicts that with the "partial unbundling or at least weakening of the national as a spatial unit due to privatization and deregulation and the associated strengthening of globalization, other spatial units or scales [such as the city] increasingly gain importance."[29]

Scholars like Saskia Sassen and Mark Abrahamson do not place value on history because of their concentration on the latest and, concededly, very spectacular developments. Hence, descriptions of the world system prior to the latest transformation towards a transnational urban system are rather rare.

All in all, the world prior to the outgoing 20th century, for them, was characterized by major industrial cities that were part of a city network within a nation state.[30] The nation state, however, was the dominant spatial unit.[31] The important shift towards a city dominated world wide urban system, according to them, took place during the late 1970's respectively the early 1980's. Ever since,

---

28 Sassen, global city, xix.
29 Sassen, global city, xviii.
30 Abrahamson, global city, p.3.
31 Sassen, global city, xviii; Abrahamson, global city, p.1.

companies in many cities of the world dramatically have increased the amount of business they conducted in other regions,[32] and many firms have become worldwide in their provision of services.[33] At one swell, the level of transnational investment increased dramatically. That means that such fields as international tourism and exports of culture goods (movies, music, styles, and fashion) increased too. And the people, products, and new ideas all suddenly moved with unsurpassed speed among the major cities of the world.[34] Those increased linkages, according to Abrahamson, became a global network, with global cities as key nodes and interfaces.[35]

For Sassen, the changing point when old economic orders were overthrown took place sometimes during the 1980's when the importance of the national as a spatial unit began to decrease as a result of privatization, deregulation, digitalization, the opening up of national economies to foreign firms, and the growing participation of national economic actors in global markets.[36] The loss of the importance of the nation state as a spatial unit paved the way for other organizational units. Sassen locates the emergence of global cities in this context.[37] Similar to Abrahamson, she stresses the emergence of a transnational urban system as a modern world system dominated and stimulated by hierarchically ordered global cities.[38]

The most important means to measure the status of a global city is to question how it has responded to the challenge of globalization. For Abrahamson, the best answer of a city on what he described as the challenge of globalization [posed by the latest wave of globalization since the 1970's] is the transformation of its economy into the "new postindustrial mode."[39] He stated that those cities that were able most quickly to attract as many transnational corporations and their specialized service firms as possible became the leading global cities and the centers of the global system.[40] Similar to Braudel, Abrahamson also detects a hierarchy among the global cities. At the center, he locates four leading cities (New York, London, Tokyo, Paris) with New York as the most important global

---

32 Abrahamson, global city, p.1.
33 Taylor, city network, p. 57.
34 Abrahamson, global city, p.2.
35 Abrahamson, global city, p.2.
36 Sassen, global city, xviii.
37 Sassen, global city, xvix.
38 Sassen, global city, xxi.
39 Abrahamson, global city, p.4.
40 Abrahamson, global city, p.4.

city leading the field of top-level global cities.[41] He further stated that the global linkages and cultural institutions do not have uniform effects within a city or a metropolitan area. Just like Braudel, he detected something like a core and a periphery. He described that foreign capital commonly targets the commercial and financial center of a city, while its fringes usually come away empty-handed.[42] On the other hand he recognizes that economical sectors and the workforce connected to international trade, finance, or tourism are also likely to benefit directly from more transnational connections. Other groups such as blue-collar workers are more apt to be adversely affected.[43] Like Braudel, he mentions also the problem of price increases.[44] According to him, a further particularity of global cities is their model role in the creation of a widely accepted culture. Although the term global culture diffuses throughout the world, the cultural industries that transmit it are concentrated in a few global cities (New York, Los Angeles, London, Paris, Tokyo). He regards the cultural industries of those cities as the major conveyers of ideas and values, influencing the way people act, think, and feel.[45] Last but not least, Abrahamson connects global cities to the term "hyperrationality". For him, hyperrationality plays an important role in shaping a global urban culture. It emerges as a trend of "demystification" in Western Societies and today has become a pervasive feature of everyday life in postindustrial global cities.[46]

For Saskia Sassen, the term global city is even more connected to the economy. She describes global cities as agglomeration economies with large companies and their corresponding specialized service firms. According to her, the mix of firms, talents, and expertise from a broad range of specialized fields creates a certain type of urban environment functioning as information center. Being in a city becomes synonymous with being in an extremely intense and dense information loop. That loop cannot be fully replicated in electronic space.[47] Because of the process of outsourcing, transnational companies attract various different specialized service firms around their headquarters in global cities.[48] She states that the "key sector, specifying the distinctive production advantages of global

---

41 Abrahamson, global city, p.164.
42 Abrahamson, global city, p.7.
43 Abrahamson, global city, p.8.
44 Abrahamson, global city, p.8.
45 Abrahamson, global city, p.15.
46 Abrahamson, global city, p.12.
47 Sassen, global city, xx.
48 Sassen, global city, xx.

cities is exactly that highly specialized and networked service sector."[49] For her, the number of firms of that sector is more important for a global city than the number of transnational corporations. These service firms need to provide a global service, which means that they had to be connected to a global network of affiliates or some other form of partnership. That results in the strengthening of cross border city to city transactions and networks. According to her, this may well be the beginning of the formation of a transnational urban system.[50] Sassen also describes the increasing inequality which is also evident in other theories. According to her, the growing number of high-level professionals and high-profit making specialized service firms has the effect of raising the degree of spatial and socioeconomic inequality in these cities.[51] As a result, the growing gap between the poor and rich led to the increasing informalization of a wide range of economic activities "which find their effective demand in these cities yet have profit rates that do not allow them to compete for various resources with the high profit making firms at the top of the system."[52]

Similar to Sassen, Peter Taylor is also focused on economic activities. For him the world system consists mainly of a network of service firms operating at at a global scale that is located in cities. He characterized them as agencies. He principally detected four actors that shape the world city network. Those actors are service firms, city governments, service institutions and nation states.[53] These actors characterize the development of cities, according to him. Hence he stated: "Many contemporary world cities bear the mark of their makers."[54] He exemplifies that the cultural agency has made Los Angeles as a world media city, political agency has made Geneva an international institutional city, and economic agency has created Hong Kong as an international financial center.[55] Like Sassen, and Abrahamson, he detected a hierarchy among the cities. "The leading world cities are the result of all of these agencies created well-rounded world cities."[56] As examples, he mentioned London or New York that are not only important media, political, and financial centers, but much more than that. Although he mentioned the manifoldness of factors responsible for the shape of a global city network, he concentrated his studies on the economic agents and

---

49   Sassen, global city, xx.
50   Sassen, global city, xxi.
51   Sassen, global city, xxi.
52   Sassen, global city, xxi.
53   Taylor, city network, p. 58.
54   Taylor, city network, p. 57.
55   Taylor, city network, p. 57.
56   Taylor, city network, p. 57.

their creation of city networks. Following Sassen's point of view, the agents he concentrated upon are advanced producer service providers. Thisapplies to the traditional urban approach of researching inter-city relations through treating cities as service center points. According to him, cities need a critical mass of firms to produce the necessary knowledge environment that global companies critically need.[57] That joint reinforcing process is most important for the definition of world cities. Like Sassen and Abrahamson, he sees the origins of a world city system in the last decades of the 20th century. For him, from the 1980's onwards, many firms have become global in the provision of services. And these firms are located in cities because only cities provide the environment the service firms need to exist.

To conclude, Abrahamson, Taylor, as well as Sassen, describe the emergence of a new world system based on transnational urban connections sometimes during the last three decades of the 20th century. For them, the importance of the national as a spatial unit decreased as a result of privatization, deregulation, digitalization, the opening up of national economies to foreign firms, and the growing participation of national economic actors in global markets. As a result, the city as another important spatial unit gained importance. The most important players in the new world system are transnational corporations and their highly specialized service firms that had spanned a world wide web of connections to other companies in other global cities. Similar to Braudel, the authors recognized a hierarchy among global cities with only a fistful of cities on the top of the system. Those cities are the leading political, cultural, economical, and social centers of the world predetermining the economical and cultural direction of the whole world system.

4. Suggested Spatial Ground Rules for an Examination of the Measurability of the Process of Globalization

So far, we have summarized some of the most important world city and global city theories. In certain respects, the authors' opinions differ widely. But astonishingly we could detect much communality too.

In this section we want to depict some characteristics that can be useful for understanding and examining globalization. In order not to get lost in the manifoldness of data and explanations, a good starting point could be a glance at spaces of compression.[58] There are many suggestions of what such spaces could be. The role of cities as important spaces of compression, however still is not

---

57 Taylor, city network, p. 57.
58 Conrad and Eckert, Globalgeschichte, p.20.

really accepted in modern world history research works.[59] The abundant global city literature, presented above, is mainly ignored in historical studies, although it would allow a concrete approach, namely the "connection of on the ground research with the interpretations of a history of interactions."[60]

The core-periphery scheme coining the structure of our world is a striking communality of global city as well as world city concepts. Such a scheme can help isolating spaces of compression for a globalization study. All of the described scholars locate an urban core area at the heart of the world system. According to Saskia Sassen, Peter Taylor, Mark Abrahamson, as well as Fernand Braudel, a fistful of particularly important cities act as epicenters of the whole system. They serve as urban centers of gravity, as the logistic heart of the system. A network of urban agglomerations connected to each other interlaminates the hierarchically structured system. A world city (Braudel, Taylor) or several global cities (Abrahamson, Sassen) are at the top of the hierarchy. Those cities are leading economic and cultural centers and creative think-thanks, attracting people from all over the system. A global or world city hence must somehow be a melting pot that affiliates different people within its boundaries. The manifoldness of live within such cities leads to the invention and consistent reinvention of a culture that integrates influences from all over the world system. For global cities are dominant within their system, more peripheral areas emulate the global city and adopt its culture. The vital effectualness of a global city makes it the main actor in the field of shaping a widespread (or sometimes even a worldwide) culture.

A further interesting commonality all authors described can be seen in the deteriorating living conditions of a city that lead to increased social segmentation. Especially increases in the costs of living worsen the living conditions of the poor and leads to a growing divide between the poor and rich. All authors blamed the phenomenon of inflation for these developments.

The term hyperrationality, according to modern global city research plays an important role in characterizing the process of globalization in a modern global or world city. Abrahamson offers a conclusive explication that fits into the long history of globalization too. For him, hyperrationality has its origins in the emergence of the trend of "demystification" that begun in Western European cities during the Renaissance period 400 to 500 years ago.[61] From that point on,

---

59 Mathias Midell and Katja Naumann, "Global History 2008-2010: Empirische Erträge, konzeptionelle Debatten, neue Synthesen," in: Comparativ – Zeitschrift für Globalgeschichte und vergleichende Gesellschaftsforschung 20 (2010): 93-133, 104.
60 Midell and Naumann, Global History, p. 104.
61 Abrahamson, global city, p.12.

magical beliefs, superstition, and rituals were playing an ever-diminishing role in most people's everyday lives. In the course of the beginning globalization and integration of more and more cities into a world wide urban network, science spread and the trend was adopted. Firstly, the automatization of manufacturing processes demanded a highly "rational control over the entire production process."[62] In postindustrial urban societies, the emphasis on rationality may have become excessive, resulting in hyperrationality that has become a pervasive feature of everyday life.[63]

Such characteristics surface in all concepts and hence could be interesting indicators for global elements in humankind's development.

5. Temporal Parameters for a Historical Globalization Study

The question when globalization actually had begun is among the most discussed within the discipline. There are as many opinions as there are authors describing the phenomenon. The following section will try to suggest a conclusive possible point of departure for a broad examination of the process of globalization.

In our view, the selection of a spatial framework depends on the definition of globalization. According to Robertson's definition we regard globalization as a process of compression of the world as well as the intensification of consciousness of the world as a whole.[64] Considering that definition, the roots of globalization's history could be detected in long 16th century. During that period, oceanic navigation made a connection of all parts of the world possible and networks between the different world economies became more and more striking. Hence some parts of the world, for the first time, got an idea what worldwide linkages are.

At that time, many parts of the world experienced an economical and cultural boom caused by enormous increases in world trade. Not only core areas in Europe benefitted from that development. To offer two small examples, Chinese trade cities increasingly adopted European and Japanese and American silver as a monetary base instead of their collapsed paper money system during that time.[65] Japanese and Chinese cities experienced population increases caused by improved diet from goods of other areas of the world brought to them by trade

---

62 Abrahamson, global city, p.12.
63 Abrahamson, global city, p.13.
64 Robertson, Globalization, p. 8.
65 Dennis O'Flynn and Arturo Giraldez, "Globalization began in 1571," in: Barry K. Gills and William R. Thompson, eds., Globalization and Global History (New York: Routledge, 2006): 232-247, 241.

activities.[66] At the same time, Indian metropolitan cultures vanished at a result of the connection of that area to the rest of the world.[67] Hence the long 16th century offers a good starting point.

Because of the diversity of humankind's history, a history of globalization is not a linear narrative of a constant growing together of the world, as Peter Stearns put it in his "Globalization in World History" book.[68] There were always certain periods when networks among the world's regions were more evident as well as periods characterized by separation and dissociation. Further more, the depiction of a continuous globalization timeline is additionally complicated because processes of connecting and separation sometimes take place at the same time. As Eckert and Conrad exemplify "economic interweaving processes sometimes went hand in hand with processes of political separation."[69] Hence a depiction of a linear development of the history of globalization within the ample framework of the world economy does not make sense. Instead, one rigorously should examine the whole period from the early 17th century until the present day in order to find out the booms and descends of the linking process of our world.

6. Conclusion

In this paper, we tried to give some insights into different understandings of the process of the increased interconnection of our world. By doing so, we tried to specify a basic approach for an examination of the measurability of the phenomenon of globalization. As we have seen above, such a complex subject needs a universal approach. For the term globalization describes compression of relations between different parts of our world[70] and the growing interweaving of different spaces[71], we recommend focusing on spaces of compression. Fields worth to consider, according to Conrad an Eckert, could be the economic integration, the changing relationship between state and market, cultural homogenization, as well as changes in the conception of time and space initiated by technological change.[72] we have seen above that world system theorists as well as

---

66   Ronald Findlay and Kevin H. O'Rouke, Commodity Market Integration, 1500-2000. National Bureau of Economic Research Working Paper 8579, 9.
67   For more information on that topic, see: Sheldon Watts, Epidemics and History: Disease Power and Imperialism (New Haven: Yale University, 1997).
68   Peter N. Stearns, Globalization in World History (London: Routledge, 2010), 159.
69   Conrad and Eckert, Globalgeschichte, p. 21.
70   Conrad and Eckert, Globalgeschichte, p. 20.
71   Conrad and Eckert, Globalgeschichte, p. 21.
72   Conrad and Eckert, Globalgeschichte, p.20.

global city analysts divide the world into world economies consisting of several spatial zones (core periphery scheme). Small but densely populated core regions dominate those spaces culturally as well as economically. (World or global) cities are such core spaces. They are highly linked informational centers where information, goods, and people from all over the world sytem(s) flow together. In other words, they are important media, political, cultural and financial centers and they shape and are shaped by worldwide connecting processes. The fields we suggest to consider above are particularly evident in those spaces. We can detect global elements more easily there. Because of their dominant role as interfaces of the whole system, global or world cities predetermine the economic as well as the cultural direction of the whole world economy. Hence, the creation of something like a global culture and the consequences of the compression of interregional relations must be best visible in such cities.

A temporal approach of an examination of globalization's history is even more difficult to find. There are many different suggestions from a variety of academic disciplines. All of them make sense for their specific research field. The choice of a temporal framework depends on the definition of globalization. For a study, we recommend the short but coherent definition of the sociologist Robert Robertson who stated that globalization "refers both to the compression of the world and the intensification of consciousness of the world as a whole".[73] According to that definition, it may seem logical to start an examination of the phenomenon of globalization with the extension of (apriori European) trade relations to the whole world during the 16th century, when networks between the different parts of the world attained global reach. Because of the diversity of humankind's history, a history of globalization could never be a linear narrative of a constant growing together of the world. There were always certain periods when networks among the world's regions were more evident, as well as periods of separation and dissociation. Instead, we suggest a rigorous examination of the whole period from the year 1600 until the present day in order to find out the booms and descends of our world's linking process. Because such a project would not be viable because of the enormous amount of data, we recommend focusing on global cities as spaces of compression. Case studies about some important global city regions in different parts of the world are an excellent starting point for such an examination that can help to finding answers to the questions, problems and challenges posed by the process of globalization.

---

73 Robertson, Globalization, p. 8.

Globalization and Global History
Two Sides of a Coin?

Bianca Winkler

While the study of global history is definitely inspired and influenced by processes of globalization, global history is neither the history of globalization nor a branch that necessarily works with a well defined concept of globalization. This paper therefore primarily focuses on the question of how the nature of the relationship between globalization and global history in theory and practice is actually constructed.

1. Definitions: What is global history?

History is an ever-changing branch of knowledge that primarily unites through a methodological angle. In practice historians work with sources – most of the time written texts; they analyze and interpret them for modern and past times. Theoretically and heuristically history has never been a united discipline – not in national borders or linguistically connected regions and of course neither so in an international context. For that reason history as an academic activity was also questioned. Sometimes the definition whether or not it can have a status among the sciences was and still is heavily dicussed,[1] while in other settings discussions focus more on the purposes and goals of history.[2] If one therefore wants to analyze historical works, schools or sub-branches – especially those as big as for

---

1   One of the classic discussions was raised by philosopher Karl Popper in the middle of the last Century through his book „The Poverty of Historicism" – more recent discussions were for example raised by american anthropologists like Robert Caneiro („The Muse of History and the Science of Culture) or in the German speaking area through the post-modernist discussions about the end of history. Compare Lutz Niethammer, Posthistorie: Ist die Geschichte zu Ende (Hamburg: Reinbeck, 1989).

2   Questions about the possibility of objectivity or the instrumentalization of history for (most of the time) political purposes have ancient roots (f.e. Leopold von Ranke famous citation that the purpose of history is an essential description of the past in the manner of Wie es eigentlich gewesen ist or the complete opposition to this position that was taken by philosopher Friedrich Nietzsche in his essay Vom Nutzen und Nachteil der Historie) still echo in the various modern dimensions of historical work but are seldom object of official discussions, because their solution is basically rooted in personal interest and choice. Philosophical discussions in an absolut dimension as they were fought out by the mentioned ancestors, therefore always had dead ends. Compare Georg Iggers, Geschichtswissenschaft im 20. Jahrhundert (Göttingen: Vandenhoek & Ruprecht, 1993).

example global history – one always needs to keep in mind the fragmented and multiperspectual aspects of history in theoretical and definitional respects as well as in and across national and linguistic borders. Global history or globalization, as a result, can in general only work as so-called umbrella terms – they might have a concrete definition for one and a completely different connotation for another historian. But despite this vagueness it can be established that for a majority of historians the terms *world* and *global* history serve synonymous functions.[3] Some voices even claim that global history is just a new and fashionable term for the longer existing tradition of writing world histories.[4] While world and global history can be used interchangeably a new sub-branch has emerged that calls itself the *new global history* and its practitioners explicitly claim that their activities differ from global/world history in important categories.[5] But however scholars talk about world, global or new global history, the fundamental similarity in all these approaches is their foundation in an epistemological concept of globalization – no matter if this concept is defined, proven or simply implied; the modern world and its special and intensified connectedness serves as the basic assumption in all kinds of world histories.

Historically as well as terminologically exists a transparent connection between global history and world system analysis or world system theory.[6] This relationship is also mirrored in the general globalization debates that started out in the discipline of sociology. There – as has been convincingly argued[7] - global-

3   Compare Peer Vries, "editorial: global history", in Global History, ed. Peer Vries et al. ÖZG 20/2 (2009): 5.
4   Especiallly American scholars seem share that sort of opinion. Vgl. Arif Dirlik, "Performing the World: Reality and Representation in the Making of World Histor(ies)", Journal of World History 16/4 (2005): 396. Or Michael Geyer and Charles Bright, "World History in a Global Age", The American Historical Review 100/4 (1995), 1034 – 1060.
5   American historian Bruce Mazlish can be counted as one of the founders of New Global History. His differentiation seems to have a postmodern influence because he bases his argument for a fundamental difference solely in the etymological connotation between the words world and global. He claims this argument quite a couple of times in his publications.
6   Lauren Benton „From the World-Systems Perspective to Institutional World History: Culture and Economy in Global Theory", Journal of World History 7/2 (1996), 261 – 295.
7   Compare f.e. Mauro F. Guillen, "Is Globalization Civilizing, Destructive or Feeble? A Critique of Five Key Debates in the Social Science Literature", Annual Review of Sociology 27 (2001): 238f. Or Roland Robertson who constructs a shift from modernization to globalization interests in sociology in the 1970s. Roland Robertson and Frank

ization became an increasingly popular and important topic as a reaction to Immanuel Wallersteins famous world system analysis that was built in the 1970`s. As well it was only after this time that global history emerged.[8] While Wallersteins theory itself was a kind of reaction to experienced outcomes that actual globalization processes had produced, an obvious connection can be stated between world-system theory and globalization studies. Since the 1970s literature concerning the topic *globalization* has steadily grown[9] – which could possibly be interpreted as a major indicator of globalization itself. But while the term is often discussed in the social sciences, in the historical discipline the word *globalization* at bottom fulfills the function of an inspirational anchor – because our world nowadays is so well connected historians are searching for similiar connections in past times or pointing out the differences between modern and past connections. Accordingly the word *globalization* in these writings is hardly ever discussed in a philosophical sense and rarely precisely defined. The english historian John Darwin represents a popular definition when he declares globalization to be a „slippery term".[10] But he – also viewable as a kind of mainstream – derives it in principle through an economic perspective with an additional modern aspect that is created mainly through modern media –especially TV and the internet. Interests in media and economy represent the heartland of globalization studies in general[11] as well as in global history. Methodologically global history approaches are in that regard manifold, but in congruence with Dominic Sachsenmaier it can be argued that global history expresses two fundamental directions: „[...] a global perspective on the human past [...or...] the history of globalization."[12]

While the theoretical aspects of global history are in no way uniform this also proves true for the field or timeframe to which global history and globalization can be applied. Peer Vries, f.e., points out the vague definitional precision

Lechner, "Modernization, Globalization and the Problem of Culture in World-Systems Theory", Theory-Culture-Society 2 (1985): 107.

8   Dominic Sachsenmaier has called especial attention to the fact that historians found the words global and globalization to be quite useful after their rise in the 1970s. Dominic Sachsenmaier, "Global History and Critiques of Western Perspective", Comparative Education 42/3 (2006): 454.

9   Guillen, "Is," (table 1) 240.

10   John Darwin, "Writing Global History (or Trying to)", in Global History, ed. Peer Vries et al. ÖZG 20/2 (2009): 60.

11   Roland Robertson, f.e., is prominent among those who critize an one sided orientation toward the „[...]hard realities (economic and political)[...]" in globalization studies. Robertson, "Modernization," 106.

12   Sachsenmaier, "Global History,"454.

in the term globalization for global historians. He shows that while Andre Gunder Frank and others view the beginning of a globalized world almost 5000
years ago, some economic historians would not even speak of a globalized
economy at the beginning of the 20th century.[13] While Wallerstein places the
rise of his conception of a world system in a time that the German tradition calls
Frühe Neuzeit beginning around the 15th century and Janet Abo-Lughod sees an
islamic world system that started to declined around the 13th century; some recent discussions place world or global history – based on a conception of globalization that roots in technology and/or financial politics – in the transition from
the 19th to the 20th century. This conception is connected to Karl Polanyis assumption of *The Great Transformation* that took place in the European lands in
the 19th century when *industrialization* began and the *nation state* arose. These
manifold interpretations and – in that context – wide implications do not solely
count for the term globalization that – a couple of times is as mentioned hardly
ever discussed – or the question when it came into being, but also for the definition of the whole branch may it be called world or global history. Mauro Guillen, who reviewed a bunch of interdisciplinary literature concerning definitions
of globalization, arrives at a similar conclusion. He divides globalization debates in three groups of scholars speaking of three different time frames: globalization starting with colonialisation processes in the 15th century; globalization
connected with modern technologies and the modern nation state beginning in
the 19th century and globalization starting in the 1970s defined as a result of the
nuclear age and the *pax americana*.[14] While the english-speaking historical tradition shares all of these interpretations, the german speaking area in general
prefers the conception of globalization starting with the beginning of the history
of mankind or in connection to the rise of capitalism in the 15th century or earlier.[15] The *new global history* also shares the assumption that globalization processes are a fundamental part of history and therefore do not dedicate themselves
to one specific period or region.[16] While important differences in scopes and in-

---

13   Peer Vries, "Global economic history: a survey", in Global History, ed. Peer Vries et al.
     ÖZG 20/2 (2009): 157.
14   Guillen, "Is", 237.
15   In Vienna the most prominent group working within the branch of global history is ar-
     ranged around professor Peter Feldbauer who edited (in international cooperation) a book
     series called Globalgeschichte: Die Welt 1000 - 2000 – which shares a very broad defini-
     tion of processes of globalization and places global history – as the title indicates – be-
     ginning around the year 1000 if not earlier.
16   So at least says a mission-statement on their homepage.
     http://www.newglobalhistory.com/mission.html accessed March, 10 2012.

terpretation can still be manifested it is an obvious side-effect of globalization itself that historians all around the globe tend to communicate more and connections are increasing.[17]

2. Historical Origins: Global history as an expression of a globalized world

Writing some kind of world history was most of the time not a tradition that was concerned with a heuristic coverage of writing about the actual world but a concentration on current circumstances and their extrapolation in the past and in the future. These approaches are generally called philosophies of history; they date back in ancient times and are proponents of different cultures. They also cover a wide range between completely ahistorical theorizations (f.e. Macchiavellis theory about the rise of states or Vicos world stages) and so called antecedents of a scientific historical method (f.e. Ibn Khalduns circle theory of nomadic and civilized life). In the 18th and 19th centuries at the foundation of new academic disciplines like economics, anthropology and sociology a lot of general theories had a kind of world-historical twist, best known examples are Adam Smith's economic theories or Marxist models about the run of world history. Therefore the inspirational influence of globalization to world and global history becomes clear through the sharp break modern historians make between traditional models of world history – that are mainly associated with universal history – and modern approaches that fundamentally try to escape determinism and eurocentrism. As Jack Goldstone points out: „In the 1970s, when I began graduate study, world history did not exist as a field of study in doctoral programs. Indeed, it had a rather bad odor about it, being associated with sprawling and abstract schemes imposed on the history of varied nations and time-periods, as in the work of Arnold Toynbee and Oswald Spengler.“[18] A dichotomie between old and new globalization approaches can also be seen in economics, anthropology and sociology where *modernization-* approaches – who also claimed a total world scope but have been discriminating in certain respects – were exchanged against more appropriate accessions to non-european histories and cultures. The inspirational influence for this shift in academic culture definitively came from anthropology where the *eurocentrism* critiques became a central theme in the 1970s and therefore motivated beginning globalization studies in important di-

---

17 Sachsenmaier, "Global History", 464.
18 Jack A. Goldstone, "From Sociology and Economics to World History", in Global History, ed. Peer Vries et al. ÖZG 20/2 (2009): 75.

mensions.[19] While Clifford Geertz critique on traditional methods of writing anthropological history became a prominent argument in eurocentrism-debates a
step into writing global or globalicing histories was only taken by a few anthropologists. The best known example is propably represented by Eric Wolf and his
book *Europe and the people without history* which has been more influential in
global history than in academic anthropology.

While in the german speaking area protagonists are only talking about
Globalgeschichte but not *Weltgeschichte*; in the English speaking world the
terms world and global history are used interchangeably – as has already been
argued. Therefore especially the American tradition hints at the differences between old and new ways of writing world history. Michael Geyer and Charles
Bright, for example, declare world history to be an always existing ambition that
was never taken seriously in academic circles but becomes fruitful and important in modern days where *globality* is an obvious condition of everyday life all
around the globe. With that argument they not only suggest the existence of an
explicit link from globalization to world history but also defend the necessity of
a global history through globalization. In their words: „[...] the world we live in
has come into its own as an integrated globe, yet it lacks narration and has no
history. [...] Global integration is a fact [...] the world before us has a history to
be explained."[20] While this appears as a pretty obvious argument the implication
is not always quite clear, for there are scholars in global history who do not
practice an integrated global accession that focuses on one world but rather defend more particularistic positions. Some of them who share theoretical ambitions do so in constructing alternative concepts to globalization – especially with
regard to the concepts of culture -, because globalization as a general worldwide
trend does not only produce directional uniformity but also new differentiations
and fragmentations. Thoughts like these stand for a general debate in globalization studies and have been mirrored in theoretical considerations, but not primarily or widely among historians. Sociologist Roland Robertson for example developed his conception of *glocalization*, which serves as a theoretical coverege
for local reactions on global phenomena.[21] Other conceptions working in the
same direction have been termed for example *indigenization, creolization, hybridization* etc. But while, or because, globalization as a theoretical concept has

---

19   Compare f.e. Benton, "From", 270.
20   Geyer, "World", 1037.
21   „[...] glocalization [...] recognizes that globalization in part features the critical construc-
     tion and reinvention of local cultures vis-a-vis other cultural entities." Richard Giulianotti
     and Roland Robertson, „Glocalization, Globalization and Migration: The Case of Scot-
     tish Football Supporters in North America", International Sociology 21/2 (2006): 172.

not really entered into theoretical discussions among historians (yet) these various terms have done neither so in a broader perspective.[22] In this regard and for the spirit of escaping eurocentrism or monocausal globalization determinisms it is quite helpful to not have a defined concept of globalization, as a lot of historians do. By adding stories of all around the world and various times global history can be constructed through some sort of practical particularity without being bothered by philosophical questions. Proponents of the Austrian tradition, for example, claim some kind of connectedness but construct it most of the time solely through adding aspects and experts.[23] In this direction globalization is neither defined nor proven, but at least it is implied. This seems to be a broad trend among worldwide historians who want to capture a kind of totality in history which is justified through the concept of globalization. Richard Grew f.e. argues, that eurocentrism or other desciminating concepts can be escaped through global history which "[...] seems to invite limitless inclusion."[24] On the other side academics also try to counterargument aspects of globalization. As Marjorie Ferguson pointed out, processes of myth making can be a way more fruitful and valid exploration in globalization studies than the assumed globality of certain „myths". Her argumentation therefore indicates that globalization is sometimes more projected and claimed than actually existing.[25]

In sum none could renounce some kind of globalization but as Guillen has shown critics are based on in solid argumentation when they criticize the circumstances, for globalization is most of the time simply assumed and not proven.[26]

---

22 Especially Sachsenmaier echoes postcolonial and postmodern criticisms on world history and calls attention to their impetus and integration. But for him this is a task to be done and not a goal that has been achieved yet. Sachsenmaier, "Global History," 459.

23 The volume collection Globalgeschichte for example includes a lot of experts, regions and timeframes and therefore creates in sum a global approach while most of the single articles do neither establish nor altercate concepts of globalization nor how the concept inspired or influenced their work.

24 Raymond Grew, "On Seeking Global History`s Inner Child", Journal of Social History 38/4 (2005): 849 + 853.

25 „[...] there is a significant aspect of globalization that goes relatively unremarked: its rhetoric is as much concerned about what should be as what is.[original italics]" Marjorie Ferguson, "The Mythology About Globalization", European Journal of Communication 7 (1992): 73.

26 Guillen, "Is", 240.

3. Origins: Global History and World-Systems

There has obviously been some kind of „global" interest in the traditional historical approaches of the philosophies of history based on grand narratives, but
the institutional origins of modern global history derive from some branches of
sociology and anthropology and show a significant connection to the world-
system theories from quite famous protagonists as Immanuel Wallerstein, Andre
Gunder Frank and Janet Abu-Lughod. Their often quoted works are historically
rooted in the economic crises of the 1970s which was caused by the globalization processes of the world economy and their various effects on national
economies and politics. All the global and world historians pay lip-service to the
fact that the connectedness of the modern world – or in other terms globalization
in all its various dimensions – was the heuristic starting point for global and
world history. In that respect Eric Vanhaute calls it a „child of its time" while at
the same time defining global history through what it is not and pointing out that
among other arguments „(i)t is not globalization studies focusing on and starting
from current processes within global society."[27] Of course some historians
would clearly disagree with that definition, especially but not only those that are
inspired by an economic perspective.

   One of the basic questions in global history is rooted in the current state of
affairs of a western economy that dominates and partially dictates the world
market and per definition asks for an explanation of this situation as well as its
historical roots – despite various critiques of this assumption as being *eurocentric*. The basic question behind world-system theories is when they came into
beeing, what their basic characteristics were and which factors might influence
and change them. While – as mentioned – Andre Gunder Frank sees the beginning of a world system interconnected with the rise of the first states 5000 years
ago and Janet Abu-Lughod posited the theory of a kind of world-system economy prior to modern capitalism in the oriental middle ages; a great tenor connects world-system theory with modernization theory and therefore with the
Great Divergence – a theoretical discussion orginally based on Karl Polanyis's
conception of different forms of societies rooted in completely contrasting
economies respectively economic politics that basically evolved in the 19th century.[28] Most of the early or traditional global historians – especially as far as they

---

27   Eric Vanhaute, "Who is afraid of Gobal History? Ambitions, pitfalls and limits of learn-
     ing global history", in Global History, ed. Peer Vries et al. ÖZG 20/2 (2009): 26.
28   While Polanyi himself was not talking about a Great Divergence – a term strongly asso-
     ciated with eurocentrism critiques -, the discussion of europoean speciality in economic
     regard is strongly connected to Polanyis assumption that capitalism is a defined phe-

made fruitful excursions into theory building – rooted their interest in the topic or the question *why Europe?* [29] This question was built on the outspoken assumption that Europe went on a kind of *Sonderweg* because it developed the potential to conquer the world through colonization.

While these questions about Europe's economic specialities also characterize Wallerstein's basic interests, his influence on disciplinary history and globalization studies pointed in a different direction. He had been especially reviewed among prominent historians and sociologists who criticized his model, his theory and the interpretations of facts that he fit into his theory; but who nevertheless appreciated the questions asked by Wallerstein and who worked in the same intellectual direction. As Theda Skocpol pointed out: „For the true contribution of *The Modern World System* will lie not in the proliferation of empirical research based uncritiqually upon it, but in the theoretical controversies and advances it can spark among its friends."[30] Wallerstein himself can hardly be mentioned among historians because his basic interest lied in the conceptualization of a macro-theory which he derived through a deductive method while historians in general methodologically stand in an inductive tradition. A lot of the basic criticisms on Wallersteins theory therefore came from a historical side that claimed his theory to not fit historical facts but theoretical defenders of a scientific approach in merely sociological sciences can always argue that a grand theory does not only not have to fit every fact – because the benefit lies somewhere else – but on the other side that no general theory can fit every particularity. Stanley Aronowitz for example defended Wallerstein's theoretical system in that manner: „The perspective that structure is prior to particular aspects is shared by social theorists, [...] who hold that the abstract is, under certain conditions, more concrete than particularities because it establishes, at least potentially, the possibility of making links between apparently disparate parts."[31] It is especially this theoretical gap between social scientists and historians – for whom the sources

---

nomenon of european culture and not a feature of every human society. This is the contrary position to modernization theories that posited a necessity for the development of modern capitalism for every society because – in their view – capitalism grants the best standard of living for humanity or – from a marxist position – it is a stage that needs to be past for achieving communism (or other „better" forms of society).

29 The quite famous Austrian historian Michael Mitterauer even titled one of his most prominent books with exactly that question.

30 Theda Skocpol, "Wallerstein's World Capitalist System: A Theoritcal and Historical Critique", Journal of Sociology 82/5 (1977): 1076.

31 Stanley Aronowitz, "A Metatheoretical Critique of Immanuel Wallerstein`s ‚The Modern World System'", Theory and Society 10/4 (1981): 505.

always have priority and who therefore claim every theory that does not stand up to the facts invalid – that caused a harsh and rapid disqualification of Wallerstein's theory in the historical sciences in general but especially in the German speaking area. While theories like Wallerstein's served as an inspirational anchor for building new world or global histories, the basic outputs of historians were in general refutations and criticisms about such kinds of general claims. Neverthetheless there existed some kind of a lobby of economic historians who wanted to solve the puzzle of european expansion and the rise of capitalism.[32] Globalization in that regard was not a theoretical concept but a fact and it was rooted in a kind of *Europeanization* and *Americanization* of the world. There was no need to define and specify globalization but an interest in explaining the roots of economic globalization. In the discipline of history the biggest recent discussion was inspired by Kenneth Pomeranz for whom Europe's special historical stance came primarily from ecological benefits and who therefore argues that it was Europe's special fate to develop this kind of capitalism and not an achievement of people or politics. Never mind what the origins where: the globalization process in economic history is a trend going from Europe outward into the world and as such is always treated as a fact and is itself never questioned.

4. Research Interests and basic questions in global history

A majority of global history approaches is directly rooted in economic history and a strong connection between global approaches and economic approaches still dominates the majority of the field. This orientation was originally based on the great question how the „West" became to abuse and dominate the rest of the world and through which mechanisms and methods this domination was achieved. In modern days these questions partially remain but the focus shifted, from the premise that the „West" through some special features dominates the world to the question whether or not one can even speak of a western domination. The so-called California school is prominent among those who deny that capitalism is a special feature of „the West" and who therefore counterargument theoretical traditions that are based on Polanyis assumption or other defenders of *The Great Divergence*. But of course this is essentially a question of the definition of capitalism that is intended. The historian Jack Goldstone is therefore right when he subsumes a dead end of these discussions by claiming that „[t]he

---

32　The huge discussions about the rise, features and causes of capitalism and its modern economic features is way out of scope of this present paper and partly way to specific to be touched hear – but for further interest I want to mention at least some important protagonists from the historical branch like Robert Brenner, Jan de Vries, Paolo Malanima, Roger Schofield etc.

patterns of capitalism seemed to go back as far as civilization, if one looked at the right places."[33] While no one would deny that some patterns of modern capitalism definitely share that feature, the word capitalism and how it is defined also always represent fluent concepts that are continuously terms of discussions.

While global history through the connection to economic world history and world system analysis has been a defined concept in the 70s today some protagonists continue in an economic and/or grand-narrative tradition, while others criticize basic economic orientations and focus their interests on cultures in global history or globalization processes. One example for the first group is represented by Peer Vries, for whom the basic impulse for global history definitely comes from the economic side. He points to the fact that „[t]alking about the Great Divergence [...] means talking about economic phenomena." But he reveals a niche for other kinds of global histories as well „Fortunately many scholars do not lose sight of the very intense interconnections between what we call economic realm and that of (geo-) politics, military, or for that matter, cultural matters."[34] Still it is a long way from mentioning various aspects and combining them in books to really working in defined new concepts – especially for the words globalization and global history this proves very difficult. Global history – it seems – only appears as a fashionable antonym to national history – that is ipso facto out of fashion. This point is represented through a couple of unprecise definitional argumentations who cover the heuristic necessity and substance of global history but cannot argue it as a theoretical discipline. An example for this kind of vague definitions is for instance Eric Vanhaute who defines global history explicitly not through globalization processes but contradictorily characterizes its innovative aspects and basic strengths as: „The added value of world history is that it provokes new questions and proposes alternative ways of looking at the past by integrating the concepts of community, comparison, connection and system."[35] These are nice catchphrases but they do not give any methodological advice. In the same manner Jürgen Osterhammel also lacks a precise definition and solely mentions that the whole project of a global history would be „[...]meaningless without some kind of a comparative approach".[36]

---

33 Goldstone, "From", 81.
34 Vries, "Economic", 156.
35 Vanhaute, "Who", 38.
36 Jürgen Osterhammel, "Global History in a National Context: The Case of Germany", in Global History, ed. Peer Vries et al, ÖZG 20/2 (2009): 43.

5. Global history proves Globalization – or vice versa?

While in sociology and anthropology the focus of current processes in globalization studies shifted from explicit premises to variable concepts that try to capture connections and reactions in a broad and additively total perspective with respect to various aspects – especially *culture* – in history the term *globalization* still mainly serves heuristic functions and therefore lacks philosophical or terminological precision. It seems transparent that the possibility of proving or to disprove *globalization* in or through historical works depends on the definition of globalization that is intended. But if globalization serves as the heuristic starting point for global history it would be a tautology to prove it solely through combining world histories – as most historians do. For them – as for a majority of social scientists – globalization serves as an implicit assumption. It is implicit because WE witness it every day – therefore proving the process as such seems obsolete. In this regard the concept of globalization or globality does not need to be argued – at least not in a theoretical perspective. It becomes valid and legitimized through the history that is written in accordance to the presence facing processes that need to be explained in historical terms.[37] This kind of history is rooted in an additive conception of scientific history – there are multiple histories to be told and the enterprise becomes fruitful by collecting them. For the question of proving global history through globalization only the economic discussions about the rise of capitalism seems to have some value. If these questions are worked out within substantial definitions and contents they can have the possibility to prove at least one direction and that would be proving globalization through global history.[38]

---

37 The fundamental argument of the positive scientific or humanitarian function that history can serve for a lot of historians lies in its explanational value for the present. Therefore world history is necessary for conceptualizing the one world we now live in. As Feldbauer et al. argue: „Wäre die Welt mit der Globalisierung wirklich in eine völlig neue, alle historischen Wurzeln kappende und folglich mit Nichts vergleichbare Epoche eingetreten, dann hätte das Studium vergangener Zeiten deutlich an Reiz verloren [...] Zum Glück – und man muss leider sagen: auch zum Unglück – ist es anders gekommen. Die ‚alten Leidenschaften' der Vergangenheit haben sich gegen das neue System erhoben, und die Welt des freien Waren-, Kapital- und Informationsverkehrs des beginnenden 21. Jahrhunderts sieht sich von zahlreichen sehr geschichtsträchtigen Faktoren gestört." Peter Feldbauer and Jean-Paul Lehners, „Globalgeschichte: Die Welt 1000 – 2000", in Die Welt im 16. Jahrhundert, ed. Peter Feldbauer and Jean Paul Lehners (Wien: Magnus/Mandelbaum 2008), 8.

38 „[...]how to actually prove the existence of world-wide economic conjunctures [...] Their existence might be a good indicator of globalization [sic!]." Vries, "Economic", 159.

6. Conclusions

I have tried to make transparent that the totality of operations and connotations sciences have projected in the word globalization is substantially reflected in the branch of global history, that per definition needs a phenomenon of globalization for legitimizing its additive value for the scientific enterprise but often counterarguments globalization through fragmented and particular histories that solely are posited in a new area or time frame. Therefore these two words are methodologically speaking two sides of the same coin. And they are so as well theoretically or philosophically – one can only be proven through the other, at least in the definitions used by historians, and are therefore rooted in a tautological circle hence posit themselves as two equal sides of a coin.

City museums in the age of globalization
Representation of metropolitan diversity

Makiko Ruike

Compression of time and space through advanced information technology and means of transportation made it possible for people, commodity, capital and information to move around the globe so fast that many parts of the world became more similar than ever. With the term 'globalization' people usually understand such unifying forces or the process of common economic, political and cultural practices spreading around the globe. Globalization certainly shows these characteristics. However, at the same time, localised commodities, surging local identities, or religious fundamentalism prove that difference still means a lot and the process of differentiation even intensified utilizing the very technology and means which propelled globalization.

One of the reasons for the equivocality of the term 'Globalization' is the difficulty to understand the dialectical relationship of these seemingly mutually opposing tendencies, universalization and particularization, or globalization and localization. As Appadurai put it, this dialectical relationship is "the politics of the mutual effort of sameness and difference to cannibalize one another and thereby proclaim their successful hijacking of the twin Enlightenment ideas of the triumphantly universal and the resiliently particular."[1] Sameness and difference, or global universality and local particularity are no longer seen as opposing dispositions, but two sides of the same coin, interacting and causing drastic restructurings of societies. In this paper, I would like to show this cannibalization of sameness and difference in the city to see the dynamic interrelation between global and local.[2] Then, I argue the centrality of identity politics in this dynamics, and city museums, as a municipal institution supported partly by private sponsors, are good case studies to see the struggle to represent diversified identities characteristic of the era of globalization.

---

1   Aryun Appadurai, Modernity at Large: Cultural Dimensions of Globalization (Minneapolis: University of Minnesota Press, 1996), 43.
2   I limit my argument only to metropolises (not global cities), as the interaction between local and global might show completely different pictures in cities in the Third World and in cities of smaller size in developed countries. Particularly, my dissertation focuses on three cities, London, Tokyo and Vienna.

1. The local and the global in a place

Treating global and local as two opposing concepts would be strategic and useful in discussing economic, political, or environmental issues. Globalization could be understood as interrelations and connectedness across national borders, and localization as an adaptation of these global flows at a particular place. However, when it comes to symbols, meanings and socio-cultural implications carried by those global flows, things are more complicated. Unlike economics or politics, which is relatively institutionalized and whose powers to decide the line between global and local is to some extent possible to locate, there is no strong cultural institutions which authorize the line.

If we look into a place, we cannot see so easily which part of it has global origins or local origins because the global and the local are relative. Certainly, there are things which can be called as global, whose activity or meaning prevail across the globe. The recent financial crisis can be called a global phenomena as most part of the globe would have been more or less affected. There are undeniable global flows of people, capital, commodities, information, ideas and technologies. However, they are not always perceived as 'global' in terms of their contents. For example, the global financial system can be seen as the domination of the West, and 'cosmopolitans' or 'managerial elites' who work in multinational corporations can be seen to be just forming a small closed society. Global flows of people, for example immigrants, certainly come from a certain place and they are recognized more with their area or country of origin, rather than as global people. Once they are uprooted and move around the globe, it can be called global. However, when it comes to be relocated in a certain fixed place, their globality has different implications, as all commodities, information and people on global flows have their own cultural connotation, which are recognized differently in different places.[3] And the local is mostly recognised in relation to the 'global'. 'Local' culture or 'local' products might have historically non-local origin, but they become 'local' because they have been adapted in the place for a long time, and they are just more 'local' than new things brought by the recent global flows. The local can be anything which does not give any feeling of threatening, in contrast to the 'global' which is new, different, and threat-

---

3   Robertson has popularized the term "Glocalization" to show the importance of locality in understanding globalization. Roland Robertson, "Glocalization: Time – Space and Homogeneity – Heterogeneity," in Global Modernities, ed. Mike Featherstone (London: Sage Publications, 1995), 28-32. See also Allen J. Scott, The Cultural Economy of Cities: Essays on the Geography of Image-Producing Industries (London: Sage Publications, 2000), 29.

ens the familiarity of the locality. Therefore, there is nothing ontologically global or local in a strict sense.

However, this is not to reject the locality of a place, "a historically produced spatiotemporal neighbourhood" and the existence of "series of localized rituals, social categories, expert practitioners, and informed audiences" which make local subjects.[4] Rather, I argue, because there is nothing ontologically global and local, it is important to know how the local is created continuously through the existing historically produced locality of places, using new resources brought by the global flows.

Borrowing Appadurai's concept of the dual character of locality,[5] I understand that locality functions as structures to control the reception of the global flows. At the same time, they also act as agencies for social changes together with the new resources brought by the global flows, and consequently restructure the locality. This dual character of locality produces transformative dynamics of places and different pictures of impact of the global flows from place to place. The re-structuring of societies under the impact of globalization therefore ramifies according to the locality. They can be an existing legal system, the composition of the population influencing the reception of the global flows, or historically accumulated social and cultural capital. However at the same time they instil some elements of the global flows, and can be a restructuring force in the local. Here we see how the global and the local are 'inextricably and irreversibly bound together through a dynamic relationship."[6] Globalization and localization is not reducible to different geographical levels, but the local is produced through the interaction of both global and local.

Local and global are always mixing up to produce new locality, and such dynamics are the motor of development of cities in their long history. However, the difficulty in the time of information technologies and mass media is that there is so much information that intermediates this mixing-up process. When new resources flow into a place, they come with countless meanings supported by symbols, images and texts and these meanings are constantly reinforced or newly re-interpreted by means of information technologies, which connect places far away from each other.[7] Especially in cities, where global flow of peo-

---

4   Appadurai, Modernity at Large, 185.

5   Ibid., 182-188.

6   John Urry, Global Complexity (Cambridge: Polity, 2003), 84.

7   Appadurai named "the nation-state, diasporic flows, and electronic and virtual communities" as sources to complicate the production of locality. Appadurai, Modernity at Large, 198. I have reservation about including the nation-state, as the relationship between the nation-state and the city can now be different from the one at the time of his writing.

ple and commodities flow in at an unprecedented scale and speed, people come from far away places and stay, while they could continue to watch the same TV programs, to read the same newspaper, to eat the same food and keep close contact with people as they did at their place of origin. Therefore, the locality of a city is no longer produced only by the people and things physically there. The sources of locality are all over the world. 'Us' and 'others' are sharing more or less the space they live in, while they imagine their living spaces in very different ways, depending on their background and information that is accessible. Therefore, producing locality involves a struggle over who decides 'local', namely, who decides what social activity should be practiced, how the local should be imagined and constructed. It is now more difficult for a place to produce a shared local sense of 'us' based on the same social practices and images of a place.

2. The Centrality of identity politics in a globalized society

However, globalization would not simply erase the local sense of 'us'. Despite the weakening power of nation-states, they are nonetheless setting the stage for powerful political borders. And, very interestingly, we see the revival of community.[8] This is because of the people's longing for a sense of security and belonging in societies where social changes are unprecedentedly fast and complex. People feel threatened when they loose familiarity or their uniqueness due to modern capitalism or globalization. Richard Sennett put it as follows, "One of the unintended consequences of modern capitalism is that it has strengthened the value of place, arousing a longing for community."[9] Hermann Lübbe also theorized the surging interests of people in museums and histories as reactions against the feeling of disorientation in societies which become more and more unfamiliar.[10] Facing uncertainty, people need a point of reference, from which they see others and recognize difference. Only through the difference to the excluded others, people can construct identities and know who 'we' are.[11] The city

---

8   Gerard Delanty, Community (London: Routledge, 2003), 158-166.
9   Richard Sennett, The Corrosion of Character: The Personal Consequences of Work in the New Capitalism (New York: Norton, 1998), 138.
10   Heinrich Theodor Grütter, "Zur Theorie historischer Museen und Ausstellungen," in Dimensionen der Historik: Geschichtstheorie, Wissenschaftsgeschichte und Geschichtskultur Heute; Jörn Rüsen zum 60. Geburtstag, ed. Horst Walter Blanke (Köln: Böhlau, 1998), 173.
11   Stuart Hall, "Who Needs 'Identity'," in Cultural Identity, ed. Stuart Hall and Paul du Gay (London: Sage Publications, 1996), 4. "[I]dentities are constructed through, not outside, difference. This entails the radically disturbing recognition that it is only through the re-

could be one of such reference points which can give people a sense of geographical attachment and meaning to their daily lives.

However, it should be questioned how a point of reference could become a steady source of a collective identity in the age of globalization.[12] With the immense amount of information, symbols and practices around us as points of reference, it is possible for an individual to have many individually customized temporal identities. We no longer have a single identity connected to one social group of a certain territorial space such as nations, but diverse, overlapping and contested identities.[13] What we see here is the deterritorialization and constant process of reshuffling of individual identities, which are to be possibly reterritorialized , using some reference points as centripetal forces. However, differences are everywhere, so are the points of reference. This re-territorialisation is a repetitive process, and political reiteration is necessary for people to form a relatively stable collective identity.

Therefore, "Whoever, or whatever, wins the battle of people's minds will rule."[14] And this does not need to be a mighty institution like a nation-state, "because might, rigid apparatuses will not be a match, in any reasonable time span, for the minds mobilized around the power of flexible, alternative networks."[15] Identity is a matter of choice, and any elements influencing people's choice are a part of identity politics. Because anything and anyone who could mobilize information and communication means could win the battle over people's minds, identity politics is now so central in organizing societies.

Moreover, identities are now so closely related to the symbolic power of things, therefore, clearer symbols and images, which carry meanings to our identities, attract capital as well as people's minds. Therefore, politics, culture and

---

lation to the Other, the relation to what it is not, to precisely what it lacks, to what has been called its constitutive outside that the 'positive' meaning of any term – and thus its 'identity' – can be constructed."

12   In this regard, Brubaker and Cooper's differentiation between "identification" as processes and "identity" as a condition with reifying connotations are very helpful. Rogers Brubaker and Frederick Cooper, "Beyond Identity," in Ethnicity without Groups, by Rogers Brubaker (Cambridge and London: Harvard University Press, 2004), 41-46. Identification can be "involving some sense of affinity or affiliation, commonality or connectedness to particular others, but lacking a sense of overriding oneness vis-à-vis some constitutive "other." Ibid., 46.

13   See Stuart Hall, Rassismus und kulturelle Identität: Ausgewählte Schriften 2 (Hamburg: Argument-Verlag, 2008), 87-88.

14   Manuel Castells, The information Age: Economy, Society, and Culture. Vol. 2: The Power of Identity (Malden: Wiley-Blackwell, 2010), 425.

15   Ibid., 425.

economics are all closely bound each other in identity politics, and cities with surging economic power and political importance with good cultural infrastructures are the best place to see its complexity.[16] And city museums reflect most vividly the complexity of identity politics as city museums are now faced with "the convergence of interests among government, cultural institutions, foundations, and corporations".[17] In the next section, I argue city museums would be a stronger actor in identity politics in the age of globalization compared to the national museums as a main actor in the age of modernism.

3. City museums representing the globalizing era

Museums are historically closely related to the identity politics, especially creating national identities. Unlike treasure rooms, which were accessible only to small groups of people, museums became public space in the 19th century. They are opened to all citizens of a nation, and nation building and its identity politics went hand in hand with national museums.

The elaborated studies of the history of museums show how nation-states have made use of museums as a tool of controlling the mass and of forming national identities. Eilean Hooper-Greenhill's "disciplinary museum",[18] Carol Duncan's "ritual of citizenship"[19] and Tony Bennett's account of how people have self-disciplined in museums,[20] all show "[T]hey have historically played significant roles in the modernist and nationalist quest for order and mapped boundaries."[21] Museums showed visitors 'their' common history, with which they identified themselves against 'exotic' others, who were at the less developed stage on the evolutionary line of history. The visitors also internalized how to appreciate 'high culture' and how to behave in public, which produced the mass belonging to the imagined community: a nation-state.

---

16   Allen J. Scott, Social Economy of the Metropolis: Cognitive-Cultural Capitalism and the Global Resurgence of Cities (Oxford: Oxford University Press, 2008), 14-15.
17   Mark W. Rectanus, "Globalization: Incorporating the Museum," in A Companion to Museum Studies, ed. Sharon Macdonald (Malden: Blackwell, 2006), 394.
18   Eilean Hooper-Greenhill, Museums and the Shaping of Knowledge (London: Routledge, 1992), 188-190.
19   Carol Duncan, "Art Museums and the Ritual of Citizenship," in Exhibiting Cultures: The Poetics and Politics of Museum Display, ed. Ivan Karp and Steven D. Lavine (Washington: Smithsonian Institution Press, 1991), 90-92.
20   Tony Bennett, The Birth of the Museum: History, Theory, Politics (London: Routledge, 1995), 28.
21   Sharon Macdonald, introduction to Theorizing Museums: Representing Identity and Diversity in a Changing World, ed. Sharon Macdonald and Gordon Fyfe (Oxford: Blackwell, 1996), 5.

Bearing in mind that national museums are more often the subjects of museological researches, it seems that city museums have not received quite as much attention as national museums until recently.[22] However, with social movements in 1960s such as feminism and post-colonial movement and the impact of globalization since the 1970s, our society and our identities have been radically diversified and destabilized. Because of such environmental changes, old national museums representing fixed images of national identity have been critically scrutinized, which stimulated new developments in museum practice and museology.[23] Although old national museums have by no means lost their splendid aura and are still attracting many tourists, it can not be denied that its power as a reference point for people's belonging is dwindling. National identity based on the clear separation between 'us' and 'others' does not reflect the reality of diversified societies, as 'others' are now often our neighbors. Great anthropological collections and archaeological collections can been seen as a manifestation of colonialism. Order and classification typical of the Enlightenment idea would be no longer tenable to understand present society.[24] National museums as a product of modernity are seeing that their rational roots are crumbling. In addition, the political power of nation-states to realize a democratic society is declining, as nation-states are now more keen on sustaining world market rather than protecting citizens' benefits from the harm of capitalism.[25] As nation-states are

22 Museological researches specially focused on city museums were still relatively limited in 1990s with some exceptions. Some exceptional works are compiled in the following volume. Gaynor Kavanagh and Elizabeth Frostick, eds., Making City Histories in Museums (London/Washington: Leicester University Press, 1998). See also Nick Merriman, "The Peopling of London Project," in Cultural Diversity: Developing Museum Audiences in Britain, ed. Eilean Hooper-Greenhill (London and Washington: Leicester University Press, 1997).
      The first symposium focused on city museums was held at the Museum of London in 1993. Max Hebditch, "Museums about Cities," Museum International 187 City Museums (1995): 7, accessed. April 16, 2012,
      http://www.unesco.org/ulis/cgi-
      bin/ulis.pl?catno=103018&set=4F999D42_1_329&gp=1&lin=1&ll=1.
23 The theoretical development in Museology is called among English speaking academics 'The new Museology".
24 Jan Nederveen Pieterse, "Multiculturalism and Museums: Discourse about Others in the Age of Globalization," in Heritage, Museums and Galleries: An Introductory Reader, ed. Gerard Corsana (London: Routledge, 2005), 171.
25 While the global movement of money is well institutionalized and put nation-states under its control, the formation of global political organizations is still underway. Recent Occupy movements could be seen as one of the examples of possible global counter politics. Appadurai also emphasises the necessity of grassroots globalization and its research.

losing its political and symbolic power and grip on people's identity, 'national museums are losing its function and become shrines of nostalgia."[26]

City museums, on the contrary, could transform themselves to represent the age of globalization. Financially, the city is a hub of the global networks, and their central roles in globalization are well researched by many urban scholars.[27] Global flows nevertheless need a strategic point to be dealt with, and capitals, managerial elites, commodities and information surge into there. To be such a point, cities need to compete with each other on the global market of cities. In order to attract capital and managerial elites, culture, symbols and images of the city play a decisive role along with infrastructures. "More than ever before, there was a need to intervene to reorganize urban space and to make urban systems function more effectively for the accumulation of capital and the management of social unrest. This brought finance capital more directly into the planning of urban space."[28] In this planning of urban space, culture plays a crucial role as culture can give unique identities or representational power to urban space.[29]

However, globalization also produces new social problems in cities. Together with the cultural differences between multicultural residents, widening gaps between the rich and the poor are causing social segmentation, which is one of the most urgent problems in cities. As Jordi Borja and Manuel Castells claims, stronger initiative of the municipal government would now be desirable as the nation-state is now too big and inflexible to handle such social problems.[30] The nature of problems differs from place to place as they all have different ways of interaction between the global and the local, and it changes constantly. With local knowledge and proximity to people's daily lives, the city could better deal with the problem, therefore, the city could mean more to people's lives than the nation-state. Under this new circumstance, "Territorial iden-

---

See Arjun Appadurai, "Grassroots Globalization and the Research Imagination," in Globalization, ed. Arjun Appadurai (Durham: Duke University Press, 2001).

26 Nederveen Pieterse, "Multiculturalism and Museums," 164.

27 Some prominent works are; Saskia Sassen, Globalization and its Discontents (New York: New Press, 1998)., Saskia Sassen, The Global City: New York, London, Tokyo (Princeton and Oxford: Princeton University Press, 2001)., Edward W. Soja, Postmodern Geographies: The Reassertion of Space in Critical Social Theory (London/New York: Verso, 1989)., and Jordi Borja and Manuel Castells, Local and Global: The Management of Cities in the Information Age (London: Earthscan, 1999).

28 Soja, Postmodern Geographies, 101.

29 For the detailed studies of this, see Sharon Zukin, The Cultures of Cities (Cambridge: Blackwell, 1996)., Scott Lash and John Urry, Economies of Signs and Space (London: Sage Publication, 1996)., and Allen J. Scott, The Cultural Economy of Cities.

30 Borja and Castells, Local and Global, 246. Castells, The Information Age, 273.

tity is at the root of the world wide surge of local and regional governments as significant actors in both representation and intervention, better suited to adapt to the endless variation of global flows."[31] Territorial identity could be a possibility as well as necessity for a city both to adapt to the new economic environment created by the global economy and tackle the social problems caused by it.

As an economic booster of a city, art galleries, especially contemporary art museums, often become a landmark of cities' redevelopment.[32] Because they create cultural space "bolstering the city's image as a center of cultural innovation", it attracts investment and elites more easily.[33] However, considering territorial identity as a way of tackling the social problems, art galleries aimed to redevelop the city's economy often have little connection with the locality of a city.[34] In city museums dealing with a wide range of objects or stories about a city, on the other hand, the representation of identities could be more elaborated as they have wider means to produce texts, discourse or images which relate to cities' history and lives. With physical closeness to the people represented in museums and relative flexible criteria in collecting materials, city museums represent better the diversity of a city. However, in practice, representing diversity in city museums is a very complicated policy involving both public and private interests groups. This makes city museums more interesting case studies than other actors to see such complexity in identity politics, such as media and popular culture, activities of which are more clearly guided by economic interests.

4. The bifocality of city museums' roles in identity politics

The complexity in representing identities in city museums lies in its bifocality. Adapting to the global economy and tackling social problems are concerned with different levels of identities; the diversified identities of individual residents with different ethnicities, gender, age or classes, and the identity (identities) of a city itself as a whole. City museums as a municipal cultural and educational institution have to bring these different levels of identities into accordance. Of course, these two do not have to be fundamentally incompatible, as a city museum could represent a city of diversity. However, as Johnson wrote, "But once it loses sight of the city itself as the central object of its responsibility and activity, it ceases to become a city museum and becomes instead a different,

---

31   Castells, The information Age, 423.
32   One of the often-cited examples of such galleries is the Guggenheim Museum in Bilbao.
33   Zukin, The Cultures of Cities, 2.
34   Graeme Evans, "Branding the City of Culture – The Death of City Planning?" in Culture, Urbanism and Planning, ed. Javier Monclús and Manuel Guàrdia (Aldershot: Ashgate, 2006), 203-205.

albeit no less valid, urban cultural centre."[35] City museums have to represent all the residents' identities without losing the city's totality as well as attractive images of the city to tourists and investors. Such a task is probably impossible. Nevertheless, city museums have responsibilities to do the best.

One of their efforts is seen in their temporary exhibitions which centre the people who are long underrepresented in city museums.[36] Such exhibitions involve enormous tasks such as creating new contacts with minority groups, collecting new objects and stories which have long been neglected, and marketing to attract people who have never visited the museum before because they feel they are not represented there. Especially city museums with long histories need reconsiderations about their collections and permanent exhibitions, as their historical collections are often the reflection of the 19th century Museology. Therefore, whole new arrangements are sometimes necessary, such as it is the case in 2010 at the Museum of London with brand new galleries which enable the museum to exhibit London's history up to present days. Wien Museum Karlsplatz also has a plan to renew the whole museum in the near future.[37] The objects exhibited are also rearranged from showing grand narrative history to presenting more people's daily life, contextualised histories, or more provocative and controversial perspectives.[38] New space for educational programs, more temporary exhibitions, and public use also show the diversification of museums' roles.[39]

Such new activities show city museums' attempts to reflect as diverse identities as possible in the museums. However, although museums have been open

---

35 Nichola Johnson, "Discovering the City," Museum International: City Museums 187 (1995): 5, accessed April 16, 2012,
    http://www.unesco.org/ulis/cgi-
    bin/ulis.pl?catno=103018&set=4F999D42_1_329&gp=1&lin=1&ll=1.
36 Early examples are the following exhibitions. "The Peopling of London: 15,000 years of settlement from overseas" (16.11.1993 – 15.05.1994) at the Museum of London and "Gastarbajteri – 40 Jahre Arbeitsmigration" (22.01.2004 – 11.04.2004) at Wien Museum Karlsplatz.
37 Curator 1, interview by author, Wien Museum Karlsplatz, December 12, 2011.
38 Curator 2, interview by author, Wien Museum Karlsplatz, December 29, 2011. For one of the early examples of the provocative presentations at the Museum of London, see Gaynor Kavanagh, "Buttons, Belisha Beacons and Bullets: City Histories in Museums," in Making City Histories in Museums, eds. Gaynor Kavanagh and Elizabeth Frostick (London/Washington: Leicester University Press, 1998), 2.
39 Wien Museum Karlsptatz created new temporary exhibition space in 1980s to be able to accommodate two or three different temporary exhibitions at the same time. Inner yard was also covered with a roof to create space for public use, café and a children's' play area.

to everyone, museums in general were (and possibly still are) the place for bour-geois identity. Democratizing museums means that some existing audiences might feel their place and a sense of security are being lost as they lose the status of majority represented. Others would not always want to see new perspectives and might feel disturbed to see more socially provocative exhibitions. Stephen Weil, citing a published research by Zahava Doering in 1996, argued that "the museum, when understood in this mode of providing individual self-affirmation, functions far more strongly as an instrument for social stability than as any kind of a lever for radical change."[40] While museums are claiming possibilities of empowering people or questioning the taken-for-granted values of society, there are still many voices which warn the risk of institutionalizing differences,[41] or doubt museums' power for social changes in reality inside and outside muse-ums.

"While there has undoubtedly been a proliferation of different, particularly mi-nority, 'voices' speaking in the public arena, the old political and cultural high ground has not simply been relinquished. On the contrary, what we have seen is an escalation of intellectual battles over the legitimacy of different kinds of rep-resentation."[42]

Not only intellectual, but also political battles are most intensive in city muse-ums, as no other places contain so diverse perspectives as cities. To do justice to all possible identities of residents is in itself already a tremendous task for city museums.

However, to make things more complicated, city museums also have to fos-ter the image of the city as a territorial unity and of museums itself in order to present the city and the museum as an attractive tourist destination on the global tourists market. Financially, although many city museums are still budgeted mostly by municipal governments, museums can no longer be free from finan-

---

40 Stephen Weil, "The Museum and the Public," in Museums and their Communities, ed. Sheila Watson (London: Routledge, 2007), 41. See also Zahava D. Doering, Andrew J. Pekarik, and Institutional Studies Office; Smithsonian Institution, "Assessment of infor-mal Education in Holocaust Museums," OPANDA Research Reports 2B (1996), ac-cessed April 3, 2012, http://hdl.handle.net/10088/17201.

41 Sheila Waston, "Museums and their Communities," in Museums and their Communities, ed. Sheila Watson (London: Routledge, 2007), 17.

42 Sharon Macdonald, "Exhibitions of Power and Powers of Exhibition: An Introduction to the Politics of Display," in Museums and their Communities, ed. Sheila Watson (Lon-don: Routledge, 2007), 187.

cial concerns and market logics.[43] In face of dwindling financial support from governments, museums are facing more serious competition to ensure the good allocation of the budget as well as attract private sponsors.[44]

To present themselves as financially successful institutions to government officers, tourists, or private sponsors, management receives now more attentions within city museums, including income-generating activities such as shops and cafes, or lending spaces for private uses. Branding and marketing also become one of the important practices. For example, a new logo for the Museum of London was created in 2008 clearly aiming at communicating London's identity and the museum's international recognition.[45] In Wien Museum Karlsplatz, the new department for marketing and public relations were created in 2003 and 2005 respectively.[46] With its presence in global media and on the Internet, city museums can now contribute to create the image of the city through their collections, exhibitions and programs.

However, such image can be a sanitized one because the image is created targeting tourist, sponsors or managerial elites. Images such as a city of diversity would contain a variety of cultures and ethnicities, but would conceal the rate of crime, drug dealing or prostitutions. City museums are well aware of such problems. When one looks at closely websites or articles on exhibitions, they are not

---

43   This varies from place to place. In Tokyo, Edo Tokyo museum have contracted with Tokyo Metropolitan Foundation for History and Culture responsible for its running.
     Wien Museum Karlsplatz is budgeted about 85 % by the city. Manager 1, interview by author, Wien Museum Karlsplatz, March 8, 2012. They would have less concern on finding sponsors than the Museum of London, which is budgeted about 60% by both the Great London Authority and the City of London Corporation. Museum of London, Annual Reviews (London: Museum of London, 2009 – 2011), accessed December 18, 2011, http://www.museumoflondon.org.uk/Corporate/About-us/ReportsPolicies/Annual-reviews.htm.

44   Since 1945, Museen der Stadt Wien had been a part of municipal government. However, through "Ausgliederung", Wien Museum Karlsplatz (renamed in 2003) now has more financial responsibilities.

45   "Since branding is not simply about re-branding with a new logo, the Museum is using the opportunity of a new visual identity to communicate its ambitions and world-class status. The identity helps us to position ourselves as fundamentally London: expert, innovative, inspiring, human, provocative and vibrant." Museum of London, Annual Report (London, Museum of London, 2007-2008): 11, accessed December 18, 2011, http://www.museumoflondon.org.uk/Corporate/About-us/ReportsPolicies/Annual-reviews.htm.

46   As a result, the publicity of Wien Museum Karlsplatz has become worldwide, reaching to South America and Asia. Manager 1.

concealed, if not specially focused.[47] However, for marketing, details are not necessary. Simplifying images by using certain objects exhibited in museums is the good strategy for publicity, which shows little about the daily lives of people in a city.[48]

Although such a simplified image is just one of the images museums have presented, it is the image, which are easily accessible to millions of people. This can create a discrepancy between the global and the local. This discrepancy would not cause any problem when the local and the global are relatively well separated. However, as is shown above, the global and the local are constantly interacting with each other. When people who have imagined a city from a distant place come to live in the city, this discrepancy might cause frustration, disillusion, and distrust. "[I]mportant tensions may arise when places that have been imagined at a distance must become lived spaces."[49]

Each city museum deals with the bifocality in different ways, as each is set in a different locality and has different ways to interact with global flows. There would be no perfect way to do it, but decisions have to be made to keep museums going. Such decisions are made considering historically accumulated social and cultural resources, cultural policies of the city, immigration policy, existing cultural infrastructures, history of the collections, and relationship between national and municipal governments. They are greatly influenced by global flows, but the degree of the influence is also different from place to place as the global flows are not even. The capital flow in Tokyo is greater than in Vienna, but the flow of people in Japan is notoriously restricted. To understand the impact of globalization, we need to look into each particular case, which clearly calls for another paper. City museums are one of such cases which could show us the complexity of representing diversified identity in the age of globalization.

---

47 For example, at Wien Museum Karlsplatz, problems of crimes and drugs at Karlsplatz are presented as a part of the exhibition, "Am Puls der Stadt – 2000 Jahre Karlsplatz", (29.05. 2008 – 26. 10. 2008) Visited by author. See also Elke Doppler, ed., Am Puls der Stadt: 200 Jahren Karlsplatz: Wien-Museum Karlsplatz, 29. Mai – 26. Oktober 2008; Katalog (Wien: Wien Museum, 2008), 494-498.

48 The Lord Mayor's coach in the Museum of London and some famous paintings of Klimt and Schiele in Wien Museum Karlsplatz are such objects.

49 Akhil Gupta and James Ferguson, "Beyond "Culture": Space, Identity, and the Politics of Difference," Cultural Anthropology Vol. 7 No. 1 (February 1992): 11, accessed November 9, 2011, doi: 10.2307/i226877.

Part Two

Functioning and Understanding

(Un) Free flowing:
Globalization and its relation
with the phenomenon of migration

Lucía Alicia Aguerre

1. Introduction

There are different ways of understanding the phenomenon of globalization. Contributions of many authors in this complex topic show different levels of approach: the "hard facts" level of the globalization of markets and finance, that is globalization from an economic perspective; the impact of globalization regarding to the symbolic different forms of life, that is globalization from a cultural perspective; the ideological level of the discourse of globalization, which refers to the use and manipulation that is made of their "facts"; the level related with population mobility, that is globalization and its relationship to migration; and the so-called "globalization from below" or "insurgent cosmopolitanism", that is a kind of counter-hegemonic globalization embodied by the social movements of resistance against the unequal terms of trade.

This contribution aims to address the phenomenon of globalization from the perspective of migration in order to make visible the tension between the discourse of globalization as a new free flowing space and the restrictions of the free flow of migrants in terms of legality and inclusion. This tension can be understood as a contradiction between free and unfree flows that are present in the definition of globalization. Attending relevant theories this paper will consider the specific role that migration plays in the logic of neoliberal globalization in order to make the phenomenon more tangible from this particular perspective.

Even when globalization implies several consequences for the traditional concept of sovereignty, nation-states continue to exercise power over the territory through restrictive immigration policies. From a perspective which combines labor market and migration, globalization appears as an ambivalent phenomenon that both obliterates and creates limits that forces people to flow clandestinely with severe consequences related to the kind of labor force that they constitute. This suggests a contradiction between the rhetoric of a supposed "globalization of humanity", in which globalization appears as a free flowing space, and the immigration laws that deny rights to migrants, showing that this flow is rather restricted and un-free.

In this sense, it is becoming increasingly necessary to undertake a philosophical critique of globalization that reveals its contradictions and the power relations under which it is governed. This perspective could bring global and supportive alternatives to these complex contradictions.

Given the massive contemporary transnational migration of people and groups in dire need, which makes them particularly liable to rejection and exclusion practices by the host societies, I will focus on the figure of the "poor immigrant"[1] whose decision to migrate is compelled since their livelihood in their home country has become unviable for socioeconomic, political or cultural reasons[2].

2. Free and Un-free flows: The ambiguous role of the Nation-State

Nation-states play an ambivalent role in the context of the globalized world, which becomes visible when examining the way in which they tackle the phenomenon of migration.

Even when different ways to approach the phenomenon of globalization have been raised, it is possible to distinguish a common denominator on their diversity: globalization cancels and devalues one of the central features of European modernity, namely, the idea of living and acting, both economic, ecological, technical, cultural and informational exclusively within the borders of nation-states and their societies. In that sense, the phenomenon of globalization involves significant changes in the exercise of global and local power. As suggested by Beat Dietschy one of the main features of the phenomenon of globalization, the sudden growth of international financial markets, jeopardized the dominant and interventionist power of the modern state. Market forces were increasingly taking place and the dynamics of globalization, led by international finance capital, now influences all areas of life[3].

---

1   Human geographical mobility in general, covering any kind of movement to another place outside the homeland for reasons of tourism, business, medical treatment or religious pilgrimages, etc. will not be treated in this contribution.

2   Fornet-Betancourt, Raúl. "La migración como condición del humano en el contexto de la globalización", in Migration und Interkulturalität. Theologische und Philosophische Herausforderungen., edited by Raúl Fornet-Betancourt, 245-257 (Aachen: Wissenschaftsverlag Mainz in Aachen, 2004); Bonilla, Alcira. "El 'Otro': el migrante", in Menschenbilder interkulturell. Kulturen der Humanisierung und der Anerkennung, edited by RaúlFornet-Betancourt, Raúl, 366-375 (Aachen: Wissenschaftsverlag Mainz in Aachen, 2008).

3   Dietschy, Beat. "Globalización: ¿hecho, destino o quimera?", in Resistencia y solidaridad. Globalización capitalista y liberación. Edited by Raúl Fornet-Betancourt (Madrid: Trotta: 2003) 11-30.

This has several consequences for the nation-state configuration and its model of citizenship. Following S. Benhabib, who combines migration and globalization approaches with the question of national citizenship and its transformations, the manifestations of the phenomenon of globalization such as the rise of a global economy through the formation of free capital, finance and labor markets, the increasing internationalization of armament, the communication and information technologies, and the development of sub and transnational political actors, have created a state of exhaustion of the Westphalian model of sovereignty[4]. This model presupposes a dominant and unified political authority with jurisdiction over a clearly demarcated territory. In this sense, globalization represents a "crisis of the territoriality of the state", as it is overwhelmed with respect to its material functions: the nation-state becomes too small to deal with economic, ecological and informational problems created by the new global context[5].

But even taking into account the collapse that globalization implies for the traditional concept of sovereignty, states continue to exercise power over the territory through immigration policies and citizenship, as Benhabib points out[6]. In this sense, "globalization" does not mean the opening or erosion of boundaries in relation to the free entry of immigrants to the territories of nation-states in terms of legality and inclusion. By contrast, globalization reinforces precarious conditions of migration, clandestine status and the utilization of this phenomenon by the economic powers.

There is a cultural dimension that should not be ignored in an analysis involving the phenomenon of migration and the role of nation-states. Most of contemporary migrants enter into nation-states that have a modern-based sociopolitical organization and a conception of citizenship whose constituent elements are cultural identity (assumed as homogeneous and easily delineable), membership policies and the allocation of rights denied to non-citizens. Benedict Anderson defined the nation as an "imagined community", in which its members perceives themselves as part of a community of fraternal values. These imagined communities have as main characteristic the territorial delimitation, represented by borders under which the political system limits its scope and is distinguished from other nations, preparing the field for the concepts of belong-

---

4   Benhabib, Seyla, Los derechos de los otros. Extranjeros, residentes y ciudadanos (Barcelona: Gedisa, 2005), 15.

5   Benhabib, Seyla, Las reivindicaciones de la cultura. Igualdad y diversidad en la era global (Buenos Aires: Katz, 2006), 291.

6   Benhabib, Seyla, Los derechos de los otros, 16.

ing and non-belonging[7]. Similarly, the philosopher Étienne Balibar in relation to the nation-state community uses the concept of "fictive ethnicity" to refer to the construction of the "nation" by the social formations. "National identity" downplays differences among citizens of the same "community" and emphasizes the symbolic difference between a constructed "we" and those assumed as "others". The mode of producing "ethnicity", so as to naturalize it and hide its fictional character, is trough two effective tools: language and race[8].

In these circumstances, the practices and politics of inclusion are severally restrictive, and exclusionary immigration laws and policies are often based on different forms of cultural racism. The kind of rejection that migrants face does not refer directly to a supposed "racial difference": biologist discourses on "races" are obsolete and currently there are anti-racism laws both nationally and internationally to de-legitimize the discourse of biological racism. Instead migrants are affected by a kind of racism which replaces the notion of "race" by "cultural affiliation". This cultural racism is based on essentialist notions of culture and defends the idea that individuals, as part of a cultural group, carry with them a single culture with firmly determined and permanent features. It also supports the idea that interaction between cultures lead to conflict. In this way, migrants are identified as a danger to the population that seeks to keep its homogeneity[9].

3. Flow exploitation in neoliberal globalization

It has been described above the way in which migrants fundamental rights are not recognized by the models of citizenship of closed nation-state communities. But in fact, it is not all about rejection: the role of migrants in neoliberal globalization must be addressed from an economic point of view, as they constitute

---

7   Anderson, Benedict. Comunidades imaginadas. Reflexiones sobre el origen y la difusión del nacionalismo. (México: Fondo de Cultura Económica, 1993) 17-25.

8   Balibar, Étienne. "¿Existe un neorracismo?" in Balibar, Étienne and Wallerstein, Immanuel. Raza, Nación y Clase (Madrid: IEPALA, 1991) 149-163.

9   Balibar, Étienne. "La forma nación: historia e ideología" in Balibar, Étienne and Wallerstein, Immanuel. Raza, Nación y Clase (Madrid: IEPALA, 1991); Aguerre, Lucía Alicia. Desigualdades, racismo cultural y diferencia colonial. Berlin: desiguALdades.net Research Network on Interdependent Inequalities in Latin America. 2011. Accesed July 20, 2012.http://www.desigualdades.net/bilder/pub-listen/WPLuciaAguerreOnline.pdf; Aguerre, Lucía Alicia. "Racismo cultural, migración y ciudadanía", CECIES, Pensamiento Latinoamericano y Alternativo (2009). Accesed July 20, 2012. http://www.cecies.org/articulo.asp?id=228

labor force both rejected and used, as they usually are not legally recognized as citizens, but are included in the functioning of the economy.

According to the political philosopher Sandro Mezzadra, globalization is an ambivalent phenomenon that both "destroys" and "reconstructs" borders and boundaries. If, on the one hand, the "globalization" sweeps away the barriers to free trade of goods and capital, "new and changing boundaries arise to curb the free movement of labor"[10]. In this sense, it is possible to distinguish a contradiction between the notion of globalization commonly associated with a "new fluid space" and what S. Mezzadra has called a "proliferation of boundaries, security systems and physical and virtual borders"[11].

However, from an economic perspective it becomes evident that migrants play a relevant role in the labor market, which is permitted due to the existence of porous borders. These barriers allow people to flow through a "differential inclusion", which implies the implementation of the "clandestinization" of the majority of migrants in order to provide docile and precarious labor force. This paradigmatic mode of control of borders is a flexible system, that rather than being dedicated to build a "fortress" is devoted to design and implement "filtering mechanisms" and "selection of mobility" according to the demands of the labor market[12].

The "differential inclusion" of migrants shows that migrations play a fundamental role in the logic of capitalist globalization. People who migrate under conditions of severe vulnerability largely do so as a result of the abandonment of forms of life and production in their places of origin, which condemn them to poverty and force them to migrate to regions where the globalization establishes the need for labor. In turn, the phenomenon of globalization reinforces the problems of capitalism, as migrants are used as an adjustment variable in the labor market, deepening conflicts with the host societies which perceive migrant workers as serious competition for jobs exposed to precariousness.

In relation to what has been identified as the ambiguous role of the nation-state, it starts to appear clearly that the very mechanisms of neoliberal globalization prevent the state to recognize migrants, since the existence of masses of human beings who are not citizens and whose rights are practically not recognized is functional to globalization mechanisms for the regulation of markets.

---

10 Author´s translation from the Spanish version of Mezzadra´s work. Mezzadra, Sandro. Derecho de fuga. Migraciones, ciudadanía, globalización (Madrid/Buenos Aires: Traficantes de sueños/Tinta Limón, 2005), 48.

11 Author´s translation from the spanish versión of Mezzadra´s work. Mezzadra, Sandro. "Confini, migrazioni, cittadinanza". Papers 85 (2007): 32.

12 Mezzadra, Sandro. "Confini, migrazioni, cittadinanza", 40.

In this scenario, poor migrant workers are exposed to severe vulnerability. Some authors, nevertheless, conceive migration as an alternative mode of globalization. Given the crucial participation of migrants in the daily construction of culture it could be possible to glimpse the emergency of a globalization of identities carried by these subjects that, through their mobility, constitute new transnational spaces and generate connections between places of origins and destination regions. S. Mezzadra, for instance, identifies this with a kind of particular globalization, namely "globalization from below" or "another globalization"[13]. He refers to the transformation that takes place both in the regions of origin and in the host societies, generated from the dual political and cultural space in which migrants live as "citizens of the borders". This kind of transformation ignores the boundaries of nation-states, and in this way could be treated as globalization.

Without detriment to this impact, it is questionable to equate the phenomenon of globalization of financial markets and their effects on various areas of life with the phenomenon of migration, which seems to be rather a consequence of globalization itself. "Globalization from below" or "contra hegemonic globalization", as described by B. De Souza Santos, refers more to the ways of organizing transnational resistance of various actors against the effects of globalization. These movements, composed by social groups that are victims of hegemonic globalization, join in concrete struggles against exclusion, subordinated inclusion, destruction of ecology, political and cultural oppression, and other ways of subjugation. They organize their resistance at the same transnational level than hegemonic globalization[14].

It is still an area of discussion that goes beyond the scope of this work to locate migrants among the actors of "insurgent cosmopolitanism". Several contemporary studies on migration call attention to the concept of "vulnerability" as an essential category for the treatment of this topic. Following A. Bonilla, the vulnerability of migrants is related to the exclusion from full citizen participation, the discriminatory treatment, and the varying degrees of violation of fundamental rights[15].

---

13 Mezzadra, Sandro. Derecho de fuga, 49.
14 De Sousa Santos, Boaventura. "Globalizations".Theory Culture and Society, vol 23 (2006), 394-397.
15 Bonilla, Alcira. "Vulnerabilidad vs. autonomía: conflictos de las migraciones contemporáneas". Passagens. Revista Internacional de História Política e Cultura Jurídica Vol 2, N° 4 (2010): 4-38.

4. Globalization as a discourse

Finally, it becomes relevant to address the discursive aspect involved in the spread of hegemonic globalization. At a discursive level, the meaning commonly associated to globalization, that is the creation of a new free flowing space without borders or belonging collides with what has been described as a system of exclusion of migrants in the so-called host societies.

In order to analyze this phenomenon I will consider the work of R. Fornet-Betancourt, exponent of the intercultural philosophy, who takes into account the contradiction between the rhetoric in support of the "globalization of humanity" and the immigration laws that deny rights to migrants. Fornet-Betancourt points out that the situation of immigrants in the context of neoliberal globalization is a situation of "institutionalized exclusion". Concerning national law and legality, there is a clear difference between citizens (nationals) and non-citizens. Political, social, economic, and cultural rights are denied to migrants, and their marginalization is legally justified by means of the concept of national citizenship[16]. In addition, exclusive citizenship works as an instrument of choice and control of immigrants, illustrated by the attempts of host societies to "assimilate" or "integrate" migrants, contrary to genuine inclusion.

Regarding the situation of migrants in this context becomes relevant to undertake a philosophical critique of globalization in order to relate and contrast the use of this expression by hegemonic powers and the reality of the migrant as evidence of the ideological character of this discourse. According to Fornet-Betancourt, "globalization" does not correspond to the meaning commonly associated to it, i.e. a system of border erosion aimed at multilateral circulation of knowledge, goods and people. On the contrary, it is a phenomenon marked by power relations that structure the flow, since this movement, far from being a spontaneous and equitable circulation, has determined directions. There is a manifest contradiction between the dominant ideological discourse about globalization of humanity in a world supposedly set as a "global village" and the immigration laws through which basic rights are denied to migrants[17].

This contradiction is a clear example that neoliberal globalization is not guided by the principles of justice and equality. Moreover, it can be understood

---

16 Fornet-Betancourt, Raúl. Interculturalidad y filosofía en América Latina (Aachen:Wissenschaftsverlag Mainz in Aachen. 2003b); Fornet-Betancourt, Raúl. "La migración como condición del humano en el contexto de la globalización", 245-257.

17 Fornet-Betancourt, Raúl. "Para una crítica filosófica de la globalización". In Resistencia y solidaridad. Globalización capitalista y liberación, edited by Raúl Fornet-Betancourt (Madrid: Trotta, 2003a) 55-79.

as the expansion of the logic of capital and hegemonic groups in order to "globalize" their interests. The discourse of globalization constitutes from this perspective an ideological offensive of the capitalist system[18], which employs the term in the sense of "integration" or "common global growth" to mask the hegemony of capitalist countries or large companies and financial centers[19]. Therefore Fornet-Betancourt proposes to refer to this phenomenon in terms of "neoliberal globalization" to depart from naives theories about globalization.

5. Globalization and migration: Un-Free flows

As a conclusion, I would like to state that the phenomenon of migration has much to say about hegemonic globalization mechanisms, since it reveals the power relations involved in this globalized flow. Globalization may represent a crisis of the territoriality of the state, but the states continue to exercise power over the territory through immigration and citizenship policies. This tension may be seen as a contradiction between the dominant ideological discourse about globalization of humanity and the immigration laws through which the states denies migrants basic rights. Assuming an economic perspective becomes possible to take into account how capital and hegemonic powers "globalize" their interest, combining boundaries, flows and filtering mechanisms.

Furthermore, hegemonic or neoliberal globalization dilutes the barriers to the movement of its own material and symbolic production while generating more strict and cruel confines. This leads to exclusive citizenships, which in many cases operate against migration in order to keep intact the "imagined community" and their strategies of cultural homogenization, while migrants arrive with different practices, languages and symbolic systems. This political exclusion is used by economic power: migrants become "adjustment variables" to make workers compete for work, reducing wages and undermining class alliances. Thereby, in the current global context there seems to be a close relationship between cultural racism, exclusive citizenship, the growth of international

---

18   Fornet Betancourt states that when the term globalization is conceived in the narrower sense of "process of creating a global market as a network without borders to trade money, commodities, industrial products and services", the phenomenon can be linked to the emergence and development of the capitalist system of production of the early sixteenth century and its relationship to the colonial enterprise. Thus, becomes manifest the intimate relationship between "globalization" and the capitalist system and can be stated that contemporary globalization is the present phase of capitalist expansion (Fornet-Betancourt, "Para una crítica filosófica de la globalización". In Resistencia y solidaridad. Globalización capitalista y liberación, 63-64).

19   Fornet-Betancourt, Raúl. "Para una crítica filosófica de la globalización", 67.

financial and labor markets, and the use of poor migrants by the economic power.

In brief, the phenomenon of migration reveals an additional face of globalization, and makes possible to distinguish between the globalization of capital, the discourse tending to legitimate these circumstances, and the reality that migrants suffer in a globalized but not so free-flowing world. Politically and ethically there is still a way to go towards a free and equitable globalization. And that is the challenge.

From System of Exchange to Globalization

María G. Navarro

This paper analyses, from a philosophical perspective, the 16th and 17th century models of currency, as well as their influence on the types of society in which the models developed. To this end, we evaluate the study by the French philosopher Michael Foucault *Words and Things* on this subject and the principal foundations of Ludwig von Bertalanffy´s systems theory. The 17th century model of currency is based on the notion of a system of exchange. The notion of a system of exchange represents a transformation of great significance, upon which the principal characteristics of our current globalised era are founded, not only in economic life, but also in relation to an understanding of the world that it implies. Furthermore, the notion of a system of exchange was the step before the current model of electronic payments of the digital era, in which large transactions (and also large data transfers) take place by pressing a button. As we will see these economic practices hold the key for a deepening of our philosophical and historical comprehension of concepts such as globalisation.

In the sixteenth century Davanzatti imagines and describes what point of view would be required to be able to contrast, according to known proportions, the reality of a precious metal and all existing things one might wish to compare it with before making an exchange. That is, its exchange; not its purchase.[1]

"Nature made all terrestrial things good; the sum of these, by virtue of the agreement concluded by men, is worth all the gold that is worked; all men therefore desire everything in order to acquire all things ... In order to ascertain each day the rule and mathematical proportions that exist between things and between them and gold, we should have to be able to contemplate, from the height of heaven or some very tall observatory, all the things that exist or are done on earth, or rather their images reproduced and reflected in the sky as in a faithful mirror. We would then abandon all our calculations and we would say: there is upon earth so much gold, so many things, so many men, so many needs; and to the degree that each thing satisfies needs, its value shall be so many things, or so much gold".[2]

---

1   Davanzatti. "Leçon sur les monnaies," in Ecrits notables sur la monnaie de Copernic à Davanzati, ed. and trans. by Jean- Yves Le Branchu (Paris: Librairie Félix Alcan, 1934).

2   Davanzatti cited in Michael Foucault, The Order of Things (London: Routledge, 2002), 187.

The question Davanzatti poses is whether there exists something like a global point of view from which to measure physical reality and its actual value. However, the author seems to want to suggest to us that there is a prior question: what would be the actual material conditions that would allow us to make such a hypothesis? During the Renaissance, investigation into the material conditions that would allow human beings to find the appropriate economic criterion to accurately value objects in the world dominated the controversy over the function and nature of currency. Davanzatti's question is topical today: both the modern and the Renaissance controversies regarding the function and meaning of currency amid the totality of economic life are old witnesses to the astonishing phenomenon of so-called economic globalisation.

In an age such as ours, in which electronic currency is associated with plasma screens or even with acoustic waves, which we use to make commercial transactions, it may seem unlikely that electronic money should be associated with exchange and its elements. Nevertheless, for all periods and cultures, and despite scant evidence, currency is a form of materiality that involves uses, appropriations and knowlege that make it possible to differentiate among periods. In order to demonstrate the difference to which I refer I shall set out the differences between the 16th century currency model and that of the 17th and 18th centuries. After that description I shall offer a reflection upon economic globalisation.

1. From Renaissance gold to the modern function of exchange

In Davanzatti's text we find a cogent reason for doubting whether it is possible for the human being to establish a total equivalence among all things, all needs and/or all work. The fundamental reason is that neither all these things nor their equivalent in gold may be considered in their entirety. However, one thing seems clear. Gold, a rare metal, highly-prized and hidden under the ground, seems to carry in itself the mark of what is appropriate to the need to exchange everything that is likewise incommensurably diverse, precious with an extension and a signification equivalent to that of the sky where its true magnitude is reflected – as if to give our amazement an idea.

The power and the reality of currency stem from its materiality, from gold's rarity and wonder, from the unanimity of how strongly it is desired, which is equivalent to the effort of extracting it. But the gold coin – to put it briefly – is not an instrument of representation of any function of exchange. A proof of this is that the coin (gold) is one more object of exchange. Gold is desired for its own sake. The coins that circulate more quickly are those that have less weight in gold, because their intrinsic value is an object of value in itself. Coins are put

away, treasured jealously and protected from the vicissitudes of loss and circulation. My aim here is not to analyse how this model of currency accompanies a
certain form of development – one that is extremely fragile due to the fact that
the currency is subject to the same fluctuations in the exchange system as other
goods. That fragility is evidenced by the fact that the abundance of gold brought
back by the Spanish expeditions and circulated throughout Europe led to an immediate rise in prices. This was the price the Renaissance *episteme* had to pay as
a result of the notion of currency understood as a kind of mark with an intrinsic
similarity of that which designates and signifies. But there was something interesting in that mark: the spirit of the Renaissance *episteme* could not grasp that
the mark of wealth (its splendour) was not vouchsafed by an element prized as
the wealth of the world. And if, as Davanzatti suggested, that world could be
contemplated in its entirety from some privileged vantage point, it would guarantee an exact and prior equivalence among all things.

The 17th and 18th centuries saw money considered as to whether it was
fundamentally appropriate to replace what had a price, and the sovereignty of
the language enshrined in the book of the world was, in a certain way, abandoned. Therefore what was being considered was whether it was appropriate for
money to occupy the place of a fixed and universally legible characteristic. That
appropriateness was no longer a question of splendour, but rather the immutable
function of exchange in the instrument of currency. Consequently, currency became a mere instrument of representation of wealth: the only wealth in the world
is what is minted. The advantage of gold or silver is that it favours the immediate representation of value that every transaction demands: both metals are materials that shine, are unchangeable and difficult to divide or break. These qualities are not the foundation of the exchange function; they favour it only from a
psychological point of view. Nonetheless, coins only have a cash value when we
succeed in replacing them with goods. Currency is therefore a sign; it represents
a distinct identity in each case. Being a sign, it is not surprising that it can return
to the hand that let it go, just as the same word can be uttered many times. The
speed with which currency, as it is exchanged, serves its purpose of representing
wealth and the speed with which it changes hands are what give rise to the generation of wealth. This was one of the great issues of mercantilism of the period.
However, it is not intuitively clear how the conception of currency-sign was able
to conquer an *immutable truth* by virtue of the exchange function. The circuits in
which currency, by definition, circulates are governed, positively, by the rhythm
of the harvests. Therefore the wealth that can be transformed into currency is,
finally, as variable as the amount of gold coined in earlier times. The advantage,
in economic terms, is that it is no longer necessary to hypothesise contemplation
of the world in its entirety or the total amount of gold hidden in the mines *in or-*

der to daily verify the rule, since ultimately the development of money as an instrument of representation of the wealth of societies freed from the yoke of agricultural labour stems from the power to represent a speculation.

2. The value of representation

In modern times the value of things proceeds by means of the *so well distributed* faculty of estimation. That implies that any object may be used as a sign in the bustling panorama created by exchange functions, in a world where desire and need are all around us. Despite this, we find a profound contradiction in that model. There is a profound contradiction between the supposed purity of the function of value (as a form of representing promoted by money amid potentially infinite exchanges) and the individualised forms of wealth that make the sign have no value in itself but only by virtue of the wealth that is its referent: gold was cursed, but money is just as bad!

The gold of modern times is not found deposited in a mine deep under the ground, where one could dig and dig until at last it was all brought up, but rather in the length and breadth of the world, throughout space. In modern times one goes from sign to referent and from referent to sign in an infinite game of representation and supposed exchange. There is another consequence associated with the contradiction with which modernity experiences wealth. Currency does not obtain its value thanks to the Renaissance gold it was made from, but in virtue of the function of value. And that fact gives rise to a deep fear. Since wealth is no longer gold qua gold, but rather the plural forms in which our desires and needs are manifested and transformed, it may be said that there is as much gold on earth as there are human beings. That fear is implicit in the well-known expression *each nation has its gold*.[3] This was one of the great themes of mercantilism. Once more the image Davanzatti spoke of appears, that of the world in its entirety, but this time from the standpoint of the chain of relations established by the tyranny of an exchange system. How could money escape the dilemma of the sign without value?

---

3   The evocation of 'black gold' (or oil) is inevitable, as is the crisis of capitalism in the mid 1970s and the rise in price of that 'cursed gold'. We should also remember the exhaustion of the economic model of the Industrial Revolution understood as a separation between the product and the process of work. The new technological revolution will consist of integrating the product and the productive process. These changes make the grandiose manufacturing groups unnecessary: once they are segmented and fragmented they make the dynamics of a system more flexible. The restructuring of the productive apparatus has its counterpart in the changes in social structure. It is not surprising that economic globalisation should be added to socio-political globalisation.

In the 16th century the increase in metal entailed an immediate increase in the price of goods, as there was a devaluation of the gold that currency placed its stamp upon. But in the 17th century the devaluation mechanism was defined by a function that was also variable, although in a sense unknown until then: because the gold of the modern era no longer has to be sought under the ground; it is above ground and it is called *commerce*. The value of currency is in its relation to the globalised totality of commerce. The old Renaissance model has been radically transformed in the modern era. In modern times it is no longer believed that proportion may be observed in the entirety of things, in that form of totality reflected in the language of mathematics that assured humankind that proportion is present everywhere. On the contrary, in modern times we think that goods bear no objective mark to vouchsafe the amount of money to be demanded. So, as Foucault suggests, modernity's dilemma is that if something's value does not lie in itself - and the need to exchange seems to support this – neither does it lie directly, in a pure and precise way, in a value function or in the totality of commerce, but rather in the originary *interior* of a *representation*. Contemporary philosophy, psychology and sociology have had a lot to say about mechanisms, impurities, paradoxes, *desires*, etc., that are present in the very body of the representation, and the economic and advertising practices of our time seem already to have learnt a lot about them. But let us address the subject of *desire*.

3. The value of desires themselves

In 1983, in *Harvard Business Review*, Theodore Levitt published an article, later reprinted with the title "Globalization of Markets".[4] That article sets out two fundamental ideas: technology exerts a homogenising force after a prior homogenisation of desires – desires for technology, presumably; and secondly, this situation is indispensable to the development of a form of production called 'economies of scale'. The article mounts a virulent and yet reserved defence – notwithstanding the contradictoriness of this description – of the economy of scale, for the sake of what Levitt called 'the globalised company'. With this term he wished to supplant 'multinational company', which was the fashionable term in the 1980s.

A multinational company contemplates the indigenous differences of the area where it is located, whether in its internal organisation or in the products with which it enters into a specific relation with its exterior or *environment*. But a globalised company does not in any sense abandon the aim of standardising its

---

4   Theodore Levitt, "Globalization of Markets," Harvard Deusto Business Review 61 (1983): 92-102.

products, because the customer does not govern her *desires*. I believe that this assertion, put forward by Levitt and many others, should not seem strange when we remember that the value function in the modern age forces upon currency a relation of abstract representation in which it measures according to a pattern. The object for which currency is exchanged does not endow itself with value but acquires it eventually within the entire apparatus of a more or less unstable system of commerce – as unstable as the desire for the products of that commerce. So it seems reasonable for globalised companies to have as one of their most important goals the manipulation of those desires that motivate a purchase. Even in the case of a model buyer who will clinically change one for the other (desire for product) we can ask: Does his desire really belong to him in the same way as that into which it is transformed? The model buyer seeks to fulfil his desire by exchanging it for the product, which is almost identical to his desire. But if many products are presented to him answering equally well to his desire or to his original need, it may be said, following Levitt, that for practical purposes the customer does not *achieve* his desire. In some way, this *interior* in each person rather resembles Renaissance gold in the sense that for an instant it relieves us of the wearisome effort of mentally representing the world's riches in their entirety.

Economies of scale represent a bid for the power of uniform desire in a world from which the former customs houses have been eliminated. The standardised construction of desire ensures the elimination of considerable production costs. This is precisely one of the differences between economies of scale and economies of focus. The latter are doomed to be eliminated by the former.[5] The economies of focus relate to an excessively complex environment; whereas the way economies of scale relate to the environment is governed by a strict principle of simplification.

The fact that the value function made the image of commerce in its entirety appear as one of the causes of price determination and that, therefore, currency went from being a good to an instrument of measurement and arbitration of the value relation, revealed a number of difficulties. To express it with Renaissance nostalgia, value is a relation and not a mark written in a friendly fashion on the flank of the world's signs. Embracing the world as a whole does not resolve the

---

5   The economies of focus involve a high degree of specificity, but this requires, from the point of view of production, a matching specificity: flexible automation of production processes without thereby foregoing the need to produce sufficient quantities to generate a profit margin. Specificity is subject to change, and this demands not only high costs of production, design, market placement, marketing, etc., but also a constant policy of product differentiation, since products are often fatally absorbed by rivals and their originators consequently have difficulty in profiting from them.

enigma of the ultimate truth about the function of exchange, because that function is intertwined with the urgency of the desires to be fulfilled in the face of such and such finite and available goods, but not its ideal whole. Both the dynamic of unfulfilled desire and the limitation of information, that is, the dynamic inherent in the partial availability of what is real in one and for one (what is available to one as a reflective individual is also partial) make this consideration immediately relevant: that the delay in transmission of information acts upon the relations of exchange. But this important factor is also an essential part of commercial activity in its entirety. The following imaginary scenario will help us to appreciate how much is at stake for a company that fails to take risks with energy and determination in the global struggle to represent reality and purport to inform afterwards:

"Let us suppose that at a given moment the price of a product in the marketplace - apples for example - falls significantly. The number of apples sold will rise as a result of this decrease in price. However, the number of apples sold will not respond instantaneously to the price variation [...] the buyers' perception of the price drop of the apples requires a certain time, which means that there is a delay between the decrease in price of the apples and the increase in apple sales".[6]

To sum up, we have seen that the transformation of the sign of currency includes a series of changes that accompany it to the point that currency (to put it in a Deleuzean way) can be understood as the surface of a practice. One of the polemics that runs through the spirit of mercantilism is precisely whether commerce as a whole is the most important referent in determining the shifting and variable value of the currency-sign. We have also wondered how to understand one of the most powerful forms of production, namely, large-scale production. After the economic impact of the transport revolution, together with large-scale production, an ostensible difference was established in the possible forms of commercial exchange at both national and international levels. Theodore Levitt said it in an affirmatory tone when he asserted that there was an association between economies of scale and globalisation. At the time Levitt asserted this the amazing effort that went into publishing and disseminating books on the term 'globalisation' was still in its gestation period, but perhaps for this very reason some things could be seen with a less standardised clarity. Not all forms of production or all types of commercial exchange have had equivalent effects on the

---

6   Javier Aracil, Introducción a la dinámica de sistemas (Madrid: Alianza, 1992), 129.

forms of social organisation. We shall now deal with the most important features of large-scale production.[7]

4. Scaling towards indiscrimination

Economists understand *economies of scale* to be the multiple ways, according to the product in question, of achieving the reduction (this is not plural, since there is only one ideal solution) of a product's unit cost by means of producing it in great quantity. Following Charles W.-L. Hill we may say: The economies of scale have a number of sources/resources, one of the most important apparently being the ability to distribute fixed costs throughout a large volume. Fixed costs are those required to establish a certain ease of production and to develop a new product that may be economically substantial. The nature of the practice contains the main themes of the idea of a globalised world.

"For example, the fixed cost of establishing a new production line to manufactura semiconductor chips now exceeds $1 billion. Similarly, according to one estimate, developing a new drug and bringing it to market about $800 million and takes about 12 years The only way to recoup such high fixed costs may be to sell the product worldwide, which reduces average unit costs by spreading fixed costs over a larger volume. The more rapidly that cumulative sales volume is built up, the more rapidly fixed costs can be amortized over a large production volume, and the more rapidly unit costs will fall ".[8]

The consequences of a satisfactory recouping of costs give rise to investment (never optional, but always necessary), especially technological investment, which is absolutely necessary and ensures the possibility of the large-scale production line. Speed is essential in carrying out the process. A further consequence of this is to create difficulties for the survival of other companies in the sector with different forms of production. Large-scale production yields comparative advantages in relation to prices. Naturally, the claim that the comparative advantage gained from an economy of scale affects the market cannot be

---

7   The phenomenon of globalisation – as a reality and as an idea – surrounds itself with so many dominant and conflicting themes that the development of each one gives rise to a different definition of a mistaken reality by definition and according to that definition, as a reality and/or as an idea. The word evokes a world in transformation. One of those dominant themes is the economic reality and its huge power over the socio-political order. That power has been increasing to the point where commerce involves forms of expansion system dynamics that provide it with feedback. It may be said that the world was destined for globalisation.

8   Charles W.-L. Hill, Global business today (New York: Irwin Mc Graw-Hill, 2007), 374.

maintained without a certain margin of confidence in the basic principle of economic rationality, which states that every agent seeks to maximise his profits and minimise costs.

One of the immediate effects of these economies of scale was the need for integration and co-ordination both at production and management levels. The aim of recouping costs in itself exceeds the restriction on enrichment imposed by nation states. Is this enrichment perhaps assured by the model of domestic and protectionist economies? No. The forms of large-scale production and indiscriminate – and thus global - selling demand new forms of management in order to direct processes with a life that goes beyond national borders. This is why the large companies are the first to earmark funds to pay for the work of researchers who investigate the transfer of large sets of signs, ways of life, products, etc. so as to install organisations subsequently in new settings.

The emphasis on organisational aspects (over and above those concerned with mere accounting, which in itself is blind) is one of the factors of change in today's companies. There are two reasons for this. Firstly, organisations are interested in achieving full adaptation to a globalised world; secondly, it is important to display a clear mastery of the medium in which adaptation to change takes place. The success with which both these things are done is a measure of the difficulty rivals will face when they try to adapt. The old patronising ideology of national corporatism, protectionism and social welfare is no longer profitable in this new panorama.[9]

Among the many descriptions found during a quick plunge into texts that reflect the new business scene, I shall offer here some of the distinguishing features of the *episteme* of our age. But meanwhile, the transformations in the sphere of business organisation are a perfect embodiment of what the German biologist Ludwig von Bertalanffy, in the 1960s, called *general system theory*. Bertalanffy coined the term with a certain degree of consistency from the 1930s onwards. The term gave rise to important research societies after the Second World War.

---

9   Many forms of company organisation and economic practices that these ideologies served have ceased to be effective in the world we live in. Thus, for example, the market economies in the 1960s were dominated by monopolised firms using mass production, which were protecting national markets and often at the same time operating as transnational corporations. There were also forms of production with a more centralised basic ideology because they produced for domestic markets. We find a good description of this in the article by Malcolm Waters, Globalization (London/ New York: Routlege, 1995 2nd ed.), 60-93.

Many authors agree in affirming that this change of organisational paradigm represents a transformation that might be called *toyotism* (from Toyota). The Japanese example has obliged many sectors to develop certain practices, above all those related to flexible accumulation and specialisation. An example of this type is, for example, the practice of flexible accumulation called *just-in-time*, which consists of minimising the inventory volume at each stage of the production process, since too large an inventory means a non-realised value. It may seem an irony of fate that this technique in the production process is the one employed by the Ford factory in Michigan where, avoiding every kind of unnecessary accumulation of stock, the components arrive only an hour before they are needed, and very seldom do they remain in the factory more than a week. The components are compulsorily stored somewhere – in case old Henry Ford should raise his head and ask for the inevitable – but not there, in the place where production occurs, which involves a high risk in itself. Rather they are stored in more than six hundred companies or subcontracted *sub-systems* in, apparently, more than thirty countries, whose purpose is to supply components to the Ford factory. [10]

This flexible accumulation may involve a flexible specialisation: each division of production into stages necessarily has its team of workers. This practice does not have the aim of speeding up manufacturing processes, but rather that of producing on the safe basis of an existing demand. First sell, then produce: this is the secret of the technique economists, for this very reason, call *just-in-time*. The reduction of the greatest elements of risk – always unnecessary in this sector – has as its counterpart the unnecessary accumulation of goods. The risk of producing components – derived from the success achieved in persuading economic agents to take up the option of buying – is partially assumed, since the other subcontracted sub-systems also assume it.

---

10 The data on the Ford factory in the USA can be found in Richard J. Barnet, Global dreams. Imperial corporations and the new world order (New York: Touchstone, 1994). One might ask which countries these are: thirty countries are producing components for a factory in Michigan! In 1991 the Levi-Strauss company subcontracted employees in Chinese prisons for its production. In Guatemala there are 250 companies that supply companies such as Sears, Gap or Kmart, where: "[...] In order to go to the bathroom, a woman needs a pass from her supervisor, which may involve sexual favours. Many women have been beaten and sexually abused. One factory [foreman] regularly beats women on the stomach every 15 days to weed out those who may be pregnant..." Barnet, Global dreams, 43.

5. The reduction of what is diverse in the economic system

The Japanese system of quality control depends on all the workers involved in production. This is the phenomenon alluded to above with the expression *flexible specialisation*, which is also commonly called *total quality management*. Concepts such as *teamwork* point towards the same reality. What it means is that a small number of workers share a specific stage in the production process that others will take charge of in the same temporary fashion. This means that knowledge of the techniques and strategies employed will predictably be transmitted by the workers among themselves, according to the requirement of maximum competence in multiple tasks as an organisational principle. The dominant feature is therefore decentralised management: let the rigid reality of centralised control give way to the image of a multi-layered hierarchy surrounded by a floating scaffold of flexible changes and practices arising in response to variations in demand on the part of consumers in the grip of an infinite and cyclical assignation.

It would be extraordinarily complex (and, in fact, of doubtful usefulness) to chronicle how these practices originated in the framework of the business organisation of production. However, to show the connection and assimilation between, on the one hand, what Levitt called 'the globalised company' and, on the other, the development of general system theory and system dynamics, would require us to point out the conceptual isomorphism between the most important concepts of general system theory and those that surreptitiously arrive at the above-mentioned practices.[11] I shall mention this briefly here.

To implement and manage in an organised way economic processes that go beyond national borders makes it necessary to invest in research and technology in order to transfer large sets of signs, ways of life, products, etc. This is because when a system is open, that is, when there is an exchange of information between a system and its surroundings, the only way of interrupting the inexorable progress of entropy is by increasing negative entropy with a process of information transfer. This is something that is present in the far from ingenuous disposi-

---

11 In the mid 1950s, a company called Sprage Electric, which manufactured electronic components and had, in turn, electronics companies as customers, realised that there were considerable fluctuations in its number of orders. This was rather strange when we consider that being a highly specialised market with very strong customers it was assured of a flow of orders. However, this did not happen. It was then that the company commissioned J. W. Forrester to conduct a study of the problem. Forrester's conclusions gave rise to the first work in system dynamics. His conclusion was that the combination of a series of delays in the transfer of information generates the fluctuations observed. Javier Aracil, *Introducción a la dinámica*, 32.

tion of the workers in what was called *total quality management*. The workers have to explain to each other the knowledge acquired during their respective assignments in designated jobs, as the various jobs are shared by everyone. But we may also observe here the presence of what R. Ashby called the *law of requisite variety*.[12] The law of requisite variety states that the variety generated in a medium – here, *medium* is not that to which the *output* of the system in question is related, but rather the medium of work in itself – must be equal to the system's capacity to absorb it. Absorption is brought about by *reduction* of semantic variety, that is, the communication among workers with interchangeable jobs. Indeed, if that reduction of variety in opinions (resulting from each individual in their fixed and untransferable job having a different opinion) did not exist, no reduction could be achieved, because the pragmatic group impulse would fail to take place since it would be acting in accordance with a common transfer of information. However, the accumulated information avoids entropy in a predictably creative way. This fact means a benefit for the system as a whole, as an excess in effectiveness or automation of information transfer reduces the ultimate effectiveness of the organisation.

Now, with regard to the description of Ashby's law in terms of a medium, which is in effect the environment that receives the system's output – this world that is us, the medium we comprise as consumers – it may be said that the *reduction* of requisite varieties becomes a simple mechanism for standardising our desires.

The importance of approaches such as this lies only in their attempt to understand the nature of the mechanisms, or rather, the systems that dominate the world. But we should not forget that there is no immanent rationality at all in the relations of production. That is why the most important questions demanded by economic globalisation are those concerned with its rationality and its justice.

---

12   William Ross Ashby, Design for a Brain (London: Chapman & Hall, 1952). We also find a classic study of the question in Oscar Johansen Bertoglio, Introducción a la teoría de sistemas (México: Editorial Limusa, 1982).

Organizational Communication
in a Postmodern Environment

Markus Gruber

Over the past few decades Globalization has become something of a refrain. Especially one aspect is globally relevant and has changed dramatically over the time. It is the rapidly growing level of specialization and integration of world's economies. This is what is affecting the social, economic and political spheres of our modern societies. The globally increasing interconnectivities and interdependencies have changed the distinctive nature of the global value chain.[1] Integration leads to the development of new markets thereby creating new places and spaces for interaction and communication and a general fragmentation of relationships. The continuously ongoing integration of the system of global relations overrides at the same time traditional patterns and rules of communication and interaction. Thus the complexity of the global environment is steadily growing and the capacity of international influence and operation is becoming a crucial factor for success. The set of interrelated developments such as the global distribution of the production of goods and services, the reduction of international trade barriers as well as the reduction of restrictions on the movement of capital and on investment can be referred to as globalization. Business units are trading increasingly transnational and not even the multidimensional financial crises in 2008 had much of a negative long-term effect on the foreign direct investment flows. The growth of world trade and investment has influenced, shaped and transformed the ground rules and institutions of the modern world we are living in. Especially during the second half of the nineteenth century the degree of integration rose up to an impressive degree.[2] All these developments had a massive impact on the global system. The traditional state-centered world order is eroding more or less slowly. "The world economy and attempts to manage and regulate it are now at the heart of international relations in a way that would have been difficult to believe a century ago and very surprising even 30 years ago".[3] Strange argues that there is a connection between the organizational transforming and learning (increasing institutional quality) and the growing

---

1 Paul Krugman, Richard Cooper and T. N. Srinivasan, "Growing World Trade: Causes and Consequences." Brookings Papers on Economic Activity, 1. (1995): 328.
2 Krugman et al. „Growing World Trade".
3 Chris Brown and Kirsten Ainley, Understanding International Relation (Palgrave Macmillan, 2005), 141.

level of integration.[4] The complexity of the global environment is steadily rising and the capacity of international influence is becoming a crucial factor for success. But what is the driving force of this development and how does it translate into the organizational and institutional architecture of global actors? What are the resources and the underlying principles of the global changes in the past?

An investigation into the structural changes and adaption of global actors needs to analyze the direct and indirect impacts of globalization on organizations from an organization-centered perspective. This provides us with an analytic framework to explore strategies adopted by business units in order to adapt to changes in their environment such as the increasing complexity of international economic relations.

The main goal will be to identify the factors determining adaption on the basis of what we know about the strategies in which organizations react (learn, innovate, transform) in response to pressures from globalization.
Starting the analysis from a wider perspective on organizations such as business units has a simple and obvious reason. Business units are usually the first socioeconomic units in the means of time and order of development that are affected from environmental changes. This way we can use them as explanatory variable to gain insights into the dynamics and effects of globalization.

- Setting the Frame: Historical Trends and the Role of Innovation

From the past million years human development went through a sequence of different employment patterns. First there was hunting and gathering, then breeding and cultivating and then modern growth of sectors like industry or services in places.[5] Employment and population structures always have been strongly related to development and progress. Progress always goes hand in hand with an improvement in economic organization, thus a higher level of institutional quality.[6] For a better understanding of progress it might be quite useful to draw a distinction between the change in technology and a change in technique. A change in technology results in more output from the same given set of

---

4   Susan Strange, "The Westfailure System," Review of International Studies. vol. 25, no. 4, (1999): 349.

5   Douglass North, Institutions, Institutional Change, and Economic Performance, (Cambridge: Cambridge University Press, 1990): 44.

6   Daron Acemoglu, Simon Johnson and James Robinson, "The Colonial Origins of Comparative Development: An Empirical Investigation," National Bureau of Economic Research Working Paper No. 7771 (2000); Robert Hall and Charles Jones, "The Productivity of Nations" NBER Working Paper No. 5812 (1996); Douglass North, Structure and change in economic history (New York: W.W. Norton & Co., 1981).

factor inputs while a change in technique is simply characterized by a factor substitution. The transition to semi-sedentary to settled agriculture was a process of integration and has to be seen in connection with the demographic transition from the flat bell to the population explosion.[7] With the growth of population people developed -out of necessity - new forms of social organization, better economic organizations and improved social institutions. This organizational transforming towards an overall better institutional quality set free new potential and work force and therefore productivity. The population grew further and more and more people changed from hunting and gathering into the cultivation sector. Another reason for the shift was that hunting and gathering depleted common property resources. This in turn resulted in harder work per unit of output.[8]

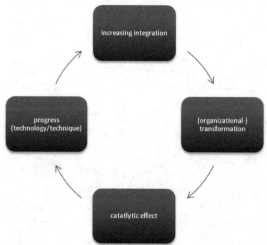

Figure 1: Innovation-Circle (Source: compiled by the author)

But this configuration became increasingly unstable. Generally systems go to equilibrium. According to the Principle of Asymmetric Transitions[9] the direction of the transition goes from a less stable configuration A to a more stable configuration B.[10] "So in going from any state to one of the equilibria, the system is

---

7 Douglass North and Robert Thomas, "The First Economic Revolution," Economic History Review, Vol 2, no. 30 (1977): 234.

8 North and Thomas, "The First Economic Revolution".

9 Ashby proposes the Principle of the Self-Organizing System (1962).

10 $P(A \rightarrow B) > P(B \rightarrow A)$ (under the condition $P(A \rightarrow B) \neq 0$).

going from a larger number of states to a smaller. In this way, it is performing a selection, in the purely objective sense that it rejects some states, by leaving them, and retains some other state, by sticking to it.".[11] Reducing the number of reachable states diminishes the complexity of the system. In order not to conflict with the second law of thermodynamics, stating that entropy in a closed system cannot decrease, von Foerster concludes that the system is not closed. Hence it does loose entropy to its environment.[12] In our case we can interpret the pressure through growth of population and its consequences (extinctions of a variety of larger animal species) as a catalytic effect for the upcoming event which North and Thomas argue to be the "First Economic Revolution"[13]. Behind the men's shift from being a hunter to become a producer of goods lies a fundamental change of the incentive: it was the evolution of exclusive property rights that account for the significantly increasing rate of human development towards a complex and highly intertwined society with a high level of specialization and labor division.[14] This change from common property rights to the new system provided a direct incentive for the acquisition of new technology and improvement of productivity and efficiency. That recursively resulted in more integration.

1. Theoretical Perspective

Systemic Approach

"A system is any organized collection of parts united by prescribed interactions and designed for the accomplishment of specific goals or general purposes. (...) Organizations can be characterized as constantly shifting states of dynamic equilibrium. They are highly adaptive systems that are integral parts of their environments".[15] Organizations are structures themselves and give structure to common economic, social and political concerns in a society at the same time. Organizations are composed of a number of interrelated people. That makes

---

11 Ross Ashby, An introduction to Cybernetics, (London: Methuen, 1964), 44.
12 Foerster, Heinz von, "On Self-Organizing Systems and Their Environments", quoted as in
    Foerster, "Understanding Understanding. Essays on Cybernetics and Cognition,"
    (Springer, New-York/Berlin, 2003: 1-20.
13 North and Thomas, "The First Economic Revolution".
14 North and Thomas, "The First Economic Revolution," 229-230.
15 Kenneth Boulding, "General Systems Theory." Management Science, 2, 3 (1956) and reprinted in General Systems, Yearbook of the Society for General Systems Research, vol. 1, (1956), 242-243.

them an integral part of pluralistic societies. An organization is a set of relationships with an identity of its own. For an organization to be effective means to develop both, the cohesion of the whole structure (vertical integration) and the autonomy of the participating individuals (horizontal integration). To measure effectiveness of an organization we can use viability as concept to operationalize effectiveness. Speaking of viability in this context means that organizations such as for instance business units have the capacity to solve problems and furthermore are able to respond to unexpected and unanticipated changes in the environment. In other terms: Organizations must be flexible in order to survive changes in their complex environment if they are to survive, in turn, virtually all of their decisions and actions affect their environment. "Systems theory views an Organization as a complex set of dynamically intertwined and interconnected elements including its inputs, processes, outputs, and feedback loops and the environment in which it operates and with which it continuously interacts. A change in any element of the system causes changes in other elements. The interconnections tend to be complex, dynamic, and often unknown; thus, when management makes decisions involving one organizational element, unanticipated impacts usually occur throughout the organizational system".[16]

Seen from a systemic point of view organizations are (sub-)systems of the societal level. You can draw a distinction between a society's organization systems like politics or the economy and formal organizations like political parties or companies. Organizations tend to act in favor or at least according to the formal (given) structures or common patterns of behavior (as an agent) of the organizational structure they belong to. Having the case that a formal organization has to process and produce an output like a common decision or binding agreement, the formal organization is constraint by the rules and conventions of the organization system to which it is related (belongs).[17] The corollaries are, first of all that the formal organizations work on their short- and mid-term performance. That is where they provide a specific service. Activities that seem not disputable for organization's nature are its primary activities. These are embedded in a specific environment. From this specific the Organization receives stimuli. As a feedback to the received input the organization produces an output. Espejo argues that the environment is a complex totality with a number of different aspects, including (1) the technological aspect, (2) the political aspect, (3) the economic aspect, (4) the socio-cultural aspect and (5) the ecological aspect.[18] These

---

16 Boulding, "General Systems Theory," 243.
17 Raul Espejo, Werner Schuhmann, Markus Schwaninger and Ubaldo Bilello, Organisational Transformation and Learning, (Chichester: Wiley, 1996).
18 Espejo et al, Organisational Transformation and Learning.

labels correspond with the aforementioned highly complex organization systems on the societal level. The inputs and outputs are usually of different nature and derive from the output flow of and to different environmental segments or institutions (organization system or formal organization). As we stated in the beginning of this analysis, due to the increase in specialization and more segmented labor division we find ourselves confronted with a global value chain, interconnectivity in almost all aspects of life and this within a setting of an environment with steadily exceeding complexity. In order to maintain viable and perform effectively within this fast spinning environmental change, organizations have to find strategies and solutions to cope with complexity and variety. Complexity is a system's property of being able to adopt a large number of states and behaviors.[19] This is the case when phenomena are not strictly linear logical context but if they influence each other recursively (loop wise, in a cybernetic way). One can express the complexity as the number of possible states of a system, call this identity variety and measure it.[20] The mathematical expression most frequently used is:

$$V = m^{\frac{n(n-1)}{2}}$$

V = Variety (the number of possible states of a system)

m = number of relations between the elements

n = number of elements

Source: compiled by the author

The level of complexity is the ratio of a system's elements and the possible relations to each other.

2. Key Concepts

2.1. Managing Complexity: Coherence and the Role of Communication

„Only Variety can absorb variety".[21] This idea is drawn from the „Law of requisite variety" and states essentially that in order to control a situation effectively, the variety level of the action response must at least be as complex as the variety of the situation to be managed. Thus the behavioral repertoire must at least correspond to or exceed the residual variety of the situation. From the „Law of req-

---

19 Stafford Beer, The Heart of the Enterprise, (Chichester: Wiley, 1979).

20 Roger Conant and Ross Ashby, Every good regulator of a system must be a model of that system," International Journal of System Science, vol 1, no. 2 (1970): 92-117.

21 Ashby, An introduction to Cybernetics, 206.

uisite variety" Ashby and Conant derived an important theorem. The Conant-Ashby-Theorem states that „Every good regulator of a system must be a model of that system".[22] Thus the theorem states, that the effectiveness of an organization is a function of the on which it is based. Usually organizations are confronted with situations that exceed their own level of variety by far. This asymmetry in variety doesn't have to be a threat to the effectiveness or viability of the organization. An organization contains autonomous sub-systems that deal with shares of the variety. The key is how to divide and delegate (orchestrate) the shares of the problem to the adequate receiver. Put together in a right way the combination of the products or problem solutions generated by the sub-systems, will provide a level of variety that is apt to deal with the variety of the initial situation the organization was confronted with. This corresponds with Aristotle's notion that the wholeness is more than just the sum of its components. As a consequence systems face a new dimension of quality requirement. The art is the arrangement of the single components (sub-systems). Each has to perform at its best, autonomously following an optimal path without affecting the other components in a negative way. The challenge is the dynamic adaption to the constantly changing environment.

Change can be seen as discontinuous function of time. Hence new organizational arrangements become necessary when the consequences of adaption to variety unfold along the arrow of time. The concept of coherence implies a high level of structural integration which needs to be logically and positively connected (thereby creating synergies). This requires structures allowing elements of the system autonomous space for action at the same time and creating coherence between the autonomous units producing larger producing agreed purposes for the larger organizations (Espejo and Harnden 1989).[23] Organizations make great efforts to achieve internal coherence through processes that guarantee the internal balance of change and adaption. This is what Espejo calls "organizational fitness".[24] To maintain the organizational fitness, the organization must realize its goals in constant adaption to the environment. These processes are based on communication. The basic functions of Communication generally acknowledged by the literature on Communication, is to affect the receiver knowledge or behavior by informing, directing, regulating socializing and persuading. Thus organizational communication fulfills specific functional communication

---

22   Conant and Ashby, "Every good regulator of a system must be a model of that system", 92-117.
23   Raul Espejo and Roger Harnden, The Viable System Model Revisited: Interpretations and Applications of Stafford Beer's VSM, (Chichester: Wiley, 1989).
24   Espejo and Harnden, The Viable System Model Revisited.

exchanges. Myers and Myers identify three primary functions of organizational communication:

- Coordination and regulation of production activities (problem-solving, decision-making): production activities require dynamic, reciprocal, horizontal communication between production workers and non-routinized, two-way, vertical communications between production workers and managers. This requires communication to have a coordinating and regulating aspect, what makes it more important, complex and difficult at the same time.

- Socialization (sense-giving, conflict management, leading, motivating, influencing, compliance-gaining): this function of communication focuses on articulating, reinforcing and reproducing organizational values and an specific organizational culture via aligning individual goals with organizational goals. In this function communication occurs reciprocally between organizational members.

- Innovation (Conflict management, negotiating, bargaining, intelligence): This function is associated with strong exchange of information with the relevant milieu the Organization is embedded. In this case the organization has an important transmission function. Adapting to the environment in order to survive within the milieu triggers and fosters organizational development and improvement of techniques and technologies used.

Any organizational structure can be characterized as a network of various communication channels between specific people and resources. Generally the contents transported via the various communication channels provide the organization with its structural coherence. Hence the coherence is the better the larger communication capacity, a common-sense of culture and the leaner the structure of each of the channels are.

2.2. Organizational Learning and Transforming

It is widely recognized that globalization imposes stresses on the organizational systems like politics, economics and the society. There are strategies to overcome these frictions. Systems tend to adjust to pressure in a process we called adaption. When structures resist a load, they do so by pushing back at it with an equal or opposite force. It was Robert Hooke (1635-1702) who realized the underlying principle behind the question how materials or structures can resist a load. This is also implicit in Newton's third law of motion which states that action and reaction are being equal and opposite. Gordon pinpoints it that way: "Thus if any structural system is to do its job - that is to say, if the load is supported in a satisfactory way so that nothing very much happens - then it must somehow manage to produce a push or pull which is exactly equal and opposite to the force which is being applied to it."[25] Hence a successful organization designs arranges and assembles its components in a way that is intended to sustain pressure stimuli like stresses from the environment. This is a process of learning and transformation. "Simon defined organizational learning as the growing insights and successful restructurings of organizational problems by individuals reflected in the structural elements and outcomes of the organization itself".[26] To be able to operate effectively and efficiently the organization strives for a logical configuration of its components. This we called coherence. It is a matter of the organization's structural design how successful an organization can match its situation. The level of "situational awareness" depends largely on the coherence a of the organization's components. The higher the level of coherence the more likely it is that the organization yields a better performance. Coherence is a prerequisite for innovative strategic choices when managing the efficiency and effectiveness of an organization. The structure of an organization is the materialized realization of the strategy. The structure is the materialized image of all the processes channels and flows of information that is the essence of the organization.

2.3. The Role of Innovation

Innovation is an important source of growth and one of the key determinants of competitive advantage for many organizations. Achieving innovation requires the coordinated efforts of many different actors and the integration of activities across specialized functions, knowledge domains and different contexts of application. Thus, organizational creation is fundamental to the process of innovation.[27] The ability of an organization to innovate is a necessary pre-condition for the successful utilization of inventive resources and new technologies. Conversely, the introduction of new technology often presents complex opportunities and challenges for organizations, leading to changes in managerial practices and the emergence of new organizational forms. Organizational and technological innovations are intertwined. Schumpeter for instance saw organizational changes, alongside new products and processes, as well as new markets as factors of "creative destruction".

---

25   J. E.Gordon, Structures: or Why Things don't fall down. (Da Capo Press, 1978), 35.
26   Marlene Fiol and Marjorie Lyles,. "Organizational Learning." Academy of Management Review. vol. 10 no. 4 (1985): 803-813.
27   Van de Ven, A.H.; Polley, D. E., Garud, R. and Venkataraman, S. The Innovation Journey. Oxford University Press Inc, Oxford, New York. 1999.

Markus Gruber

3. Adding a Dimension of Analysis

From an international political economy perspective, the international political system of states claiming exclusive authority and the monopoly of legitimate violence within their territorial limits - the so called "Westphalian System"[28] - is inseparable from the prevailing capitalist market economy which also first evolved in Europe. Each was a necessary condition for the evolution of the other. To prosper, production and trade required the security provided by the state. To survive, the state requires economic growth, hence the credit creating system of finance, provided by the economic system that the state has to protect in return. The reduction of trade barriers leads on the long-term perspective to the convergence of prices of goods and factors. Relatively scarce factors in each country are declining in their nominal, real and relative reward. "Nowadays, most governments in the world which do not rely on direct physical coercion to stay in power (as well as some that do) understand that their well-being and survival in office is more or less directly determined by their success at economic management, and this is task that cannot be understood in isolation from the international economy. This, it is worth remembering, is a relatively new state of affairs".[29] International fragmentation and interdependencies are eroding the traditional state-to-state-system.

„Globalization is not a phenomenon. It is not just some passing trend. Today it is an overarching international system shaping domestic politics and foreign relations to virtually every country and we need to understand it as such".[30] As indicated above the international system has transformed and adapted. By shifting the focus away from a state-centered analysis to an organization-centered perspective we can eliminate a blind spot resulting from the market-state-asymmetry. This market-state-asymmetry is an effect of the globalization and can be described as the gradual change of communication patterns and therefor relations between the elements in the international system. The system has changed in so far that there are new actors (e.g. regions - particularly in the EU-context), supranational actors (EU, WTO etc.) and non-state actors (NGOs, business units), which are all interconnected in a very complex relational context. The actors are over different systemic levels and through different channels

---

28 "The post 1648 system of international relations in which states - secular, sovereign, independent, and equal - are the members, and stability is preserved by the balance of power, diplomacy and international law." (Berridge and Alan 2001).

29 Chris Brown, and Kirsten Ainley, "Understanding International Relations," (Palgrave Macmillan, 2005), 141.

30 Thomas Friedman, The Lexus and the Olive tree: Understanding Globalisation. (Harper-Collins, 2000), 3.

in different constellations interlinked (Hooghe and Marks 2001; Putnam 1993).[31] In the wake of the transformation of the international system, the political organization is not able to transform and adapt as fast as it is possible for business organizations. A few decades ago diplomacy was "the term given to official channels of communication employed by the members of a system of states".[32] While states used to be the basic units in the international system with a gatekeeper-function when it came to communication and interaction in general there are now functionally differentiated units such as business units that are managing the transcending issues.[33] That calls for a coordinated approach that pays attention to the vertical and horizontal tension lines caused by multidimensional differentiated stakeholders. There is a rising number of issues that can't be dealt with on national level or without including societies from other regions, cultures or countries. The eroding blocks of national structures make space for new functional arrangements. This gap is usually filled by new channels of organizational communication spanning the boundaries of the subsequent logically linked subsystems, which can be for instance business units that are organizing and institutionalizing their interactions with their relevant environment. In the multi-level reality of an integrated and specialized world economy a business unit that is active on a global scale are adapting to the market-state-asymmetry by filling the structural gap and might address its communication to a whole lot of different actors in different countries and different contexts. This postmodern model (Figure 2) allows us to understand changes, developments and growth as function of organizational sophistication.

Organizational learning and transforming can be seen as the driving force and nurturing basis for innovation. The main challenge in this context is to manage the coherence of the organizational communication flow. That way the communication transcending out of the organization - becoming public - can be channeled properly and materialize in the relevant environment such as the political system of a country for regulatory issues etc. It is important to note that all the elements are in recursive relation to each other.

31   Gary Marks and Lisbeth Hooghe, Multi-level Governance and European Integration. (Rowman & Littlefield: Boulder. Colorado, 2001); Robert Putnam, "Diplomacy and Domestic Politics – The logic of Two-level Games," In: Evans, Paul, ed. "Double-edged diplomacy. International bargaining and domestic politics," (University of California Press, 1993)

32   Berridge, G. R. , Keens-Soper, Maurice and Otte T. G., "Diplomatic Theory from Machiavelli to Kissinger," (Basingstoke: Palgrave, 2001): 26

33   Brian Hocking and David Spence, "Foreign Ministries in the European Union: Integrating Diplomats," (Palgrave Macmillan Press, 2005)

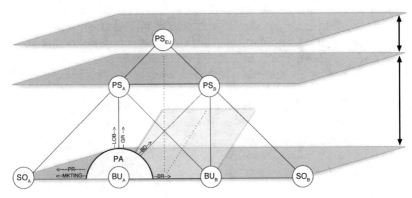

The graphic shows a model of the supra-territorial postmodern system of integrated international relations where relations between the elements of the system are transcending the traditional layer-hierarchy.

Abbriviations

SO = Society (Index: Country A/B)   PR = Public Relations
PS = Political System (Index: Country A/B)   LOB = Lobbying
BU = Business Unit (Index: Country A/B)   GR = Government Relations
PA = Public Affairs Sphere (corresponds to the   BD = Business Diplomacy
external dimension of organization communica-
tion with its different operational channels and
instruments)
MKTING = Marketing   BR = Business Relations

Source: compiled by the author

Figure 2: Postmodern multi-level multi-actor system

3.1. Concluding Remarks

This analysis has repeatedly referred to the rapidly growing level of integration and specialization of the world's economies as the main aspect that is fundamentally changing the social, economic and political spheres of our lives. Issues that are relevant to these spheres are no longer contained in a two-dimensional level of analysis. The postmodern environment has to be explored in a three-dimensional space of analysis. The functional accuracy of the institutions of the classic "Westphalian" political system is not able to fulfill its requirements. We witness a process of adaption to the new requirements in the international system. Issues that require higher levels of coordination (above the state-level) are transcending. Business units are translating these pressures and requirements from a changed environment into their organizational architecture. The international system is differentiating. The new channels of communication and interaction will develop further and institutionalize. The better the "quality" of the institution resulting from the organizational transformation and learning process, the more innovative the business unit can be, which will result in a higher degree of integration and specialization (change in productivity) and so on and so forth. This emphasizes the complementary nature of coherent organizational transformation (learning, adaption) and an the increase of integration.

Cities and Architecture in a Time of Globalization

Jasna Cizler

Globalization is leaving an undeniable mark on cities and architecture. The world today experiences expansive forms of urbanization, a spatial expansion of the city, which is not just a consequence of globalization, but also its driver[1]. As the world urbanizes, cities become globalized. Under such circumstances, architecture and cities act as a mirror in which the image of society is reflected.

Globalization in architecture first emerged as a collaboration. A need for new, modern architecture in the early 20th century as a response to new industries and technology, mobility, and the existing social and political order led to the birth of the International Style. Based on standardization, mass production, functional logic and aesthetic composition deprived of ornament, this style was in use in different countries - Le Corbusier built in India, Khan in Bangladesh, and Foster in Japan. This meant that if they have similar use, buildings in South Asia may be the same as those in America. Architect Rem Koolhaas talks about the beginnings of globalization in architecture: „UN was a building that an American could never have *thought* and a European could never have *built*. It was a *collaboration*, not only between two architects, but between cultures; a cross-fertilization between Europe and America produced a hybrid that could not have existed without their mating, however unenthusiastic."[2]

Architecture is today deeply affected by globalization and its orientation to private rather than public interests. The construction market is led by the needs of consumers and typical architectural manifestations in a city of globalization are banking skyscrapers, shopping malls and chains of standardized hotels and restaurants: „Today's architecture is subservient to the market and its terms. The market has replaced ideology. Architecture has turned into a spectacle. It has to package itself and no longer has significance as anything but a landmark."[3]

Market pressures force designers to create objects that look unusual. Even big cities that have their identities established a long time ago now aim at creating unusual architecture in order to stay attractive. Despite being critical towards many characteristics of global architecture, Koolhaas designed a CCTV building

---

1 Urbanization is an increase in the proportion of the total population that lives in urban areas, Michael Pacione, Urban Geography: A Global Perspective (London and New York: Routledge, Taylor & Francis Group, 2009), 88.

2 OMA, Rem Koolhaas and Bruce Mau. Small, Medium, Large, Extra Large (New York: The Monacelli Press, 1998), 363.

3 "Evil Can also Be Beautiful," Spiegel, March 3, 2006.

in Beijing that is no exception in these terms. Does this mean that architects are becoming servants of private interests and interests of the market, instead of creating a good architecture for the public? 40% of buildings with over 12 floors all over the world were built after 2000. This is particularly evident in Asia where cities are full of contrasts - traditional blocks are being demolished to accommodate new lifestyle. With 16.5 million people, Shanghai is today one of the largest metropolitan areas in the world, the biggest and most globalized city in China and a city that experiences the fastest globalization in the world. Urban redevelopment began to accelerate in the 1990s with the city aiming to become one of the international economic, finance and trade centers. In 1980 Shanghai had 121 buildings with over 8 floors and there are now more than 10,000 of such buildings in the city. Such development has demographic and social implications - immigrants from rural China make one fifth of the total population, often coming to work on construction sites despite being unqualified and inexperienced[4]. Beijing's panorama was once dominated by the Forbidden City and monumental, uniform public buildings. The city until 1990 did not have a central business zone. In recent years it was turned into one of the largest construction sites in history, with thousands of new projects, mostly skyscrapers, being realized. Half of the world's annual production of concrete and one third of steel production was spent on the Chinese architectural boom during the preparation for the Olympics. Technology associated with cheap labor has turned China into a playground and testing place for foreigner architects. Low paid Chinese workers enable them to design buildings whose construction would be impossible in another country.

1. Global City – Positive Trend or a Problem?

The world's largest cities are major places of globalization. The term Global city, coined by Saskia Sassen[5], indicates urban centers where major companies

---

4   It is estimated that 150 million people in China left villages, mainly to find jobs in industrial towns on the coast. In 1970s less than 20% of the population of China lived in cities, today the figure is around 40%. Many villages in China disappear due to the emigration, or only the old and children remain in them, Peter Hessler, Inside the Dragon. National Geographic, May 2008.

5   Saskia Sassen is one of the leading sociologists who contributed to the study of relation between cities and globalization and is credited with having coined the term global city. Sassen has a critical perspective on global cities particularly for its social polarization. She concluded that global city formation results in a dual and highly polarized labor market – with global corporate elite earning high salaries and having high standard of material well-being on one side, and low-wage service workers, many of whom immi-

and plenty of financial, technical and consulting services are located (such as Tokyo, New York and London). Global cities are faced with many challenges and the question is how to plan their development efficiently. One of the biggest challenges is the increasing number of inhabitants. For the first time in history, more people live in cities than in villages. It is anticipated that in 50 years over 75% of the population will be living in cities. Globalization causes mass migration from the developing regions of Africa, Asia, Latin America and some parts of Europe, thus transforming the global cities of the North (Europe, North America) into heterogeneous and multicultural settings. More than 50% of the population of New York and Toronto were classified as ethnic minorities or foreign-born, while the percentage of foreign residents in London is 29%, and in Paris above 15%[6]. As a result emerges a spatial and social segregation between residents. Global cities are characterized by high levels of inequality - simultaneously with wealth there is extreme poverty, and a slum is a phenomenon typical for contemporary urbanism in Africa[7]. Globalization changes the relationship between large urban centers and areas around them that remain on the periphery of economic growth. Moscow and peripheral regions of Russia are an example of the disparity between the global city and the rest of the country. Almost all new foreign investments are concentrated in a capital, and with the increasing importance of global cities connecting, decreases the importance of connections between the city and region.

Rem Koolhaas has introduced a concept of *Generic city* as a critique of global cities. He compares modern cities with airports that are all the same: "The street is dead... ...The Generic City is on its way from horizontality to verticality. The skyscraper looks as if it will be the final, definite typology. It has swallowed everything else. It can exist anywhere: in a rice field, or downtown – it makes no difference anymore."[8] There is a conscious rejection of the identity and shift from diversity to the similarity. Some cities even have to set aside their past, history and heritage in the name of economic survival: "Some continents, like Asia, aspire to the Generic City; others are ashamed by it... ....Sometimes

---

grants, on the other side, Douglas Yang, "Sassen, Saskia," in Encyclopedia of Urban Studies, ed. Ray Hutchison (Thousand Oaks: SAGE, 2010), 687-688.

6   Anar Valiyev and H. V. Savitch, "Globalization," in Encyclopedia of Urban Studies, ed. Ray Hutchison (Thousand Oaks: SAGE, 2010), 318.

7   It is anticipated that in 2020 1.4 billion people will live in slums. This number today is about one billion, meaning that one out of seven inhabitants of the Planet lives in a slum.

8   OMA, Koolhaas and Mau. Small, Medium, Large, Extra Large, 1253.

an old, singular city, like Barcelona, by oversimplifying its identity, turns Generic. It becomes transparent, like a logo. The reverse never happens..."[9]

London, 2011 – an image that could easily be located in any other city
(photo by author)

The generic city is characterized by the absence of history. Still, international tourism based on sites visits is a growing phenomenon. Every year 15 million tourists visit Paris, 11 millions visit London and 6 millions New York[10]. This makes tourism a major urban industry, but it also turns cities into centers of consumption, entertainment, the service industry and infrastructure for accommodating tourism needs. Simultaneously with destroying of historic quarters and local identity, selling places and attracting tourists is easier when there remains a semblance of historic continuity: "In spite of its absence, history is the major preoccupation, even industry, of the Generic City. On the liberated grounds, around the restored hovels, still more hotels are constructed to receive additional tourists in direct proportion to the erasure of the past... ...Tourism is now independent of destination."[11]

This turn towards the commercial, and similarity can be seen in most global cities. Many Asian cities today seem like copies of Western models – with cen-

9   OMA, Koolhaas and Mau. Small, Medium, Large, Extra Large, 1250.
10   Valiyev and Savitch, "Globalization," 318.
11   OMA, Koolhaas and Mau. Small, Medium, Large, Extra Large, 1256-1257.

tral business zones, air-conditioned skyscrapers, McDonald's restaurants and shopping malls selling the same products. Remains of the original city fabric, temple, mosque or small shops are withdrawn in small enclaves or preservation zones. That way experience of being in cities in different parts of the world threatens to become the same. In such a system, democratic models of decision-making that involve smaller interest groups such as local communities, ethnic minorities, immigrants, the elderly and the poor, are being neglected. This is closely connected with a term gentrification, indicating a process of physical, economic, social and cultural transformation of the area, resulting in an extension of the property system of the private ownership of domestic property, resettlement and possibly even marginalization of former residents, by introducing individuals who share the same cultural lifestyle and consumer preferences. Its negative effects are mostly felt by the less well-off and displaced households and businesses[12]. Moral questions could be raised here - why should people be forced out of their low cost homes? The Chinese construction boom destroys most of hutongs, old urban districts with traditional homes, whose inhabitants are often relocated to make way for new projects. As Deyan Sudjic pointed out before the Olympic Games, the new Beijing will present China as an economic superpower, but it will also serve to highlight the gap between rich and poor[13]. Income in Chinese cities is more than three times bigger than in rural areas. The expansion of the global economy narrows and replaces local economy, that way marginalizing some parts of the population. Aside from destroying smaller communities, these processes have ecological consequences: –the growing number of factories, farms, dams and cities causes pollution and destroys nature.

Valuable city spaces are under the pressure of investors. Market-led development is one of the major threats to public spaces and heritage. A need to promote the city in an increasingly competitive market stands in contrast with development of projects that the local community needs most. Clearly, new uses and spaces can be lucrative for the owners, but completely irrelevant to the interests of citizens. A question is whether they will be properly used and whether the new function will contribute to the preservation of values such as local democracy, public control, heritage, the urbanity of cities and the quality of its public places. After selling public services and property to global companies, less power is left to local representatives to respond to the problems such as social inequality. Typical consequences are dominance of private places and increasingly corporate-owned cities, with controlled, monotonous developments

---

12   Andrew Tallon, Urban Regeneration in the UK (Oxon: Routledge, 2010).
13   Deyan Sudjic, "The City that Ate the World," The Guardian, October 16, 2005.

denying engagement and interaction with passers-by (gated communities are one of the manifestations of this). At the same time, less controlled public and green spaces and places that do not bring income, stay neglected. This is followed by production of places that are identical in cities of different cultures, such as shopping malls or airports. One of the results is exclusivity, as spaces of consumption are accessible and open only for selected people and closed for many marginalized groups. Local culture and diversity of natural landscapes are repressed. It is obvious that a different approach is needed in order to relate to the problems that cities face today.

Leeds, 2011 – dominance of roads and a lack of public spaces are typical for global cities, but also for many residential areas in cities around the world (photo by author)

2. Exploring Development Alternatives. Is a different approach possible?

Discussed phenomena are just some of the changes that have occurred in architecture and cities in the global era. With urban areas growing and attracting new residents who rush to them in search of a better life, the city remains the most common model of urban development. But is it the best one we know? Cities need changes and turn towards more sustainable ways of functioning. There is a need for a more integrated, holistic and innovative approach and ideas for this could be followed in concepts that emerged in the last few decades. Being critical towards the influence of private interests on the production of cal towards the influence of private interests on the production of space, Henry Lefebvre introduced the concept of The Right to the City and suggested occupation and creation of spaces free of capitalist influence. Lefebvre explains that the right to the city as the right to urban life, to spaces of encounter and exchange, right to inhabit and conquer the space regardless of the ownership[14]. David Harvey writes about the equal right to the city and decision-making that all actors should have. He describes the right to the city as a collective right to influence the process of creating cities[15]. A number of modern movements, including the squatter movement and a number of artistic movements, have accepted this idea as a basis of its functioning. A city and its public spaces could be understood as a public good - a value that all people have a right to without paying and exclusion. Involvement of people outside formal governmental decision-making processes through different citizens' associations and initiatives can be significant for indicating the importance and meaning of urban space. Even a small degree of autonomy of social actors can encourage initiative and self-organization, and a small group of innovators can demonstrate how things can be done differently. Participation is important because it provides the ability to translate potentially destructive conflicts in urban development into constructive ones on the basis of associations, cooperation, compromise and consensus. Such an inclusive approach would make space for non-elitist culture and production of community and working class. Site-based resistance movements, with artist and community intervention in the regeneration process, activation of unused buildings, DIY culture of squats and participatory architectural and urban design are manifestations of these concepts and they clearly stand in contrast with big projects of urban regeneration and gentrification. Flexibility in urban planning, rather than a rigid, rational approach, could create a context in which actors can be involved in the process of transforming the environment through learning, experimenting and engaging in a dialogue[16].

Localization occures as a counterbalance to globalization. In cities of mixing cultures, social inequalities and the dominance of private interests, localization could be significant as a mean of bringing back the power to residents to influence and plan their living spaces. Helena Norberg-Hodge[17] believes that a long-

---

14   Henry Lefebvre, Writings on Cities (Oxford: Blackwell Publishers, 1996).

15   David Harvey. Social Justice and the City (London: Edward Arnold, 1973).

16   Michael Burayidi, ed. Urban Planning in a Multicultural Society (Westport, USA: Praeger Publishers, 2000).

17   Helena Norberg-Hodge, "Shifting Direction: From Global Dependence to Local Interdependence," in ed. Jerry Mander and Edward Goldsmith, The Case Against the Global Economy: and for a Turn Toward the Local (San Francisco: Sierra Club Books,

term solution to prevent social and environmental problems requires a large number of small, diverse, local initiatives, and describes a number of initiatives directed towards creating new types of economy based on the community. What is more, Norberg-Hodge draws attention to the fact that urbanization is often mentioned as a response to overpopulation, which implies that centralization is more efficient because the urban population uses less resources. But, according to her, when costs of urbanization are considered more closely, it is clear that large-scale centralized systems use resources more intensively and are more harmful for the environment than small-scale models. For example, food and water on which the population is dependent are continuously transported over long distances, thus spending a lot of energy and creating large amount of waste. Norberg-Hodge writes that it is necessary to support models based on the under-standing of the diversity of places and to support the remaining rural communities and small farmers because they are a key to rebuilding a healthy and strong economy. Another step that can be taken is the use of renewable, locally available energy, which would reduce pollution, ease the pressure of large-scale energy installations, and reduce dependence on oil. Also, measures for the protection of rural households, small local companies and local businesses can have important role in providing equivalent development of cities and rural areas, thus narrowing the gap between the rich and the poor and stopping excessive migration to cities. Initiatives and campaigns of ordinary people, such as Buy local, help small, local businesses to survive and prevent the outflow of money from the local economy. Similar models are *Community-supported agriculture* (in USA), *Subscription farming* (in Europe) and *Linking farmers and consumers* (in UK), innovations in agriculture in which consumers associate directly with farmers from the surrounding thus getting closer to the production process of the goods they use. This also means less unnecessary transport typical for globalization - the longest distance that food travels in these systems is 320 km. The movement for the creation of ecological villages which brings together communities from all over the world who seek a more sustainable, environmentally cleaner way of life through the development of a local economy by using renewable sources of energy is based on similar ideas. All these ways enable people to remain in villages or towns in which they were born, to preserve their cultural and personal identity, and thus contribute to the maintenance of more sustainable ways of life even in times of globalization.

Part Three

Case Studies

The Role of Globalization in the Process of Singlezation

Ana Tajder

One phenomena of our postmodern society is the continuously increasing number of people choosing to live alone, outside of a long-term partnership - a process I have named *singlezation*. As American sociologist Eric Klinenberg noted in his interview for PBS Newshour on 27 March 2012, "this is the biggest social change of the last 50 or 60 years that we have failed to name or identify." According to him, while in 1950, 22 percent of American adults were single, today this number has risen to more than 50 percent. The marriage rate in the EU-27 declined from 7.9 marriages per 1,000 inhabitants in 1970 to 4.5 marriages in 2009, an overall reduction of 34 %. In the same time, the divorce rate doubled from 1.0 divorce per 1,000 inhabitants in 1970 to 2.0 divorces by 2008[1]. The same trend is so obvious in Asia that The Economist of 20 August 2011 featured a title page with a story named, "The Flight From Marriage".

There are many questions to be answered when analysing this new process: Where does this phenomenon come from? Is it connected to other aspects of social change such as modernisation, globalization, individualization and medialization? Is it a by-product of postmodern capitalism? What role do media play in this process? I am trying to find the answers to these questions, and more, in my dissertation, "Singles as a Construct of Postmodern Capitalism – the Role of the Media in the Context of Social Change".

It is indeed a combination of various forces of social change that encourages people to choose a life outside of a long-term partnership. And globalization is undoubtedly one of the strongest of these forces. In this paper, I will analyze the role of globalization in the process of *singlezation*. I will do so by concentrating on its aspects 'hypercapitalism', the emergence of new communication technologies, and the construction of new global identities - all of which have a surprisingly strong influence on our romantic and family lives.

1. What is Globalization?

Powerful and ambiguous, globalization is a widely disputed phenomenon. While globalists regard it as the most important fact in contemporary history, ultra-

---

1   "Marriage and Divorce Statistics," Eurostat, accessed March 7, 2012,
    http://epp.eurostat.ec.europa.eu/statistics_explained/index.php/Marriage_and_divorce_st
    atistics

sceptics dismiss any theory about globalization as a myth.[2] Scientists disagree about whether it is a new idea or has existed for centuries. They also argue about its form, chronology, driving forces, and its role in social change. Different conceptions of globalization have been developed and now include internationalization, liberalization, universalization, westernization/modernization and respatialization. According to Scholte, the disputes and confusions begin with the very definition of globalization.[3] In this whirl of complex ideas, let us adopt a simple but valid definition of globalization as: "[...] a reconfiguration of social geography with increased transplanetary connections between people".[4]

Globalization might be one of the most important developments in contemporary world history, but it is not isolated – it happens parallel to and in conjunction with other major social trends such as the liberation of familial forms, individualization, the rise of new technologies, and the changing form of capitalism. Working together, these developments result in major social changes with a strong impact on our everyday lives.

Many of these continuous social changes are caused by the tight relationship between globalization and capitalism. We are witnessing the emergence of a new, global form of capitalism which has introduced a new world division of labour and increased inequalities, the rise of regionalism, a greater concentration of production in large corporations, more accumulation through consumerism and finance capital, and a move towards post-Fordist regimes[5]. Scholte sees globalization as responsible for the occurrence of hypercapitalism:

"Accelerated large-scale globalization in contemporary history has been closely associated with several important turns in the development of capitalism, but globalization has by no means been the midwife of a post-capitalist society. On the contrary, thus far globalization has left capitalism as entrenched as ever, if not more so, to the point that one could even speak of an onset of 'hypercapitalism'".[6]

This "hypercapitalism" brought about huge issues of flexibility and insecurity. While enthusiasts have emphasised gains in efficiency and economic growth including trade, investment and technological advances, for the critics, globalization has had harmful consequences for economic security. While both sides

---

2   Jan Aart Scholte, Globalization – A Critical Introduction (London: Palgrave Macmillan, 2005), 17.

3   Scholte, Globalization, 15.

4   Scholte, Globalization, 16.

5   Birgit Mahnkopf, "Zukunft der Arbeit: Globalisierung und Unsicherheit," Kurswechsel 3 (2003): 71.

6   Scholte, Globalization, 24.

seem to be right, the global economic crisis, which started in 2008, seems to have proven that, as William Greider claims: "Global capitalism appears to be running out of control toward some sort of abyss".[7] In these times of all encompassing insecurity, avoiding responsibility for a family seems to be the safest solution.

Globalization also means new global cultures and identities. In a world where all forms of barriers are rapidly disappearing, traditional forms of culture and identity have lost their relevance. We are witnessing a creation of new, hybrid cultures and identities that cross borders and compile aspects of different identities[8]. Looking for some guidance in times of fundamental change, we are turning towards the strongest and the loudest: The West. The result is a number of new hybrid identities that are cross-cultural but reflect strong western influences.

For both its admirers and opponents, Globalization is strongly associated with new technologies such as the Internet, global capital markets, air travel, communication and entertainment technologies, news, and quick deliveries over very large distances.[9],[10] New communication technologies have drastically changed our romantic lives: whereas before the Internet, we would have chosen a partner among the people we met face to face, now we have a choice of millions of people regardless of their geographical location, connection to us, nationality or social status. As good as choice may seem, it brings unprecedented problems into our romantic lives: indecisiveness, unwillingness to commit, and expectations that cannot be met – all good reasons to stay single.

2. Globalization as Hypercapitalism: Flexibility & Insecurity

While at its peak, capitalism provided the environment and the security that encouraged family life, at its current stage it does not only make it difficult to form a family but actually encourages staying single. The generation which is today increasingly choosing a life outside of a long-term relationship was born into the generation of baby-boomers who, during the golden era of both capitalism and socialism, took basic socio-economic securities for granted. They taught their

---

7   William Greider, One World Ready or Not: the Manic Logic of Global Capitalism (London: Allen Lane,1997),12.

8   Jan Nederveen Pieterse, "Globalization as Hybridization," Working Paper Series 152 (1993).

9   Richard Sennett, The Corrosion of Character: The Personal Consequences of Work in the New Capitalism (New York: W.W. Norton & Company, 1998), 25.

10   Emma Rotshield: "Globalisation and the Return of History," Foreign Policy 115 (1999): 107

children to see security as a prerequisite for starting a family life. But since then, things have drastically changed.

The interconnection between work and security, which used to be one of the biggest achievements of industrial modernity, is rapidly disappearing, leaving a growing number of people all around the world without basic socio-economic security.[11]

During the golden era of capitalism (between the end of Second World War and collapse of communist states) political institutions offered people who had no other property but their labour, the security and possibility to plan ahead, build houses, receive predictable loans and acquire qualifications to increase their competences. This basic security enabled people to make long-term plans both for their professional careers and their family lives. Changes in the 1970's, and especially the collapse of communist states in 1989, started destroying this connection between work and security. We witnessed a growth of the informal sector and gray zones between formal, informal and illegal work. At the macro-economic level, the idea of security became detached from the idea of economic growth. According to Mahnkopf, this development went so far that security is now seen as a barrier to economic growth.[12]

The early 1990's introduced a steady growth of informality in work forms (manifested in illegal, informal, precarious, short-term, low-paid, insecure jobs which offer no social or economic security and no stability). This trend, which first started in third world and transition countries, quickly moved to the developed industrial countries of North America and Europe. Today, Mahnkopf claims, the situation in developed countries has become grim: ¼ of employees work illegally or in precarious jobs.[13] Global transformation processes are introducing new transnational and supranational norms, which challenge our established (work and social) norms.

Informalization partially may be a political project[14], as Mahnkopf claims, but more than that, it is a result of the fight for continuous economic growth, ever increasing profits and global competitiveness at any cost. Mahnkopf agrees that insecurity and informalization are logical results of increasing unemployment caused by increased productivity and automation, cutting costs and increasing flexibility. She calls insecurity a shock absorber for globalization, ex-

---

11   Birgit Mahnkopf, "Zukunft der Arbeit: Globalisierung und Unsicherheit," Kurswechsel 3 (2003): 63.
12   Mahnkopf, "Zukunft der Arbeit," 64.
13   Mahnkopf, "Zukunft der Arbeit," 65.
14   Mahnkopf, "Zukunft der Arbeit," 69.

plaining that the informal sector acts as a "sponge" for the workforce that became redundant as a result of the global competition for production locations.[15]

This new insecure *Lebenswelt* clearly has a large impact on every aspect of our existence, including our familial forms. Sociologists are busy discussing the influence of capitalism on human character.[16],[17] They will agree that this 'hypercapitalism'[18], as Scholte calls it, is putting enormous pressure on the individual, while exchanging traditional values such as persistency, obligation, commitment and responsibility (all prerequisites for family life) for new values such as flexibility, adaptability, and risk-taking - all better dealt with when single. Even with secure jobs, individuals are now forced to be flexible with their time and space (working over time and travelling for business) and to erase borders between their work lives and private lives. New communication technologies, for example, allow them to always be online and ready to solve job related problems. Mahnkopf perfectly describes this process:

"Kennzeichen der Erwerbsarbeit in den Industrieländern zu Beginn des 21. Jahrhunderds ist die große Fluidität und Elasitzität. Neue Formen Prekärer, nicht existenzsichernder Arbeit sind ebenso verbreitet wie 'Hybridformen' zwischen abhängiger und selbstständiger Erwerbstätigkeit. Doch selbst innerhalb der stabilen Kerne der formellen Ökonomie wird Beschäftigunssicherheit oft nur durch Zugeständnisse im Hinblick auf räumliche Mobilität, zeitliche Flexibilität und gesteigerte Leistungsintensität gewährt: sie geht mit einer wachsenden Defizit bei der Arbeitslatz- und Einkommenssicherheit einher. Ein Zeitregime, das die Grenzen zwischen "Arbeit und Leben" verwischt, zwingt "flexible Individuen" dazu, in einer Grauzone zwischen Arbeitszeit und " freier Zeit " die eigene Arbeitskraft marktfähig zu halten, selbstverständlich auf eigene Kosten durch wiederholte Qualifizierungsanstrengungen, Selbstmanagement und Selbstvermarktung."[19]

Sennett claims that it is the dimension of time (specifically the short-term, 'just-in-time' aspect of new capitalism) that most directly influences people's emotional lives outside the workplace: "Transported to the family realm, 'No long term' means keep moving, don't commit yourself, and don't sacrifice."[20] He sees an incompatibility between new 'hypercapitalist' work ethics and durable

---

15 Mahnkopf, "Zukunft der Arbeit," 70.
16 Sennett, The Corrosion of Character.
17 Lisbeth Jerich, Burnout: Ausdruck der Entfremdung (Graz: Grazer Universtitätsverlag, 2008): 36-78.
18 Scholte, Globalization, 24.
19 Mahnkopf, "Zukunft der Arbeit,",72.
20 Sennett, The Corrosion of Character, 25.

relationships: "This conflict between family and work poses some questions about adult experience itself. How can long-term purposes be pursued in a short-term society? How can durable social relations be sustained? How can a human being develop a narrative of identity and life history in a society composed of episodes and fragments? The conditions of the new economy feed instead on experience which drifts in time, from place to place, from job to job."[21]

3. Globalization as Identity-Construction: Singles

As recently as the 1950s, being single was seen as undesirable and a sign of failure, especially among women. Today, through the freedom to construct their own identities and through new identity patterns spread by and legalized by global media, it has become a legitimate, and even desirable, global identity.

As Giddens argues, self-identity is a modern project in which individuals construct their personal life story to create a feeling of control over their lives.[22] Identity is not anymore inherited through family, nation, culture or work – today, we are free (or even more so: obliged) to construct ourselves, to create a "project draft of our own lives" (»Projektentwurf des eigenen Lebens«).[23] We have turned into "managers" of our lives and sociologists will agree that this is a daily, continuous and never-ending process.[24]

According to Jenkins, this continuous process of constructing our narratives and our identities is being commercially used: "The advertising industry has long understood that selling things to people often means selling them an identity too: a 'new look' may be synonymous with a 'new me,' and the path to that new identity is likely to pass through the local shopping centre"[25]. Not only goods, but also entertainment became an important aspect in the process of constructing new identities. As both these industries - goods and entertainment - are global industries, the "new me's" we buy from them have become global "new me's."

And we need those global identities: stripped of traditional definitions of identity, we must construct new identities to reflect the globalized world and transcend geographical, class and language borders. Globalization has caused a

---

21 Sennett, The Corrosion of Character, 26.
22 Anthony Giddens, Modernity and Self-Identity (Stanford: Stanford University Press, 1991).
23 H. Keupp, T. Ahbe, & W. Gmür, Identitätskonstruktionen. Das Patchwork der Identitäten in der Spätmoderne (Hamburg: Rowohlt, 1999), 30.
24 Keupp and Gmür, Identitätskonstruktionen, 67.
25 Richard Jenkins, Social Identity (London and New York: Routledge, 2007), Chapter 2.

rise of intercultural constructions of being and belonging[26] and we are now creating identities that are cross-cultural and hybrid. Our new identities are based on similar experiences or lifestyles. Giddens will define lifestyle as a "more or less integrated set of practices which an individual embraces, not only because such practices fulfil certain needs, but because they give material form to a particular narrative of self-identity." [27] A modern phenomenon, lifestyle is not handed down, but chosen. It is freely adopted through wearing certain clothes, consuming certain goods, services or entertainment, acting in certain ways or choosing certain environments for encountering others.

Today, a single woman in Croatia will identify with a single woman in New York (as pictured in "Sex and the City"), just as much as (or maybe more than) with her mother or her fellow Croatian. She can do this now because of the liberalization of familial forms, made possible largely by women's emancipation, but also because global mass media help spread and legitimize new lifestyles. Giddens claims soap operas offer new narratives, suggesting models of the construction of the self.[28] But soap operas are only one building block in this "patchwork identity"[29] assembled from various experiences, inputs and materials. Being a single woman is only one of multiple identities she nowadays has the freedom to adopt. Pieterse will recognize this as a "contemporary phenomenon of multiple identities and decentering of the social subject. [...] Thus globalization is the framework for the diversification and amplification of the 'sources of the self.'"[30]

It was Western media in the early 1990's that started spreading the attractive image of singlehood globally through TV series such as "Sex and the City", "Ally McBeal," or "Two and a Half Men," books like "Bridget Jones" and "Quirkyalone," and films like "Singles", encouraged construction of "single" as a new identity. (It must be mentioned here that the protagonists are always on the search for the perfect partner, but as long as they found him or her, being alone seemed like a great stage in life). As Giddens argues,
"Mediated experience, since the first experience of writing, has long influenced both self-identity and the basic organization of social relations. With the development of mass-communication, particularly electronic communication, the in-

---

26   Scholte, Globalization, 26.
27   Giddens, Modernity and Self-Identity, 81.
28   Giddens, Modernity and Self-Identity, 199.
29   Heiner Keup, "Identitätskonstruktionen in der spätmodernen Gesellschaft," Zeitschrift für Psychodama und Soziometrie 2 (2008): 297.
30   Pieterse, "Globalization as Hybridization,"7.

terpretation of self-development and social systems, up to and including global systems, becomes ever more pronounced."[31]
Together with new economic developments and other global social changes, media helped this new identity, this new lifestyle, to spread across the globe. "The Economist" recognized this trend of *singlezation* in Asia as so powerful that the magazine gave the story a cover page. The subtitle reads: "Asians are marrying later, and less, than in the past. This has profound implications for women, traditional family life and Asian politics."[32]
Yes, globalization gave birth to various new cross-cultural identities – and "Single" is definitely one of them.

4. Globalization as New Communications Technologies: Choice

Internet and new communication technologies have revolutionized our world. The changes are so fundamental they have transformed our private lives, influencing our behaviour in romantic relationships and helping us to stay single – by creating a feeling of endless choice.

The Internet plays a central role in globalization, as it is rapidly accelerating the effects of globalization by using technology to blur all borders – geographical, national, cultural, and social. This new technology has quickly become an integrated part of our work, our daily lives and our social and romantic lives, changing the way we communicate, construct our identities and make choices.

Since the early 1990s, social networks and online dating sites have revolutionized our romantic lives, primarily by globalizing the pool of potential partners. As Eva Illouz describes it:
"No technology I know of has radicalised in such an extreme way the notion of self as "chooser" and the idea that the romantic encounter should be the result of the best possible choice."[33]
Meeting people over the internet quickly became popular for its many charms. First, people who are lonely or socially anxious in traditional face-to-face interaction settings feel better able to express their true self on the Internet.[34] Second, the Internet helps us manage social relationships wherever we are, whenever we want, and whatever else we might be doing. This instantaneity perfectly satisfies

---

31   Giddens, Modernity and Self-Identity, 4.
32   "The flight from marriage", The Economist,accessed August 20, 2011, http://www.economist.com/node/21526329
33   Eva Illouz, Cold Intimacies: The Making of Emotional Capitalism (Frankfurt am Main: Suhrkamp Verlag, 2007), 79.
34   Katelyn McKenna, Arnies Green and Marc Gleason, "Relationship Formation on the Internet: What's the Big Attraction?," Journal of Social Issues 58(1) (2002), 9-31.

our postmodern need for flexibility, as Sennett recognised it.[35] Finally, the Internet removes one of humans' most feared feelings - the feeling of loneliness - in the blink of an eye (even to the level of connectedness turning into an addiction). One of my interviewees illustrated this by stating he uses social network sites when he feels lonely to "feel connected with the world when you're not".

Illouz argues that one of the most revolutionary aspects of the Internet is the increase in one's choice of potential romantic partners.[36] Dating sites and social networks play the most important role in this process as they create virtual global pools of millions of new partners who are just a click away, thus turning users into what Illouz calls "choosers."

What was traditionally a relatively small pool of potential partners constituted of people we knew personally, now also includes millions of people from all over the world, from all classes and/or backgrounds. This new social technology is creating a completely new genre of interpersonal relationships. [37]

As positive as it may seem, psychologists have argued that extended choice hides various problems – a theory easily applicable to romantic relationships. For a start, too much choice blocks humans from making a decision. An interviewee in my last research compared dating sites to the confusion when shopping:

"Like in supermarket where there are 10 different shampoos and you leave without buying one because you can't decide or you want one which does what all 10 can do"

This negative effect of too much choice was proven in a study by Lyengar and Lepper, in which consumers were offered either 6 or 24 flavours of jam to taste and make a purchasing decision. Whereas those with more choice (24 jars) were more attracted to testing different jams, only 3% purchased a jar. Out of the group with less choice (6 jars), 30% purchased a jar. The same study proved more dissatisfaction and regret with the choice made when the sample was larger.[38]

When faced with extensive choice, we create rational filters and more complex decision-making processes. A study by Thimoty Wilson and Jonathan

---

35   Sennett, The Corrosion of Character, 46-63.
36   Illouz, Cold Intimacies, 79.
37   Erich R. Merkle and Rhonda A. Richardson: "Digital Dating and Virtual Relating: Conceptualizing Computer Meditated Romantic Relationships," Family Relations 49 (2000): 190.
38   Sheena S. Iyengar and Mark R.Lepper: "When Choice is Demotivating: Can One Desire Too Much of a Good Thing?," Journal of Personality and Social Psychology, Vol. 79, No. 6 (2000): 995-1006.

Schooler has shown that extensive analysing leads to non-optimal choices and to all options seeming more equal.[39] Other research has shown that extensive choice has a negative effect on the process of choosing and especially on the satisfaction with the choice made.[40] Should we then wonder why we are staying single with so much choice out there?

The feeling of endless choice made us start treating relationships with the same consumerist mindset with which we treat material objects. People become goods. Relationships are "produced on an assembly line, to be consumed fast, efficiently, cheaply and in great abundance."[41] Users are "checking-out" the Internet when unhappy with their current relationship, using it as a convenient "market place" for potential partners. One of my interviewees said, "When you hit a rough spot in a relationship, your mind wonders what's out there, and you do check the Internet". Why repair when you can get a new one? This very postmodern attitude has used the Internet to enter our romantic lives.

On top of it all, the feeling of having an indefinite choice creates a problem with expectations. As Koselleck puts it:

"My thesis is that in modern times the difference between experience and expectation has increasingly expanded; more precisely, that modernity is first understood as a new age from the time that expectations have distanced themselves evermore from all previous experience."[42]

Why be satisfied with second best when somewhere, among all that choice, there must be the "ideal" (partner)? Presenting only the positive sides of one's life and identity, virtual profiles on dating sites and social networks create a false perception of an endless number of interesting people with whom one could eventually become romantically involved. Due to so much choice, the idea of the "perfect" is constructed by adding all preferred aspects of the potential partners – he/she should look like X, be fun like Y, as successful as Z, and earn as much as A. And we forget that according to our experience, there is no such a thing as the "perfect" partner.

Online dating sites and social networks inverted the process of choosing a partner, re-introducing the issue of rationalization into what, since the start of

---

39   Timoty D. Wilson and Jonathan W. Schooler: "Thinking Too Much: Introspection can Reduce the Quality of Preferences and Decisions," Journal of Personality and Social Psychology 60(2) (1991): 181-192.

40   Iyengar and Lepper "When Choice is Demotivating" and Wilson and Schooler "Thinking Too Much".

41   Illouz, Cold Intimacies, 91.

42   Reinhart Kosselleck in Jürgen Habermas, Moral Consciousness and Communicative Action (Cambridge: Massachussets Institute for Technology,1990), 12.

modernization, used to be a very irrational realm. Users are now analysing the information about the potential partner online before deciding to take the relationship to the next level and to include more person-to-person communication. Merkle and Richardson have observed this development in their research:
"Thus, the development of face-to-face romantic relationship moves from initial encounter, based on special proximity and physical attractiveness, to discovery of similarities and to self-disclosure. In contrast, most Internet romantic relationships progress through an inverted developmental sequence."[43]
This inverted process of deciding on the potential partner based on his or her virtual profile puts huge emphasis on the topic of self-presentation and self-disclosure. The Internet has turned into a technological tool for moulding, constructing and presenting our newly constructed, global, virtual identities. All in the hope of finding "the perfect one" in the sea of perfect ones – a long search during which it is better to stay alone and have some fun with the choices.

5. Conclusion

The new, global postmodern world needs people who are fast, flexible, rational, risk-loving, free and ready to be who they have to be at any given moment. Globalization and 'hypercapitalism' have radically changed our work life and work ethics, introducing new aspects such as an ever-increasing emphasis on flexibility, competition, risk-taking, rationalization, and short-term commitment, while at the same time diminishing socio-economic security. All of these contradict our traditional idea of a family and make it more compelling to function as a single. And today, in our postmodern world, in which we are free to create new global identities, "single" has indeed become a legitimate identity. This process was encouraged by mass media, which projected a picture of singlehood as desirable. And then finally, there is the Internet to offer a safe space for singles as it helps to feel connected and erase loneliness while it also introduces the idea of an endless choice of perfect partners, making it harder to choose – and stick to - one's choice. Agreeing with Eric Klinenberg, I will conclude that singlezation is the biggest social change in last 50 or 60 years. And that globalization indeed is one of its strongest agents.

---

43   Merkle and Richardson: "Digital Dating and Virtual Relating," 189.

Unequal Globalization: North and South Divide

Mattew Okeyim, Innocent Okoronye

Why do we have unequal globalization and divisions between the North and South? The discussion on this paper Africa (Nigeria) where global forces in some peculiar situations have had negative effects on the provision of a healthy environment in the Niger Delta region of Nigeria. Although we are not going to downplay the benefits of globalization, the world's attention in Africa has increased new opportunities where African leaders accept liberalization of their economies as an option for development. The aim of this paper is threefold:(a) evidences of inequality between the various nations of the world; (b) creation of the conditions of economic diversities in Africa (Nigeria) through their investment in the areas of energy and natural resources (c) global countries generate huge revenues from Africa but labor, wages, and technology transfer are not complimentary (d) Global institutions have weakened the sovereignty and authority of African states through democratic process. The key question is how can we achieve a complimentary relationship in the process of globalization? The theoretical framework is drawn from the theories of globalization. The empirical questions are drawn from the activities of the Multi- national oil companies in the Niger Delta. Method of data collection is the analysis of case studies with unstructured interview method administered on members of the public, and key oil company officials. The paper concludes that globalization has created divisions and inequalities between the North and the South.

1. What is Globalization?

Globalization involves the interconnection of sovereign nations through trade and capital flows, harmonization of the economic rules that govern relationship between these sovereign nations, creating structures to support and facilitate dependence and interconnection and creation of a global market place.[1]

It is the process of shifting autonomous economies into a global market. In other words, it is the systematic integration of autonomous economies into a global trading environment.

The key elements of the process are: the interconnection of sovereign nations through trade and capital flows, harmonization of the economic rules that govern relationships between these sovereign nations, creating structures to sup-

---

1   Kwanashie, M. 'The Concept and Process of Globalization' in CBN Economic and Financial Review. (Vol. 36, No.4, Dec, 1998), p. 341.

port and facilitate dependence and interconnection and creation of a global market place.[2]

Globalization has many dimensions such as economic, social, political and environment, cultural and religious. These dimensions affect people, institutions and countries positively or negatively. Economic globalization is a process of change towards greater international economic integration through trade, financial flows, exchange of technology and information and movement of people. Economic globalization is also seen as the contemporary internationalization of major financial markets, of technology and certain important sectors of manufacturing and services.

Khor sees economic globalization as the external liberalization of national economies by breaking down national barriers to economic activities, resulting in greater openness and integration of countries in the world markets.[3]

Our submission is that globalization is simply a process of breaking down the national barriers to international influences and the integration of countries into the international world order.

2. Globalization and the North and South Divide

We have seen that globalization is basically the intensification of the interconnection and interdependence between all parts of the world, particularly at the levels of the economy and communication, such that former national barriers to the movement of information, finance, goods, services and entrepreneurship are being drastically reduced and everybody now has to compete with everybody in what has now become a global village and single global market.

However, this notion of globalization which appears on the surface to be convincing and attractive does not capture the actual realities of the contemporary world economy.

There is the illusion of a free global trade and free market. Some examples include:

- The overwhelming majority of mankind who lives in Africa, Asia and South and Central America produce and live from commodities derived from agriculture including livestock-rearing and fisheries. The barriers to international trade in these goods in the form of the heavy subsidies and

---

2   Okon, E.E. 'Foreign Investment and National Security in Developing Countries under the Globalized Environment: The Nigerian Experience"(paper presented at a round table on international trade and globalization) Lagos, Nigerian Institute of Advanced Legal Studies, 18th June 2002, p. 7.

3   Khor, Martin, Globalization and the South: Some Critical Issues (Ibadan, Spectrum Books, 2000), p. 1.

other protectionist policies and practices of the United State of America, the European Union and Japan are still as high as ever. If the commodities which are actually produced by and which sustain most of the human race are actually barred from being freely traded around the globe, then globalization of trade are just a myth.

- There is also this debt issue. Most developing countries face serious external debt problem and have gone through economic/financial crisis. Obviously, states which are hindered by debt and are lacking in finance for development cannot be expected to be actively involved in international trade.

- In respect of trade and investment developing states are deficient in this area and consequently have to import from abroad. Capital importation is difficult for the developing state due to its scarcity. While it is true that globalization has resulted in massive investments in developing states by the multinational corporations, the developing states in most cases have not been able to benefit from the investments. Such foreign direct investments have instead resulted in environmental degradation and impoverishment of rural dwellers who depend on their farms and rivers for sustenance. A good example is the Niger Delta region of Nigeria where oil was discovered in commercial quantity in 1956. since then, exploration and production activities have continued with the attendant environmental degradation and pollution.[4]

According to Fekumo,[5] between 1986 and 1992 alone, approximately 407,588 barrels of crude oil were spilled into the Niger Delta environment from the eastern operations alone. Two major spills took place in 1998. The first was on January 12 when more than 40,000 barrels of crude oil leaked from Mobil's platform in Akwa Ibom State with the Spill traveling 'hundreds of kilometers'. On March 27, a further spill of 20,000 barrels took place at Shell's Jones Creek Flow Station in Delta State killing large numbers of fish.[6] These spills have continued unabated as there were cases of oil spills even in 2011. Apart from oil spills, there are also the

---

4   Mamby Bronwen, "The Price of Oil. Corporate Responsibility and Human Rights Violations in Nigeria's Oil Producing Communities' in Environmental and Planning," Law Review 2 (No.1, March, 2005): 9.

5   Fekumo, F. "Compensation for Oil Pollution in Nigeria'. A New Agenda for Sustainable Development," in (ed) Struan Simpson & Olariwaju Fagbohun Environmental Law and Policy, (Lagos: LASU Law Centre, 1998), p. 338.

6   Unsworth, E. 'Mobil Covered for the Nigeria Spill' in Business Insurance (Jan. 26, 1998).

problem of gas flaring, emission of chemicals and effluents that are discharged into the environment by the oil companies.
While the people of Niger Delta have faced the adverse effects of oil extraction, they have in general also failed to gain from the oil wealth. The Region remains poorer than the national average and the degradation has been aptly described as a tragedy of the commons.[7]
- The technological gap between the North and South again makes globalization a tool for the exploitation of the developing states by the advanced nations and their multinational corporations. There is brain drain which results in the migration of skilled labor from the south to the North. Thus developing states are deprived of the human capital as these skilled workers migrate to Europe and America to develop already developed nations and giving their host states a greater pace in the technology race.[8]
- At the level of the World Trade Organization (WTO) one of the consequences of globalization was the adoption of the Trade Related Agreements on Intellectual Property Rights (TRIPS) aimed at protecting intellectual Property in inventions, products, literary works etc.
Article 27(1) of the TRIPS Agreement provides that patents shall be for any inventions, whether products or processes, in all fields of technology, provided that they are new, involve an inventive step and are capable of industrial application. Two points emerge from this provision. Firstly, it makes clear that there are three common criteria for patentability. Second signatory states are obliged to make protection available for any inventions in all technological fields. This has required significant changes to the law in numerous states which previously did not have strong patent system or specifically excluded certain types of invention from protection such as pharmaceutical products. Criticism especially from developing countries immediately greeted TRIPS especially as regards access to drugs from multinational companies for the treatment of HIV/AIDS disease. In order to address its own chronic public health problems, South Africa enacted the South African Medicines and Medical Devices Regulatory Authority 1998 which allowed the Ministry of Health to determine that the rights with regard to any medicine under a patent granted in the Republic shall not extend to act in respect of such medicine which has been put onto the market by the owner

---

7   Emejuru, C.T. & Okpara, J.O. "The Niger Delta Problem.' A Tragedy of the Commons,"
      in: Ebonyi State University Law Journal 2 (No. 1, 2007): 126.
8   'Globalization of World Trade and Developing Countries' paper presented by the Faculty
      of Law, University of Benin, Nigeria and Published in (ed) Ameze Guobadia, & Azinge
      Epiphany. Globalization, National Development and the Law, (Lagos, NIALS, 2005):
      106.

of the medicine or with his or her consent. This law would give South Africa the power to manufacture patented pharmaceuticals under compulsory license and or import cheaper generic drugs from abroad. This Act never saw the light of the day as Pharma filed a suit against it and the US imposed economic sanctions through the removal of preferential tariff treatments, making imports from the US economically unviable.

Consequent upon the disputes, the WTO Fourth Ministerial Conference in Doha in 2001 came up with the Doha Declaration[9] which stressed the importance of balance in intellectual property protection. It further provides that the implementation and interpretation given to TRIPS must be in a manner *'supportive of public health, by promoting both access to existing medicines and research and development into new medicines'.*

In Further articulation of this Declaration the WTO Public Health Declaration[10]10 provides that TRIPS does not and showed not prevent members from taking measures to protect public health, and that WTO members have the right to use to the full flexible provision found in the Agreement itself to support the right to public health and promote access to medicines for all. Such flexible provisions are found in article 5 of TRIPS and include the right to grant compulsory licenses and the freedom to determine the grounds upon which such licenses are granted. The Declaration however did not solve the problem as the right to grant compulsory license. Under Article 5 of TRIPS extends only to producing drugs for a domestic market. Thus many developing countries who lack the ability to manufacture drugs locally could not benefit from this provision.

In order to solve the problem, the General Council of TRIPS Decision of August 30, 2003, on the Implementation of paragraph 6 of the Doha Declaration on the TRIPS Agreement and Public Health was adopted. The decision which essentially is a waiver of obligations under Article 31(f) of TRIPS established a system under which countries with no or little capacity to manufacture essential drugs could import such drugs. The waiver operates to the extent necessary for the purpose of production of pharmaceutical products and its export. Other conditions include notifications to the TRIPS Council of specific needs for drugs and the tailoring of license terms accordingly, labeling requirements to set these products apart from others in the market and a public disclosure requirement through the internet disclosing the quantities and distinguishing features to be

---

9   Made on 14 November 2001. See Adewole Ayodele 'Globalization, the TRIPS Agreement and their Implications on Access to essential Medicines for Developing Countries. A Case Study of Nigeria in NIALS JOURNAL OF LAW AND DEVELOPMENT, (Lagos, NIALS, 2011), p. 181.

10   Made on 20th November, 2001.

exported. Essentially, the 2003 Decision made it possible for any member state to manufacture and export pharmaceutical products under compulsory license for public health reasons.

Notwithstanding the 30 August 2003 decision some challenges still remain. Example it is important to reach an agreement on how to determine that a country lacks manufacturing capacity such that it can rely on the waivers. Again, there is need for a provision creating obligation on the part of an importing member state to take reasonable measures within their means to prevent re-exportation and a duty on all members to ensure that effective legal means are in place to prevent the import of goods made under the scheme which have been unlawfully diverted to their market.

The foregoing shows that globalization is only a tool in the hands of developed economies to further exploit the developing and poor nations of the world.

The Council of European Municipalities and Regions

An Essay on Shared Governance
in a World Featured by Globalization Issues

Manfred Kohler

This article answers the question of how European cities, municipalities and regions[1] within the Council of European Municipalities and Regions (CEMR) tackle some of the issues concerning all of us in a world featured by increasing globalization. It may appear odd at first sight to write a conference contribution on local and regional authorities, while the topic of the conference in November of 2011 was the role and function of the global city. However, legally speaking, global cities can also be categorized as being local and regional authorities, despite their global reach and influence. Since the 19th century, the world has seen an unparalleled increase in the formation of international organizations. In times of economic, cultural, and technological globalization, just to mention three forms of globalization, the conventional nation state alone is not able to sufficiently control and influence cross-border transactions and interactions anymore. As a result, there were about 251 International Governmental Organizations (IGOs) in 2001, such as the United Nations Organization (UNO) or the European Union (EU), and more than 5,000 International Non-Governmental Organizations (INGOs) like Greenpeace or Amnesty International.[2] Along with the North Atlantic Treaty Organization (NATO) or UNO, the CEMR was among the first international organizations formed after the Second World War.

The globalization issues looked at in this contribution are employment, energy and climate as well as urbanization. I will do so by focusing on the CEMR, which is the umbrella organization founded already in 1951 for a wide range of national associations of local and regional authorities (LRAs), which goes beyond the territory of the European Union (EU). Although European local and regional authorities are the oldest and most persistent forms of political organi-

---

1 For reasons of simplicity, cities, municipalities and regions will be collectively called local and regional authorities (LRAs) in this article, as this is the conventional term according the United Nations Organization (UNO).

2 Wichard Woyke, Wichard, "Internationale Organisationen," in: Wichard Woyke, ed.: Handwörterbuch Internationale Politik (Opladen & Farmington Hills: Verlag Barbara Budrich, 2008), 202-209.

zation thus far[3], they are nowadays facing multiple pressures from above, e.g. the nation state, the European Union (at least for those who form part of EU member states), and other global forms of political organization, coordination and governance overall.[4] It is true that the big decisions are increasingly made at supra-communal and supra-national levels. However, it is LRAs only which can give teeth to decisions - because they are the ones to implement decisions. After all, we all live in and are governed by LRAs, and they are the ones we refer to in our everyday lives.

Before the author specifically explains how LRAs within the Council of European Municipalities and Regions tackle the four globalization issues mentioned above, one will first make a short introduction of the CEMR for the reader to understand what it is and what its goals are. Then one will locate the position of the CEMR in the EU system of governance, because only then can one understand the constraints and limits of political action LRAs are facing currently in the European Union political system. That means that one will first describe the European system of governance and then show how the CEMR places itself in this EU governance system. After all, local and regional authorities can only act upon delegated competences and responsibilities as a result of being part of greater governing frameworks, such as nation states and the EU here. Ultimately, the author will give concrete examples of how LRAs within the CEMR tackle certain globalization problems like the interrelated energy and climate issues overall, employment or unemployment, as well as urbanization.

1. What is the CEMR?

The Council of European Municipalities and Regions was founded in 1951 by a group of Federalist European mayors. It is today the biggest umbrella organization for local and regional political authorities in Europe. Its members are 53 national associations of cities, municipalities and regions from 39 countries. Taken together, these associations represent close to 100,000 local and regional authorities. CEMR's budget amounts to 2 million EUR, mainly comprised of contributions made by the national associations. The remaining funds, approx. 10%, are annual contributions made by the European Commission in the framework of its *Active European Citizenship* program. The current President of the

---

3   Aristotle was one of first great philosophers who said that people naturally organize their lives in communal entities, see Aristoteles, Politik (Düsseldorf: Artemis & Winkler, 2006).

4   For information on global forms of political organization, see, Johannes Varwick, "Globalisierung", in: Wichard Woyke, Wichard, Ed.: Handwörterbuch Internationale Politik. Opladen & Farmington Hills: Verlag Barbara Budrich, 2008) 166-177.

CEMR is Wolfgang Schuster, mayor of the city of Stuttgart in Germany. The CEMR has two governing bodies – the Policy Committee and the Executive Bureau. The Policy Committee meets generally twice per year; it is for most purposes the main governing organ. It is based on national representation, ranging from two places for states of less than 5 million, to 6 places for states of more than 60 million in population. The Executive Bureau is a smaller body; it takes decisions between Policy Committee meetings. It also meets normally twice a year. CEMR's President, and other members of its Presidency are elected by the Policy Committee for a three year term. It has nine vice presidents.

The CEMR is also active at a global level. It forms the European section of the global organization of United Cities and Local Governments (UCLG). This worldwide association is the most important partner to the United Nations Organization whenever it comes to matters concerning local and regional political authorities. Upon recommendation of the CEMR and today's UCLG, UNO established the United Nations Advisory Council of Local Authorities=UNACLA) in 1999, which is designed to include cities and municipalities in UN deliberations on communal issues. In April 2007, the United Nations adopted a resolution on the *Guidelines on decentralization and the strengthening of local authorities*, thus strengthening the idea of local self-government and democracy.

The most important goal of the CEMR is to support a united and strong Europe based upon local and regional self-government and democracy. The CEMR advocates an EU governance system which includes all policy-stakeholders at local, regional, national, and EU levels as equal partners. It advocates a Europe in which decisions are tangible and plausible to citizens while at the same time recognizing the principle of subsidiarity. With this in mind, the negotiations on a European Constitution in 2003/04 led to the first mentioning of the role of local and regional authorities in the Member States and to the fortification of the principle of subsidiarity. The reformed Lisbon Treaty of 2009 absorbed all of these provisions for local and regional authorities.[5]

---

5   For the political and legislative inclusion of LRAs according to the subsidiarity principle, look at Article 5 of the Lisbon Treaty or Protocol 2 attached to the latter on the application of the principle of subsidiarity, which stipulates, among other things, the inclusion of LRAs in the EU's legislative process in the form of consultations by the European Commission. Article 8 of Protocol 2 to the Lisbon Treaty even gives the Committee of Regions (CoR) the power to call upon the European Court of Justice (ECJ) when it sees its right to be heard by the EU legislative institutions and its subsidiarity rights infringed upon, see Bundeszentrale für politische Bildung (Hg.), Vertrag von Lissabon (Bonn: BPB, 2008).

One of the main tasks of the CEMR is to influence EU policy-making. EU legislation in the fields of environment, public procurement, structural funds, state aid and competition has a major impact on local and regional authorities. Exerting influence upon EU legislation is thus a key task of the CEMR. Based upon and strengthened by the Lisbon Treaty, the CEMR and its national member associations draft positions to be tabled at the European Commission through the new legislative dialogue and consultation mechanisms in place. It also tries to influence legislation thrashed out between the European Parliament and the Council of the European Union, thus trying to effectively represent the interests of local and regional authorities in a wide range of policy areas.

Another task of the CEMR is to exchange information and experience. Local and regional authorities have great experience in their sphere of competences, be it education and training, economic development, environment or transport. The CEMR supports the exchange of experience and information among its members in order to increase their capacities. To this end, the CEMR organizes working groups, seminars and conferences for members to exchange views and ideas.

The third important mission of the CEMR is to support town partnerships in the form of twinning. The CEMR invented the concept of town partnerships, the idea of which is to promote a united and peaceful Europe from below, that is through its citizens. There are currently more than 26,000 so-called town twinning projects at work in Europe, and it remains a primary objective of the CEMR to further invigorate this unique movement, especially by coordinating the work done by representatives dealing with town twinning. The CEMR closely cooperates with the European Commission as well as the European Parliament in order to secure the constant funding and political support for town twinning projects.[6] Before explaining certain initiatives taken by the CEMR in the framework of the globalization-related issues of energy and climate change, urbanization and employment mentioned in the introduction, the author would like to outline the possibilities, constraints and limits the CEMR faces in the EU governance framework.

---

6 For further information on the activities of the CEMR, see, CEMR (ed.), Ein Europa für unsere Gemeinden und Regionen! (Brussels: CEMR, 2011).

2. The EU governance structure

Simon Hix does not conceive the European Union as a state, but more as a political system.[7] This remains true up until today. The European Union is neither an international organization per se-because of its supra-national structures and competences-nor is it a state in the sense of a nation state. It is not based upon the idea of one people forming a state with a monopoly on violence on its exclusive sovereign territory. The EU has no true government with an exclusive monopoly on violence. For instance, there are no genuine EU police or military forces to enforce compliance. Even in exclusive EU domains such as competition and internal market, the EU is very much relying on the compliance of EU member states when it comes to implementing and enforcing policy. However, the member states of the EU have developed a political culture of overall compliance with EU treaty law. They have also legally installed a quasi-government in the form of the European Commission. The latter has the exclusive right to initiate policies within the EU legislative triangle formed together with the Council of the European Union and the European Parliament. However, member states have made sure that their influence remains strongest in the EU political system. They made sure that the European Council of heads of state and government is now an official EU body with strongest power tools at hand. It provides the guidelines for EU policy-making and remains the body to decide upon major treaty changes.[8] In fact, no major steps towards further European integration can be made without the heads of state and government.[9] Indeed it remains to set the major guidelines at the cost of further parliamentarization of the EU governance system. Indeed, the EU sometimes equals a medieval empire, with the heads of state and government acting as electoral princes who decide upon major political steps in European integration. This can be very well seen in the current sovereign debt crisis, in which national leaders ardently thrash out major deals and bargains on EU economic and monetary governance. The directly elected European Parliament remains to be bound to react to these major developments, without being able to drive the process of treaty change in the EU in the sense of genuine parliamentarism. Overall, the EU remains in the hands of its member state leaders.

---

7   Simon Hix and Bjørn Høyland , Eds., The Political System of the European Union. (London: Palgrave Macmillan, 2011).

8   Article 15 of the Lisbon Treaty defines the role and competences of the European Council, see Bundeszentrale für politische Bildung (ed.), Vertrag von Lissabon (Bonn: BpB, 2008).

9   Moravcsik, Andrew, The Choice for Europe: Social Purpose and State Power from Messina to Maastricht (Ithaca, NY: Cornell University Press, 1998).

However, the strive for peace in Europe and increasing globalization have led European leaders to increasingly delegate competencies to the EU level, with internal market, competition, and customs union issues, among others, being quite firmly in the hands of the European Commission. They did so because nation states alone could not tackle overall globalization alone anymore. Indeed the globalization of markets happened much too fast for politics in the sense that political systems remained national. However, indeed the number of international organizations has enormously increased as a result of increasingly globalized markets and communication structures, with the EU being the most developed international organization.

Overall, one can maintain that the EU governance system remains to be firmly controlled by national leaders in the European Council and the Council of the European Union. However, the globalization of the markets, especially the financial markets, increasingly put national leaders under pressure to further strengthening political union in the EU, and a further strengthening of political union goes hand in hand with a decrease in power of EU member states. The EU is a political system without true government. Neither the European Commission nor the EU national leaders are in full control of things, especially right now in times of the sovereign debt crisis, in which markets dictate political decision-making, not the other way round. The EU is thus, as Beate Kohler-Koch maintains, a network system of governance, in which competencies and hierarchies are blurred and in which many more actors have a crucial saying, from the local, regional, national and EU-levels to NGOs, private and public sector lobbyists and associations, and so forth.[10] The Lisbon Treaty has additionally strengthened the role of regional and local authorities, granting them the right to be consulted in all the major policy areas.[11] If not even the EU and its composite nation states can tackle globalization problems like those resulting from the global financial crisis, who is able to tackle them then? There is no clear-cut answer to this question, but one thing is certain, the EU and its composite nation-states will need local and regional authorities on their sides to tackle global issues.

The CEMR has come to terms with the need to include local and regional authorities, and thus pursues an EU political system of shared, instead of delegated, governance. The new Lisbon Treaty has at least guaranteed that local and regional authorities must be heard and that their input must be taken seriously, as is illustrated by the possibility of the Committee of Regions to file charges at

---

10   Beate, Kohler-Koch and Rainer Eising, eds, The Transformation of Governance in the European Union (New York: Routledge. 1999).
11   See footnote 5.

the European Court of Justice against a member state or the EU when they breach the subsidiarity principle.[12]

The CEMR has seized the initiative upon these new treaty changes in order to introduce its new idea of shared governance or governing in partnership, as CEMR President Schuster calls it.[13] Schuster maintains that, given the fact that local and regional authorities are ever more needed when solving problems that cross boundaries, all levels of government including civil society and social partners have to govern in partnership, not in a hierarchical system that does not take account of the needs of its citizens. Indeed the CEMR supports the EU 2020 strategy including its 5 goals[14:]

- 75% of the population aged between 20 and 64 should have a job
- 3% of GDP are to be spent on R&D
- The 20-20-20 climate-energy goals are to be achieved.
- Reducing the school drop-out rate to below 10% and increasing the rate of people with a tertiary degree aged between 30 and 34 to 40%
- Reducing the amount of people endangered by poverty by 20 million.

President Schuster wants these goals to be implemented in a system of shared governance, in which networks between all political levels, universities, as well as private and other civil society associations are created to implement the EU 2020 strategy from below. According to Schuster, these networks should be composed of a steering committee headed by a Commissioner in charge of a certain policy area. Additionally the steering committees should be supported by working groups on specific issues, including all stakeholders in a certain policy area. The newest proposal by the CEMR wants the seven flagship initiatives of the EU to pursue the EU 2020 strategy to be implemented by such networks so that all actors are included, including European citizens. The CEMR mentions a number of such networks funded by the European Commission that are already in place, such as the networks created in the framework of the Baltic Sea Strategy aimed at increasing territorial cohesion between cities, regions and countries, such as Denmark, Poland, Germany, Estonia, Latvia, Finland, Lithuania etc. Another example is the EU Alpine Space Programme called Interreg III B that aims at finding sustainable transport solutions in the Alpine area. Anyways there are already such networks in place that cover a wide range of policy areas.

---

12 See footnote 5.
13 Wolfgang Schuster, Governing in Partnership: An EU Governance Model. City of Stuttgart (Stuttgart, 2001).
14 European Commission (2012): "Europe 2020 targets," online at: http://ec.europa.eu/europe2020/reaching-the-goals/targets/index_en.htm (accessed on 27 February 2012).

The overall idea behind these networks is that all actors are needed to tackle cross-boundary issues in a network type of governance structure.[15]

Let us now look at actions taken by the CEMR within the EU framework to tackle problems related to globalization, such as the issues of (un)employment, energy and climate as well as urbanization.

3. Tackling the globalization-related issues of climate change and energy

One of the networks or movements that were strongly supported by the CEMR is the so called Covenant of Mayors initiated by the European Commission in 2008 in the framework of its integrated energy and climate package. The CEMR is part of the Covenant of Mayors Office. The Covenant of Mayors is an official European agreement consisting in 2011 of around 2,800 signatories, mainly cities and towns, that voluntarily commit to exceed the EU 20% CO_2 reduction objective through increased energy efficiency and the development of renewable energy sources. The signatories of the Covenant have all issued formal declarations to implement Sustainable Energy Action Plans (SEAPs) at local level to reach the EU 20% greenhouse gas reduction goal. These plans also require annual reports and bi-annual implementation reports by local and regional authorities in order to ensure compliance with the goals set out in the community-specific SEAPs.[16] All these actions are accompanied by constant knowledge exchange among local and regional authorities and European citizens in the framework of the sessions and conferences organized by the Covenant of Mayors Office, among others. Indeed the Covenant of Mayors is widely considered a prime example of multi-level governance, helping local and regional authorities to reach EU goals, and vice versa. Unlike Germany, which can muster 32 local SEAPs (of which 7 are approved by the European Commission), Austria seems to lag behind in drawing up and implementing SEAPs. Currently there are only two municipalities, Lassee and Laxenburg, which have turned in SEAPs at the European Commission, of which none have been approved yet by the latter. However, this does not mean that Austrian municipalities and towns are lazy. Many Austrian municipalities, above all those from the state of Vorarlberg, already participate in energy efficiency schemes. Out of 600 towns and munici-

---

15 Schuster, Governing Partnership; and CEMR (ed.), Response to the European Commission's Consultation on the Future EU 2020 Strategy COM (2009) 647 final (Brussels: CEMR, 2010).

16 For information on SEAPs, see ICLEI (ed.): LG Action: 3. und abschließendes Positionspapier der europäischen Kommunen über Klima und Energie (Freiburg: ICLEI, 2011).

palities in 10 European countries, 3 municipalities from Vorarlberg - Langenegg, Zwischenwasser and Mäder - rank among the top three in terms of energy efficiency, thus receiving the European Energy Award in 2010, which is the most significant award for energy efficiency achievements. The SEAPs by Lassee and Laxenburg are still quite promising, since both of them show that their CO2 reduction potentials far exceed the 20% EU benchmark.[17]

4. Tackling the globalization-related issue of (un)employment

In a world in which labor markets are strongly affected by the global strive of capital and firms to look for cheap factors of production, it is ever more important for the EU to ensure that labor markets are attractive and growth-enhancing. The EU 2020 strategy's goals are strongly related to the issue of employment: it sets out that, until 2020, 75% of all EU citizens between 20 and 64 should have at least a job. Indeed, all the goals set out in the 2020 strategy are aimed at promoting employment: spending on R&D can lead to more qualified employees, greening the economy can offer jobs in totally new industries, and social inclusion in terms of reducing poverty would also lead to more employment in the EU labor markets.

In January 2010, CEMR issued a response to the Commissions' Communication on the EU 2020 Strategy.[18] In this response, the CEMR contends that the EU 2020 Strategy is too vague. It thus proposes an action plan and concrete indicators to monitor the implementation and outcome as well as the involvement of all levels of governance when it comes to meeting the 2020 goals in terms of employment. It can thus be clearly seen that the CEMR tries to involve local and regional authorities in European policy-making and implementation wherever possible. Shared governance is pursued at all levels. The CEMR also calls upon the EU to further support the infrastructure needs of many local and regional authorities in order to promote employment and business attraction. After all, it is the communal level that strongly contributes to make infrastructures work for more employment. The CEMR also pronounces its dissatisfaction with the fact the EU 2020 Strategy does not sufficiently address the spatial or territorial cohesion dimension when it comes to meeting the employment and overall 2020 goals. The CEMR contends that social and economic cohesion can only be achieved when creating more territorial cohesion in the EU, only then would

---

17 For detailed information on the SEAPs of Lassee and Laxenburg and other European LRAs, Covenant of Mayors (2012): "Sustainable Energy Action Plans", online at: http://www.covenantofmayors.eu/actions/sustainable-energy-action-plans_en.html (accessed 27 February 2012).

18 CEMR, Response.

people more identify with EU goals. When it comes to the 2020 social inclusion goals, the CEMR also points out that local and regional authorities are often the key players in providing services to promote active inclusion of young and old people on the labor markets through training and education, welfare services and so forth. The CEMR thus wants the EU to take account of that fact and to stronger support local and regional authorities in their function as job creators. The CEMR points out in its response that, as a result of the financial crisis, it is especially young people living in local and regional communities who are most affected by unemployment. Focusing on local and regional authorities when meeting the 2020 employment goals must therefore be a main priority of EU policies. The CEMR finally highlights that it supports the EU goals of greening the economy which lead to more jobs and a reduction in greenhouse gas emissions. However, it holds that, if Europe wants to create new jobs through greening the economy, it has to stronger involve the communal level which has better knowledge of local conditions and the needs of people. Indeed the EU has recognized this fact by initiating the Covenant of Mayors outlined above.

5. Urbanization

One of the aspects of globalization is increasing urbanization. One of the effects of urbanization is rural exodus. Indeed urbanization has positive and negative impacts, modernization on the one hand, but also impoverishment and a brain as well as skill drain for local and regional authorities. The author does not want to talk too much about urbanization in general here, because this topic has been covered extensively by other researchers in this conference volume.

Austria and many other countries are very much featured by rural communities, and one way to mitigate the negative impacts of increasing urbanization is to increase the territorial cohesion of Europe. Linking rural and urban areas is a key interest of local and regional authorities in the CEMR. Indeed the CEMR welcomes EU efforts in the form of the EU *European Territorial Agenda and the Leipzig Charter on Sustainable European Cities*, as the CEMR outlines in a 2007 response to the *European Territorial Agenda and the Leipzig Charter on Sustainable European Cities*.[19] Integrated urban development should be applied throughout Europe and, in order to be able to do so, the appropriate framework for this should be established on a national and European level, including above all local and regional authorities with their knowledge of local conditions. Deprived urban and rural neighborhoods must increasingly receive political atten-

---

19 CEMR (2007)

tion within the scope of an integrated urban and rural development policy. According to the CEMR, Europe must reach all of its citizens.

6. Conclusion

One has clearly seen that local and regional authorities are indeed important actors in tackling globalization problems. Indeed the EU more and more addresses these topics in close cooperation with local and regional authorities, also within the CEMR. Because only the latter can really guarantee that EU goals tackling globalization-related issues can succeed, and this is why the CEMR pursues a new EU system of shared governance where all levels are included in policy-making and enforcement. The examples of network cooperation between CEMR, other local and regional authorities and the EU institutions indeed show that the EU is moving towards a political system based less on central government but on network governance including all levels of political decision-making.

Who's Afraid of Twitter?![1]
The Egyptian Revolution going Global

Sarra Moneir Ahmed

Readings that deal with the role of new mass-media as a tool of political communication are certainly plenty, particularly in the European and US based academia. One must highlight in that regard, that globalisation and capitalism have primarily been associated to these two regions, on the political, economic as well as the cultural levels, in spite of the fact that "third-world" countries have been significantly drawn into coping with the wide-open doors of globalisation and "mingling" in the "global society". A particular shift, however, took place in the break out of the Arab revolutions that got the world to freeze their calculations and pre-tailored stereotypes of Arab citizens, the power of the Arab streets, the will of the underprivileged and "nationalism" as a concept in general. Keeping this in perspective, the question that rises to stimulate the writing of this paper is: how does a people ruled by tyranny and despotism for decades create its own escape towards a world and destiny it creates on its own; making its own contribution to the global community of physical networks and its own version of what is to go "global"?

In tackling this question, the paper will be presented in a form of merging theory with practice. By that, it means that the paper will resort to three main ideas or theories to explain the Egyptian reality. These are namely: Gramsci's dominant culture, Gustave le Bon's crowd psychology and George Katsiaficas' eros effect. While knowing the wide scope of these theories, resorting to them will only be for the sake of elaboration and analysis of the Egyptian Revolution, rather than going into methodological depth related these theories. This is made clearer throughout the next sections of the layout, tackled questions and concepts.

- Layout: Constants and Variables

In that respect, this paper will be focusing on studying the employment of new social-media as an output tool used for mass empowerment and political communication in the case of Egypt since the beginning of its revolution on January

---

[1] Title taken from one of the posters held by a female protester during the first Tahrir Revolution wave from 25th January until 11th February 2011. For the photo see link: http://tinyurl.com/br66yvs

25, 2011. This being the locus of the research, the paper tries to map-out this topic through covering the following points:

Part I: Translating virtual dreams into physical spaces

Part II: Identity shaping of the self and the perception of the "other" towards the "actor", the balances and imbalances of power

These three parts will be dealt with as general themes or topics throughout the paper, in order to cover the general framework at hand: how did the Egyptian local influence the traditional understanding of the "global"?

In that respect, the three topics or aspects mentioned will be dealt with through a set of three constants in assistance to the three theories mentioned earlier. By that, it is meant the constant/ fixed elements: 1) the shaping of group and mass psychology, 2) communication tools used by both the masses versus the tools of the former regime ("the old generation"[2] and "the new generation"[3] dilemma), and 3) the formation or birth of new concepts and norms - that were suppressed and unfelt during the former regime - will be observed and analysed while looking at how the virtual space became physical, how this affected the shaping of the identity of the self and the perception of the other, and how the world in return sympathises and participates in this process of a vigorous struggle of a people.

- Tackled Questions

The locus of this paper can also be crystallised through the following question:
    - How did the Egyptian local influence the traditional understanding of the "global"?

---

2   The concept "the old generation" is depicting the generation born, advocating and striving to get the old regime, as in Mubarak's regime back. This, however, does not denote that the word "old" is associated with age. On the contrary, a large proportion of the supporters of the former regime are either young adults associated or affiliated to the old regime either through family ties, employment or party affiliations to the former NDP (National Democratic Party – the ruling party for 30 years during Mubarak's era), or members of the Ministry of Interior or the Egyptian Intelligence, to mention the least.

3   "The new generation" is employed in this context to explain the new stream of thought, the strife to impose new blood into the country and to bring in new concepts and notions, fundamentally speaking that of freedom and justice. Ones again, the concept "generation" does not associated itself with age as a variable. It denotes the idea of a new generation of thought and norms and patriotism against a military state and the rule of the SCAF (Supreme Council of Armed Forces in Egypt).

In answering this, a set of sub-questions have been identified to guide the way throughout the paper. They are as follows:

- *Is the impact of globalisation through social media only visible or acknowledged when measuring the influence of the use of social media by the "domestic" to reach the "global" or "the international"?*
- *Does not the interconnectivity of the people within one region or one nation through social media count as "global"; their own "global"?*
- *Is not the birth of the "global" originally given on a domestic or national level, which is then exported into the world through the "soundwaves" of globalisation and new mass-media? How did that take place following the starting up of the Arab Spring (Egypt in particular)?*
- *How do the home-made events create a globally intertwined society surrounding an issue or an event?*

- Concepts

Concepts such as "incivility", "outrage"[4] and "the Eros effect"[5] translated through the use of new social media and internetworking both nationally, regionally and consequently also internationally, are serving as the central concepts in this paper. In other words the research is based on the presumption that people's use of mass or social media since the January 25 Revolution in Egypt, similarly to the case in Tunisia, was a tool to express their acute outrage towards ancient and decayed institutions, Mubarak's un-representative government of three decades and the abusing, if not the demolishing of the Egyptian dignity. It was through this, that the shout out of *Bread, Freedom and Human Dignity* became the trademark of the Egyptian Revolution. This long indebted feeling of outrage and incivility was and still is accompanied by a complicated construct of emotional and psychological motivation, mainly referred to here in this paper as the Eros effect, as introduced by George Katsiaficas[6]. The Eros Effect, or the

---

4   Sarah Sobieraj and Jeffrey M. Berry. From Incivility to Outrage: Political Discourse in Blogs, Talk Radio, and Cable News. Political Communication, 28:19-41, London: Taylor and Francis Group, 2011, p. 20.

5   George Katsiaficas, The Eros Effect, American Sociological Association National Meetings, Wentworth Institute of Technology: San Francisco, 1989.

6   George Katsiaficas is a professor of Sociology at Boston University specialised in uprisings and social movements in the 20th century in Asia (particularly South Korea, Philippines, Burma, Tibet, China, Taiwan, Nepal, Bangladesh, Thailand and Indonesia). Katsiaficas, along with being the author of a set of books on his specialisation, he is the founder of the concept of "the eros effect" which is particularly found in his latest work on Egypt "The Real Egyptian Revolution is yet to Come" published on February 14, 2012. See his homepage www.eroseffect.com/

emotional bonding and belonging of a group of individuals unfamiliar to one another, entails the sense of a particular mission that harmonises the people, is perceived to be born "on the field" or during marches and riots by the individuals[7]. This sense of "Eros mood"[8] that is sensed in the place the protesters occupy, let it be squares or streets, is in return exported to the world through Twitter and Facebook via YouTube. This in return triggers the sense of, not just the original idea of Katsiafias' Eros Effect, but a "universal Eros Effect"[9] that when "digitising the physical and the emotional"[10] experience through expressions of outrage, automatically the Egyptian actor (the protestor) becomes a global actor which in return constitutes the Egyptian version of what is to be globalised.

Based on this, it is important to define how globalisation will be employed in the research. Apart from the well-known characteristic that globalisation is a rather wide concept that cannot be limited and confined into one single description; this research depicts the "global" as the concepts, ideas and impacts the Egyptian Revolution experience had on the national level, that through the use of mass media became internationalised and had a significant contribution to the globalised world.

1. Part One: Translating Virtual Dreams into Physical Spaces

While discussing the idea of the globality of the Egyptian revolution, it only makes sense to synthetise this through starting with the position or the role of the virtual world in the revolution throughout its stages: the formation and birth of the revolution, the stage of struggle between the people or the masses and the SCAF (Supreme Council of Armed Forces), the struggle towards presidential elections on a popular basis and a constitution and the after effects and future speculations between the success and failure scenarios of the Egyptian revolution.

The Egyptian revolution, one could confidently argue, broke out by chance after a long period of patience and a deeply engraved outrage within the minds and being of ordinary Egyptians towards Mubarak and his government puppet-

---

7   Ibid., p.2.
8   The "Eros Mood" is a concept created by the researcher of this paper, Moneir. It resembles the stage of mind and psychological setting of the subject of analysis, it being the groups or the individual. This Eros Mood in return constructs the Eros Effect of Katsiaficas.
9   Concept created by the researcher of the paper. The Universal Eros Effect resembles in this context the impact of the Egyptian revolutionaries in the creation of their own version of contributions in globalisation; through their experience in the Revolution.
10   Concept developed by the researcher.

eers. As a matter of fact, the random imprisonments, detentions and brutality against ordinary civilians for shouting out their needs and protesting against the regime were more than enough to lead the Egyptian people to the highest level of despair. Seeing that neither the government nor the Ministry of Interior affairs were serving the general well-being of the masses[11], people had to resort to a place where they were less likely to be caught, less likely to be limited, less likely to be detained. Most importantly also, a place where an individual could easily categorise him or herself as a political activist and staying anonymous at the same time, if they were to wish to do so. The only means to do so was the virtual space through the new social media channels of Facebook, Twitter and YouTube.

The fact is, though, resorting to the new generation of communication tools started a while before the break out of the Egyptian revolution. We can look back further to May 2010 to the death of Khaled Said, a young Egyptian from Alexandria beaten to death by a couple of police officers ordered to detain anyone who seemed to be "marked as rebellious" and charged him with drug abuse in order to get away with his murder[12.] As a result, and after a very long time of silence (not forgetting bloggers being detained even before Khaled Said's murder but were not all too often mentioned in the media and the press), the Facebook page of " We are all Khaled Said"[13] was established by political activist Tarek Ghoneim (#WaelGhonim)[14] on 10 June 2010. Today, We are All Khaled Said is one of the leading politically related homepages on both Facebook, with approximately 2 million followers and Twitter (#El-Shaheeed)[15] with 178000 followers, it is acknowledged that this was the bullet that finally triggered the revolution of an oppressed people against their tyrannical regime.

It is important to note that followers of these groups, whether on Twitter or on Facebook, are not only Egyptians or even Arabs. On the contrary, by observing the followers' list, a long list of international journalists, newspapers, news broadcast networks like BBC and the CNN. One of the strongly observed examples was Stephania Zamparelli[16], founder and director of Community Awareness Through Arts Inc. in Brooklyn, an Italian independent photographer and expressionist artist. Zamparelli was present during most of the Tahrir events, taking

---

11   Naila Hamdy and Ehab H. Gomaa, Framing the Egyptian Uprising in Arabic Language Newspapers and Social Media, Journal of Communication 62 (2012) p.195.

12   Ibid. p. 199.

13   Official Facebook homepage: www.facebook.com/ElShaheeed

14   See his homepage on Twitter www.twitter.com/Ghonim

15   See www.twitter.com/Elshaheeed

16   See Zamparelli's homepage: www.zamparelli.us/gallery/main.php

photo shots of different instants and moment that represent the intense feelings of protesters and the Egyptian people who assist and support them whether in Egypt or abroad. In fact, the photos taken by Zamparelli will be resorted to throughout the paper. The prime reason, is that her work has reached not only the Egyptians through her Flickr[17] account and Twitter, but her publications of these photos in New York, where she is currently based, or in Italy as well as Germany have contributed to raising the awareness of what we may call "the global observer"[18]. In addition to this fact, her pictures were also chosen by the researcher of this paper in order to explain what new norms and concepts were brought about through the Egyptian revolution, that were taken global through the use of new social media. This is discussed and elaborated upon in Part II of the paper.

Perhaps one of the most dominant photos that were "shared" on Facebook since the outbreak of the revolution was that of an Egyptian man protesting in the USA, holding a big poster with "EGYPT" written on it. Just to note, and for the benefit of the topic of globalisation, he used the letters of different new social media networks and internet sites to write the word "Egypt": the letter "e" using the Internet Explorer abbreviation, "g" from Google, "Y" from Yahoo, "P"| from PayPal, and "t" from Twitter. (See image below)

Image 1: Taken by Stephania Zamparelli, Presented on Beirut Spring Blog[19]

Another photo, not taken by Zamparelli, was published by the Huffington showing a young man holding a white poster marked in both Arabic and English stating: "Facebook against every unjust"[20].

---

17   See Flickr by Zamparelli: www.flickr.com/photos/zamparelli/
18   Concept by the researcher.
19   See homepage of the blog www.beirutspring.com/blog/2011/02/04/if-you-still-think-egypts-revoltuion-has-nothing-to-do-with-social-media/

Image 2: By Catherine Smith for the Huffington Post

The simplest way to explain image 2 is by noting the fact that the message written on the poster is not only in Arabic. The reason behind this was to send out a message not just to the Egyptians and the former regime, but also to the whole world that the Egyptian dignity and self-determination of the people has come back to the surface through the use of unconventional channels to get their rights and dignity back[21]. The success of the intentions behind this message is evident as it was published in international blogs and spread on Twitter as well as Facebook, making the international community aware of the role the Egyptians are playing and the messages they are portraying through peaceful means in their revolution against tyranny and dignity abuse. The fact that this poster was also carried by a very ordinary Egyptian young man shows how widespread the use of new social media is in Egypt – especially at the grassroots level. It is in fact the prime method for young Egyptians to communicate, get access to international news and information. This is also a symbol, showing how deep the Egyptian revolution runs and how diverse it is. A clear and straightforward statement can be made in that regard that the Egyptian revolution is "social-status-less", "genderless" and "technological".

Having spoken about 'We are All Khaled Said', it is worth mentioning the degree of "globality" that this Egyptian story reached. In fact, Emanuella Degli Esposti, a freelance journalist living in London, introduced the news about 'We are all Khaled Said' winning the BOB Award in Germany (Deutsche Welle Blog

---

20 Catherine Smith, Egypt's Facebook Revolution: Wael Ghonim Thanks The Social Network, The Huffington Post Online, www.huffingtonpost.com/2011/02/11/egypt-facebook-revolution-wael-ghonim_n_822078.html.
21 See Naila Hamdy and Ehab Gomaa, p. 200 for more examples.

Awards). This article was written in June 2011 on the homepage of the German-Arab Chamber of Industry and Commerce[22]. As Esposti is stating in her entry, *"One year on, and the mangled corpse of a young man has arguably resulted in the overthrow of an entire governmental system in Egypt, and a wave of civil unrest rippling out from North Africa across the Middle East...one year may be long enough to change the world, but only time will tell whether this change will be for the better."*[23]
Moving on from the international level of recognition for the Egyptian Revolution through the use of new social media, one must not ignore the impact the regional level has had since January 25, 2011.

Image 3 by Stephania Zamparelli on Flickr[24].
A Tunisian man holding a poster saying "Leave & Let us Live"

Image 3 clarifies the bond between the Tunisian and the Egyptian revolution. This picture was taken during the 18 day revolution, from 25th.January until 12th February 2011 in Egypt. In basic terms, it symbolises the continuation of the Arab revolutions; in fact, the nature of the Arab Spring is of being a continuous process, which cannot be completed with only one country, but rather a unity. However, in that regard and this time, it is not a unity between governments, it is a unity of masses across the Arab region using Facebook and Twitter and getting their voices heard internationally, the attention of international media drawn to them, and the sympathy and support of the "international masses"[25] through either protests or active participation on new social media networks. Furthermore, adding to the globality of the Egyptian revolution, the Tunisian

---

22 Emanuella Digli Essposti, We are all Khaled Said wins BoB Award, Deutsche-Arabische Industrie und Handelskammer, www.ahkmena.com/node/179.
23 Ibid.
24 See Zamparelli's Flickr account for image: www.tinyurl.com/79cwdem
25 Concept by the researcher

protesters were sharing their experience in resisting the Zein Al Abedine regime on both Twitter and Facebook.[26] Experiences shared, as depicted on a clip called "Tunisian Cyber Activists take on Egyptian Cause", and on Twitter as well, were related to how to resist attacks by the military, or in that regard also how to deal with tear gas by using Coca-Cola to wipe the face or using dissolved yeast in water. Through personal experience at al-Tahrir as well, protesters would be gathering all this information and searching techniques, medically, on the internet to see how to best deal with the type of gasses the protesters were attacked with and the type of wounds as well. It is a solid fact that the internet, social media and the experience of sharing information between protesters through the Arab world, that the protesters in the Egyptian revolution were able, at least the surviving number of them, to deal with the SCAF and gain stability on the battlefield at al-Tahrir.

In connecting this section to what was earlier introduced as the Katsiaficas' Eros effect and the concepts of "outrage" and "incivility", the reason why the Egyptian experience in is revolution can be seen as going global is through the international level of the "group feeling" or the Eros effect stimulated through the new social media networks, as well as the regional and international protests.. This Eros effect, one might well add, not only means the global influence or popularity of the Egyptian revolution but it was a prime factor in increasing the confidence and solidarity of the Egyptian protesters. This positive energy not only made the protesters gain a sense of confidence in their actions and demands, but also in the fact that finally the Egyptian citizen is an international actor, and that the Egyptian masses are of significance for the international community after long decades of degradation by their own regime. One might add, as a final point in that regard, that the outrage and acts of incivility, criticised and demeaned by the former regime and advocates of the former regime, were powered and charged by emotional motivations, anger, and psychological gears, without which and in spite of the 1000 martyrs, would not have gotten the Egyptian people as far as queuing in the middle of the summer to elect a president for their nation with pride.

These examples, to mention a few, are all samples of how influential the Egyptian revolution was and how recognised it has become, both regionally and internationally. It is now also important to imbed this experience within a theoretical framework that serves the message of this section in the paper. Anthonio

---

26 See YouTube clip: Tunisian Cyber Acitvists take on Egyptian Cause.
www.youtube.com/watch?v=uCVBXuO3HrE

Gramsci's dominant culture and physical space is seen to serve this notion at best along with Gustave Le Bon's crowd psychology.

2. Part II: Identity Shaping of the Self and the Perception of the "Other" towards the "Actor", the Balances and Imbalances of Power

This section was first introduced by Moneir and Massoud in their paper *Revolution, Cyber Culture and "New Identity": Egyptian Political Changes as a Model*[27]. The following section is the contribution of Moneir and taken from the paper of *Revolution, Cyber Culture and "New Identity"* and is found to be rather useful with respect to the topic of this paper. Antonio Gramsci's dominant culture and physical space is important when it comes to looking at how the culture of the former political system in Egypt was predominant over the behaviour of the masses or the Egyptian people. It is the struggle between generations and cultures, the old versus the new (the protesters), that marks as the prime motives behind the break out of the January 25 Revolution in Egypt. The following explanation is found to be particularly useful in understanding how Gramsci's dominant culture and physical space are related to the use of mass media or new social media in expressing the state of outrage and incivility by the protesters.

A common agreement among scholars revolves around the idea that the revolution is deconstructing traditional patterns and thoughts by the layman in any society. As a result to challenging those traditional patterns, the ruling class in most cases begins to lose its commonality and its dominant, or to put it correctly, its leading culture on people. Hence, it would be weakening the master slave patron. The new emerging social and political identity is formed, but this time the creator is not the "master" in order to maintain his authority and preserve his "master identity", but rather the great masses who are struggling severely to invent their new mass identity. Revolution in that case means a new identity and a new "dominant" culture that invalidate the legitimacy of the former dominant order. This should be taken into consideration while observing both the first and the second waves of the revolution in Egypt that had the master – obedient struggle in focus:

"If the ruling class has lost its consensus, is no longer "leading" but only "dominant", exercising coercive force alone, this means precisely that the great

---

27 Sarra Moneir and Amany Massoud, Revolution, Cyber Culture and "New Identity": Egyptian Political Changes as a Model, a paper prepared and handed in to the Extremely Close and Incredibly Slow International Conference at the Amsterdam School for Cultural Analysis: University of Amsterdam, 28-30 Mach 2012.

masses have become detached from their traditional ideologies, and no longer believe what they used to believe previously"[28].
In this context, it may be methodologically proper to argue that Tahrir square in the Egyptian case denounced the old identity of the previous ruling system and created a new concept for mass identity (although it was produced virtually and related to internet users) within the Egyptian society. It is seen that the situation which Gramsci and Wolfe refer to is the gathering of vast groups of individuals facing common threats to their daily life's set of basic needs for over three decades at a place that, as the name implies, symbolizes emancipation and freedom … Tahrir.

This takes us to further understand the idea of the physical space and its creation with respect to the situation, as was the case in Egypt. Acknowledging that the cyber space was the prime mover of the first wave of the revolution in Egypt would enable us to perceive how the virtual identity of the masses or laymen was gradually translated into reality through bringing the virtual connections and emotional and psychological construct into the "physical" or al-Tahrir square. This certainly did not exist in a vacuum. The earlier on revolutionary experience by Tunisia enabled: (1) networking between revolutionary partners (2) facilitating communication and shared experiences (3) minimizing the sense of space and distance (4) the sensual ability to translate virtual knowledge into the physical space (5) widening up the public space which was invaded by the "closeness" and "highly exclusive" features under the pre-revolutionary system which was Mubarak's regime.

This can be clearly understood through Gramsci's *Quaderni del Carcere*[29] in which he evokes the significance of self-critique and awareness of the self and the other that in return will lead to automatic and collective assembling of the masses rather than being silent to a hegemonic knowledge; in Egypt's case the

---

28   Alan Wolfe, The limits of legitimacy: political contradiction of contemporary capitalism (New York: The Free Press, 1977) 340.

29   Esteve Morera,"Gramsci and Democracy", Canadian Journal of Political Science (Mar. 1990): 25. "In the Quaderni del Carcere, Antonio Gramsci provided the foundations for a socialist theory of democracy. This theory can be drawn from some of Gramsci's most important concepts: his views of intellectual activity on the one hand, and the conceptions of hegemony and civil society on the other. The former provides a general conception of a non-bureaucratic relationship between leaders and the led, the latter points to a participatory model of political activity. This thesis, however, is formulated within the framework of a realist epistemology in which the class structure is conceived as the long-term determinant of the general historical process. Hence, although Gramsci's thought sheds new light on a non-class domain of political activity, it is constrained by both socio-economic conditions and the realism of available knowledge."

hegemony was through the ruling elite, their progressive and consistent mass oppression as well as the final explosion of the silence of the masses. Gramsci explains this by stating:

"A philosophy of praxis cannot but present itself initially in a polemical and critical manner, as superseding the preceding mode of thinking and of the existing concrete thought (or existing cultural world). Therefore, first of all as a critique of "common sense" (after using common sense to demonstrate that "everyone" is a philosopher and that it is not a question of introducing from scratch a science into "everyone's" individual life, but of renovating and making "critical" an already existing activity)"[30]

Ironically, Gramsci's dominant culture concept, prior to the 25th January, had the upper hand in determining the nature of the physical space, who can use it, the identity of those involved in the public space, as well as the nature of information and media used and disseminated to the masses to shape their awareness and position them in the appropriate identity frame, namely "passive and reactive"[31]. In addition, Gramsci further explains how the subaltern (in this case the Egyptian masses in a generalized term) are not homogenous by nature, which is proven by history. Only the unification of a common goal would lead to a clear unison and ability to face the commonly agreed on "evil other".

"The history of subaltern social groups is necessarily fragmented and episodic. There undoubtedly does exist a tendency to (at least in provisional stages) unification in the historical activity of these groups ... It therefore can only be demonstrated when a historical cycle is completed and this cycle culminates in a success."[32] - Antonio Gramsci

These two previous quotes by Gramsci are translated by the transitional phase or boiling point at which the Egyptian streets burst out into self-determining their fates through the revolution. The howling down of this hegemonic dominant despotic culture was only feasible via the use of new media and becoming proactive. Hence, claiming the identity of the master which is the "creator".

This analysis, using Gramsci's explanation, can also be further applied with respect to the first Egyptian presidential elections in modern Egypt. Although this sentence sounds rather over-exaggerated, history proves that this presidential election is not only the first election where the people actually leave their

---

30 Ibid, 26.
31 Robert Fatton Jr., "Gramsci and the Legitimization of the State: The Case of the Senegalese Passive Revolution", Canadian Journal of Political Science (1986): 729.
32 Harry E.Vandan, "Social Movements, Hegemony, and New forms of Resistance", Latin American Perspectives: No.2, Globalizing Resistance: The New Politics of Social Movements in Latin America (2007): 17.

homes to vote. In fact, this election is the first, no matter which candidate will win, where the voter or the masses actually feel they are citizens of a nation with rights and being acknowledged. Apart from the political game that is being played behind the scenes between the SCAF and the MB (the Muslim Brotherhood) and former, yet currently severely active, members of parliament and business and politicians during Mubarak's regime, the Egyptian individual has finally deconstructed what was known as the "pharaonicisation" of the leader, and the "fear" of who is ruling has diminished. One may well say, that still a considerably large proportion of the Egyptian population is still politically unaware and ignorant, yet the larger scene depicts the changes in the political culture which was not only manifested and clear domestically among the youth, school children and university students as well as the adults and families, but also regionally and in particular, internationally.

In proving this, one must look at the rise of the "occupy movement" that first started right after the rise of the Egyptian revolution in Madrid, Spain in May 2011 and now includes more than 23 countries from Spain to New York's Wall Street to Washington DC and Tel-Aviv. This inspiration of what a people can do and hence spread internationally is not to be taken lightly nor simplified to an intifada, as some may argue who are affiliated with the former tyrannical regimes.

2.1. Gustave Le Bon's Crowd Psychology

In addition to Gramsci's dominant culture and the physical space, Gustave le Bon's theory on "crowd psychology" and, as a contribution of the researcher (primarily also evident in her PhD project) comes the notion of "the political psychology of the masses" are further theories or central notions to be presented.

Gustave Le Bon in his book The Crowds: A Study of the Popular Mind, used the concepts of "herd behavior" and "the crowd psychology". He utilized these central ideas to explain how the crowds, serve as interactive groups that are primarily constructed through the context of their respective circumstances and societies.[33] Le Bon moreover proceeds in explaining that the changes that come about by the people are rather complicated in process, seeing that people are tied by culture, as well as political and religious constraints. In that regard, when agreeing or coincidently gathering while serving a certain purpose, this requires a closer observation since that in its self is out of the norm. The birth of

---

33   Gustave Le Bon, The Crowd, p.iii.

this crowd construct is a new structure of crowd psychology that deserves greater observation[34].

In applying this to the Egyptian revolution one should primarily focus on the birth of new concepts this revolution has resulted in through the "herd feeling" generated by the masses. With that respect, there will be a focus on one main scene accompanied with images supporting them also taken by Zamparelli: Egyptian Manners while Protesting Against the Mubarak Regime

2.2. Dignity and Rage

While protesting during the first phase of the Egyptian revolution, from 25th January until 11th February, two main concepts were crystallized through al-Tahrir: the dignity of the Egyptian man, and the civility of the Egyptian citizen. In order to avoid making this point theoretical and methodological, it can be easily depicted through the following image taken by Zamparelli[35] also on her Flickr account:

Image 4 By Zamparelli

Image 4 depicts not only resistance, but as previously mentioned also the failure of the Mubarak regime from planting in fear and submission within the Egyptian people. Perhaps it makes more sense to say, that this scene shows the breaking free of the Egyptians from the political cuffs that were there for thirty years during Mubarak's rule. Not only are the three men in the picture being beaten by the police men, but one of them is resisting in spite of the difference in numbers and weaponry used.

---

34   Ibid., p. x.
35   See Zamparelli's Flickr account under: www.tinyurl.com/6t4qv59

2.3. Civility and Spontaneity

The Egyptian revolution was marked by being the first revolution in history where the protesters clean after protesting and finishing their sit-ins. This fact hit the tabloids internationally to raise the awareness of the people as to how civilized the Egyptians really are. The truth is, not only was the international community astonished, the Egyptians themselves were so as well. One can say that this act of spontaneity depicts the level of purity and peacefulness this revolution really is based on and driven by what gave the Egyptians their long lost pride.[36] This is particularly supported by the general nature of the Egyptians to be supportive and standing beside each other in times of crisis and struggle, as asserted by Dr. Gehad al-Atta in the Huffington Post Blog.[37] She also added that during the revolution, hospitals, in particular the Cairo University Hospital, was receiving a large amount of blood donations on a daily basis and the treatments at the hospital as well as the field hospitals at Al-Tahrir or in any other city in Egypt were for free and based on donations and volunteer work. This in return explains Le Bon's theory on crowd psychology as well as Katsiaficas' Eros Effect, of a collective sense of responsibility and bonding that is naturally transmitted without particular historical background between the individuals or any particular common experiences.

Image 5[38] By Zamparelli

---

36   The Egyptian Protesters Volunteer to Clean Up Streets. www.huffingtonpost.com/2011/01/31/egypt-protesters-voluntee_n_816465.html
37   Ibid.
38   Zamparelli's Flickr account: www.tinyurl.com/chjwuez. Image showing a young man standing in line with his fellow protesters protecting the Egyptian museum and wearing white medical masks for cleaning and against the tear gas.

3. Conclusion

The Egyptian revolution is indeed a very exquisite experience of its own. Not only has it impressed the Egyptians as to how the will of the streets can influence their destiny, but it has also astonished the world. The Egyptians have started to pave their own path towards regaining their dignity through national recognition, the presidential elections, the constitution in the making and international recognition as a people being able to make their future and be proud of their past at the same time. It is the group feeling and the Eros effect that was present, without knowing it, throughout the days of the revolution until today, that is keeping the streets, the people, the protesters and the families sitting at home unable to protest but heartily supporting the mission of the masses, pumping new blood into the veins of the country that was buried and long lost through the disasters practiced by the former regime of Mubarak and his clan. New social media has played a fundamental yet unexpected role in bringing the will of the people and the revolution into the light. However, this is only the beginning of the track towards democratisation made by a generation that has deconstructed the tyrannical temples of the former regime and is striving to build a more representative one.

The Impact of Market Globalism on Urban African American Communities

Dawn Kremslehner-Haas

The twenty-first century's global economic order has led to increasing economic inequality. As markets have extended their reach around the world and gigantic flows of capital combined with technological progress have intensified economic stratification, the global economic playing field has become increasingly uneven. The same trend towards growing inequality has also manifested itself within national borders. In the US, workers involved in manufacturing have been affected most by the new economic order. The loss of jobs in metropolitan cities has had devastating effects on minority residential areas. Particularly African American communities in urban centers have been vulnerable to the new forces in the economy.

In the following, the socio-economic decline of urban African American communities over the last few decades shall be considered in the context of market globalism and technological advancement. It will be argued that the disproportionate rates of social dislocations in impoverished black urban neighborhoods such as crime, family dissolution, and substance abuse are linked to these global changes. The dire state of urban African American neighborhoods, which had been racially segregated since their formation following the Great Migrations and which were severely impacted by the exodus of the black middle class in the 1960s and 1970s, has been exacerbated by the loss of work under the new global economic order.

1. The US Urban Economy Transformed by Global Changes

Under the driving twin forces of international competition and technological change, the urban American economic profile has metamorphosed. In the large agglomerations of the U.S. such as New York, Chicago, and Los Angeles manufacturing has ceded place to a different set of activities centered around information processing and the transaction of business deals. As the new urban economy shifted from goods to services, it relegated smokestack cities to the past and altered its occupational profile. White collar positions replaced the unskilled and low-skilled jobs which had been essential to the former industrial, capital and labor intensive economy. As a result, "growing disparities in income and employment across the U.S. economy [have manifested themselves], with highly educated workers enjoying more opportunities and workers with less education

facing declining employment prospects and stagnant incomes," economist and
Nobel Prize winner Michael Spence notes.[1]

The effect of the new economic order on the U.S. labor market has been
compared to the shape of a pear with most of the new jobs created in the last few
decades clustered at the high and low ends of the income scale. While professional and managerial jobs, which require at least a college degree, have increased "at the top," employment opportunities "at the bottom" are now limited
to minimum wage jobs in the retail and service sector. Meanwhile, the middle
section of the employment scale, formerly constituted by manufacturing and
technical jobs, is conspicuously absent. The U.S. Congressional Budget Office
estimates that the manufacturing sector has lost more than three million jobs between July 2000 and January 2004 alone.[2]

The biggest winners of the new economic order are those at the very top.
David Cay Johnston notes in his essay for the New York Times Company entitled "Richest are Leaving even the Rich Far Behind" that "[t]he hyper-rich have
emerged in the last three decades as the biggest winners in a remarkable transformation of the American economy characterized by, among other things, the
creation of a more global marketplace, new technology, and investment spurred
partly by tax cuts. The stock market soared; so did pay in the highest ranks of
business".[3]

Pay in the lowest ranks, however, has dwindled. While wages for the average American workers have stagnated and the "middle-class squeeze" has affected the majority of the American population, cities have borne the brunt of
these large scale transformations. Harvard sociologist Julius William Wilson
reports that job growth in the rustbelt cities of the North has been lagging far
behind national average in the last two decades. "While national employment
increased by 25 percent between 1991 and 2001, job growth in these older central cities either declined or did not exceed 3 percent".[4] And the job growth that
did occur in the cities affected primarily highly-qualified white collar employ-

---

1   Michael Spence, "The Impact of Globalization on Income and Unemployment: The
     Downside of Integrating Markets," Foreign Affairs 90/4 (2001): 35.
2   Qtd. in Beth Shulman, "Making Work Pay," in Ending Poverty in America: How to Re-
     store the American Dream, ed. John Edwards et al. (New York: New Press, 2007), 114.
3   David Cay Johnston, "Richest are Leaving even the Rich Far Behind," in Class Matters
     (New York: Times Books, 2005), 186.
4   William Julius Wilson, "A new Agenda for America's Ghetto Poor," in Ending Poverty
     in America: How to Restore the American Dream, ed. John Edwards et al. (New York:
     New Press, 2007), 91.

ment. The urban poor therefore find themselves in a precarious situation which exacerbates their economic marginalization even further.

These changes had a profound impact on African American communities in northern city centers. Millions of blacks who had migrated north from the rural South in search of employment opportunities were laid off as the new urban reality took shape. The proportion of African American workers employed in manufacturing decreased from 23.9 percent in 1979 to 10.1 percent in 2006.[5] Having to compete against workers around the world, American laborers have watched their wages stagnate and their prospects shrink. This trend is significant since manufacturing jobs, especially those in the auto industry, used to be a primary source of well-paid employment for black Americans since World War II.[6] Wilson notes that the decline in demand for unskilled labor was most severe in the older central cities of the North. "The four largest (New York, Chicago, Philadelphia, and Detroit), which in 1982 accounted for more than one quarter of the nation's central-city poor, lost more than a million jobs in manufacturing, wholesale, and retail enterprises between 1967 and 1976 alone."[7] By 1980, "nearly half of the adult male population [in those cities] had only tenuous connections to the city's formal labor market."[8] The inner-city manufacturing jobs, for which the minority poor had been recruited in earlier decades, were thus irrevocably gone.

In his sociological study of the economic and political forces in postwar Detroit, Thomas Sugrue points out that "the deproletarianization of the city's black population had far-reaching consequences: it shaped a pattern of poverty in the postwar city that was disturbingly new. Whereas in the past, most poor people had had some connection to the mainstream labor market, in the latter part of the twentieth century, the urban poor found themselves on the economic margins."[9] It seems almost ironic, therefore, that the urban magnets of opportunity which had attracted the greatest number of black southern migrants during the first half of the twentieth century developed the largest impoverished minority communi-

---

5   William Julius Wilson, "The Economic Plight of Inner-City Black Males," in Against the Wall: Poor, Young, Black, and Male, ed. Elijah Anderson (Pennsylvania: University of Pennsylvania Press, 2008), 60.

6   Schmitt and Zipperer in Wilson, "Black Males," 60.

7   William Julius Wilson, The Truly Disadvantaged: The Inner City, The Underclass and Public Policy (Chicago: University of Chicago Press, 1990), 101.

8   Thomas Sugrue, The Origins of the Urban Crisis: Race and Inequality in Postwar Detroit. (Princeton: Princeton University Press, 1996), 262.

9   Sugrue, Urban Crisis, 262.

ties in the second half of the century since these older, manufacturing-dependent cities were hit hardest by the economic transition.

With regards to African American residential areas, the effects of large-scale economic changes have reinforced and cemented the structural factors which had previously contributed to the construction of poor black neighborhoods in the inner cities, such as racial segregation and the outmigration of middle-class blacks in the 1960s and 1970s, thereby compounding a widening gap in wealth and class between mainstream America and the urban poor. And the rift is deepening. Wilson points out that "[d]espite increases in the concentration of poverty since 1970, inner cities have always featured high levels of poverty, but the current levels of joblessness in some neighborhoods are unprecedented.[10]" The consequences of long-term unemployment are reflected in the patterns and norms of behavior in these socially isolated communities which deviate from society at large, as will be elaborated on in the following section.

2. The Nexus of Class and Work

"The consequences of high neighborhood joblessness are more devastating than those of high neighborhood poverty," Wilson argues. "A neighborhood in which people are poor but employed is different from a neighborhood in which people are poor and jobless. Many of today's problems in the inner-city ghetto neighborhoods—crime, family dissolution, welfare, low levels of social organization, and so on—are fundamentally a consequence of the disappearance of work."[11]

The culture which is created as a result of wide-spread and long-term unemployment creates a self-perpetuating cycle which adversely affects the socioeconomic situation of a community. Wilson suggests that neutral terms, such as "lower class" or "working class," do not adequately capture the social changes which have occurred in these communities. Instead, he uses the term "underclass" in describing communities of urban African Americans whose culture has been severely impacted by the effects of joblessness and isolation. He defines this group as "families and individuals who inhabit the cores of the nation's central cities. Unlike in previous years, [they] represent almost exclusively the most disadvantaged segments of the urban black community."[12] Wilson explains that the term suggests that a fundamental social transformation has taken place

---

10   William Julius Wilson, When Work Disappears: The World of the New Urban Poor (New York: Vintage, 1997), xiii.
11   Wilson, Work, xiii.
12   Wilson, Disadvantaged, 143.

in ghetto neighborhoods since the groups represented by this term are collectively different from and much more socially isolated than those that lived in these communities in earlier years. Norms and sanctions against aberrant behavior, a sense of community, and positive neighborhood identification as essential features of social organization have almost completely been lost in these deserted inner-city pockets.

One central aspect of "the new urban poverty," as Wilson has termed it, pertains to family structure. He suggests that the high percentage of single-parent households in impoverished urban areas is directly related to the labor market status of black males. Since black men are often not in a position to support their families, incentives to marry in inner-city communities are low, resulting in high numbers of female-headed households.

Another important effect of long-term joblessness in inner-city neighborhoods is related to the underground economy. With the decline of manufacturing employment, which had offered unionized, relatively stable and well-paying jobs, employment for low-skilled workers in the postindustrial urban economy are almost exclusively minimum wage retail and service jobs. Christopher Jencks remarks that "no native-born American male can imagine supporting a family on [minimum wage]. If that is the only 'respectable' alternative, he will usually conclude that respectability is beyond his reach and slip into crime, alcohol, or [drugs]."[13]

It does not come as a surprise, therefore, that the number of ex-offenders has swelled over the past several decades. Wilson quotes an estimate according to which "as many as 30 percent of all civilian young adult black males ages sixteen to thirty-four are ex-offenders"[14] and Betty Pettit and Bruce Western estimate that "among [black] male high school dropouts the risk of imprisonment [has] increased to 60 percent, establishing incarceration as a normal stopping point on the route to midlife.[15] Kalais Chiron Hunt is one of many black males who serves time in the Cook County Correctional Facility in Chicago "for the typical reasons: drugs, crime, and gangs."[16] In an interview with the prominent African American scholar Henry Louis Gates, Jr. he describes his background, an impoverished inner-city community, as a place where "it is easier for me to,

13 Christopher Jencks, Rethinking Social Policy: Race, Poverty and the Underclass (New York: Harper, 1993), 127.
14 Wilson, "Black Males," 62.
15 Qtd. in Wilson, "Black Males," 62-3.
16 Henry Louis Gates, Jr., America behind the Color Line: Dialogues with African Americans (New York: Warner, 2004), 407.

say, sell drugs than to go and get a job."[17] This holds true for most of Hunt's friends:

[G]uys like me that don't have job training and don't know how to fill out an application coming out of these places or coming out of the penal institutions.... [N]ine times out of ten, that means you are either selling drugs or you are doing something that's against the law. It ain't something that you want to do, but if you be around it so much growing up, that's something that you start to take on. You start saying, okay, well, I think this is the norm. It's as easy for me to sell drugs as to expect to go to school. It's as easy for me to sell drugs as it is to expect to play basketball. That's the pain of it all.[18]

Hunt demonstrates how closely class and work are related by pointing to the absence of role models in most isolated urban communities. Emulating the role models who are present and who influence the choices of the inner-city youth usually leads to the perpetuation of inter-generational poverty. "The average kid growing up on the West Side or the South Side of Chicago, they tend to look at drug dealers, hustlers, players—so-called players—and pimps in their neighborhood. They don't look at the schoolteachers, the firemen, the police officers, or the professors. They don't look at that because they're not around in the neighborhood."[19]

For black male ex-offenders, of course, it is exceedingly difficult to find employment. This predicament has been exacerbated by the recent economic trends. Since most of the low-skilled jobs available are offered in the service sector, black inner-city males, who are usually perceived to be threatening or dangerous, are at a definite disadvantage. This applies especially to black men with a prison record. The chances that a potential employer will offer them a job in the retail sector are extremely low.[20]

Given these limited options, how then do low-skilled inner-city residents stay economically afloat? A phenomenon which has grown under the new economic order and which has increasingly attracted attention in recent years refers to workers in low-wage jobs, usually called the working poor. Their solution to the economic inner-city dilemma shall be presented in the following section.

---

17   Gates, Color Line, 407.
18   Gates, Color Line, 407-8.
19   Gates, Color Line, 408.
20   See Wilson, "Black Males," 62.

3. The Working Poor

Most Americans associate poverty in the U.S. with black long-term welfare recipients. Yet, a closer look at statistics will show that this image is not correct. In her study on the working poor in the inner city, sociologist Kathrin S. Newman reports that "the largest group of poor people in the United States are not those on welfare. They are the working poor."[21] They are part of the more than 30 million Americans in low wage jobs, who do not earn enough to secure the basic necessities of life.[22]

Millions of these workers were "pushed into a region of adversity by federal welfare reform's time limits and work mandates" enacted in 1996, author and journalist David K. Shipler reports.[23] The welfare reform act was passed during a time of economic growth and is "credited by many welfare recipients for inducing them to travel beyond the stifling world of dependence into the active, challenging, hopeful culture of the workplace". Many more, however, Shipler notes, "are stuck at such low wages that their living standards are unchanged. They still cannot save, cannot get decent health care, cannot move to better neighborhoods, and cannot send their children to schools that offer a promise for a successful future."[24] The earnings of these men and women do not cover more than the immediate basic necessities for their daily living and sometimes even less.

It does not come as a surprise, therefore, that minimum wage does not allow workers to enjoy amenities considered basic (and often necessary) in the American mainstream: "The man who washes cars does not own one. The clerk who files cancelled checks at the bank has $2.02 in her own account. [And] the woman who copyedits medical textbooks has not been to a dentist in a decade."[25] Incidents which merely inconvenience an affluent family—car trouble, illness, disrupted child care—often turn into a veritable crisis for those "moving in and out of jobs that demand much and pay little," causing them to "tread just above the official poverty line, dangerously close to the edge of destitution."[26] "Harlem's working poor are perpetually one paycheck away from disaster," Newman confirms and explains that "almost half of Americans who work under

---

21   Katherine S. Newman, No Shame in My Game: The Working Poor in the Inner City (New York: Vintage, 1999), 40.
22   See Shulman, "Pay," 114.
23   David K. Shipler, The Working Poor: Invisible in America (New York: Vintage, 2005), 4.
24   Shipler, Working Poor, 4.
25   Shipler, Working Poor, 3.
26   Shipler, Working Poor, 3.

the poverty line lack health insurance of any kind."[27] For those who do qualify for Medicaid, the quality of the care has greatly suffered after major budget reductions in 1996. Meanwhile, as Newman points out, "the need for health care among the poor continues to grow. Chronic asthma rates are rising at alarming rates among ghetto residents [and] diabetes is also far higher among African Americans."[28] Newman calls this condition "a national disgrace in its own right," which, however, creates further problems as it perpetuates the cycle of poverty for the working poor by setting "the stage for employment instability as parents struggle to cope with the endless rounds of hospitalization and doctor visits that treatment for chronic asthma requires."[29]

Barbara Ehrenreich, bestselling author and *New York Times* columnist, has published her firsthand account of life in low-wage America working as a waitress, hotel maid, house cleaner, nursing-home aid and Wal-Mart associate in her book *Nickel and Dimed*. She observes that the psychological costs that come with performing low-wage duties not valued by society add to the burden of barely making ends meet. Working as a "temporary" cleaning maid, Ehrenreich describes the feeling she derived from her job as doing "an outcast's work, invisible and even disgusting. Janitors, cleaning ladies, ditchdiggers, changers of adult diapers—these are the untouchables of a supposedly caste-free and democratic society."[30] She further observes that low-wage labor is not part of American culture at large. It does not appear in the political rhetoric, public intellectual discourse, or daily entertainment. Perhaps it is this lack of representation, Ehrenreich concludes, that makes the low-wage worker feel "like a pariah."[31]

Thus, returning to the pear as an image for the transformed economy, lawyer and activist Beth Shulman suggests that it is time to return to the days in American labor policies in which the national employment structure offered jobs in the middle section as well: "Millions of manufacturing and technical jobs [used to] practically guarantee a hardworking American a good wage, decent health insurance, vacation time, and even a pension...." It is therefore necessary, Shulman insists, to turn today's "bad" jobs into "good" ones since "nothing intrinsic in a particular job chains it forever to low pay and miserable conditions". With broad support and political will, today's low-wage service jobs—which fortunately cannot be shipped overseas—can easily become the "good jobs of the

---

27 Newman, Game, 53.
28 Newman, Game, 54.
29 Newman, Game 54.
30 Barbara Ehrenreich, Nickel and Dimed: On (Not) Getting By in America (New York: Holt, 2008), 117.
31 Ehrenreich, Dimed, 117.

twenty-first century [ensuring] that America's economic growth and profitability translates into a better life for all working Americans."[32]

4. Mounting Inequality

As the economic order of market globalism increasingly spans the entire globe giving rise to uncertainty and fear, economists have sought to paint a comprehensive picture of the new economic order. Michael Spence voices the general consensus among globalization researchers when he declares that "the massive changes in the global economy since World War II have had overwhelmingly positive effects. Hundreds of people in the developing world have escaped poverty, and more will in the future. The global economy will continue to grow— probably at least threefold over the next 30 years."[33] Yet, most economists also agree that market globalism is cause for concern since it is creating new levels of distributional inequality, especially in advanced economies. "Not everyone is gaining in those countries, and some may be losing," Spence remarks in reference to those on the lower rungs of the economic ladder, who have been affected most by the restructuring of the economic order.[34]

David K. Shipler confirms Spence's assessment with regards to the United States. Addressing the economic disparity within the country, he reports that the richest ten percent of the nation increased their wealth by 6.1% between 2001 and 2004, averaging their net worth at $3.11 million, while the poorest 25 percent, "whose assets equaled their debt in 2001, dropped to a net worth of minus $1,400 in 2004," plunging them headlong into debt.[35] The trend toward hardening class stratification continued throughout the last decade. Referring to the economic crisis and post-crisis period, Political Science Professor Robert C. Lieberman notes that "the average income of the top five percent of earners went up, while on average everyone else's income went down. This was not an anomaly but rather a continuation of a 40-year trend of ballooning incomes at the very top and stagnant incomes in the middle and at the bottom."[36]

In fact, many economists would consider the situation in the U.S. labor market today to be "the greatest challenge since the Great Depression," as Richard

---

32   Shulman, "Pay," 115.

33   Spence, "Impact," 41-1.

34   Spence, "Impact," 41.

35   David K. Shipler, "Connecting the Dots," in Ending Poverty in America: How to Restore the American Dream, ed. John Edwards et al. (New York: New Press: 2007), 14.

36   Robert C. Lieberman, review of Winner-Take-All Politics: How Washington Made the Rich Richer—And Turned Its Back on the Middle Class, by Jacob S. Hacker and Paul Pierson, Foreign Affairs, 90/1 (2001), 154.

B. Freeman phrases it.[37] Economic disparity has been rising steadily since the New and Fair Deals were implemented. Douglas Massey notes that "by the end of the twentieth century all of the declines in inequality achieved [earlier in the century] had been wiped out and the United States had unambiguously returned to levels of inequality not seen since the laissez-faire era of the 1920s."[38]

"This inequality is the ill that underlies all the others," George Packer, staff writer for *The New Yorker*, laments. "Like an odorless gas, it pervades every corner of the United States and saps the strength of the country's democracy."[39] The New Deal as a social compact that guaranteed that the benefits of economic growth were distributed widely has thus been obliterated by the economic forces of market globalism compounded by "public policies that have concentrated and amplified the effects of the economic transformation and directed its gains exclusively toward the wealthy," Lieberman explains in a review essay on Hacker and Pierson's recent study *Winner-Take-All Politics*.[40]

Given this politically unfavorable situation and the tightening grip of global economic structures, the prospects for advancement in urban African American communities are bleak. Locked into the spiral of decline of concentrated poverty combined with a lack of employment opportunities, the situation in these racially and socially isolated urban areas is worsening. What is needed, according to economists concerned about the situation in urban minority communities, are effective policy measures which allow everyone to share in the economic growth generated by market globalism. In fact, an unmistakable tone of urgency informs the advice of scholars addressing the situation of inequality in the context of global economic forces. "[W]hen up against state capitalism and the potent force of global markets, the Western democracies have little choice but to engage in strategic economic planning on an unprecedented scale," Charles Kupchan, who teaches International Affairs at Georgetown University, notes[41] and Michael Spence confirms with regard to the U.S: "The [...] government

---

37 Richard B. Freeman, "The Great Doubling: The Challenge of the New Global Labor Market," in Ending Poverty in America: How to Restore the American Dream, ed. John Edwards et al. (New York: New Press, 2007), 55.
38 Douglas S. Massey, Categorically Unequal: The American Stratification System (New York: Russel Sage, 2007), 36.
39 George Packer, "The Broken Contract," Foreign Affairs 90/6 (2011): 29.
40 Lieberman, "Richer," 155.
41 Charles Kupchan, "The Democratic Malaise: Globalization and the Threat to the West," Foreign Affairs 91/1 (2012), 67.

must urgently develop a long-term policy to address [the] distributional effects [of market globalism] and their structural underpinnings."[42]

5. Suggesting Policies

Most analysts agree that effective reforms to meet the challenges of the new economic structures are based on the two prominent pillars of expanding rewarding employment opportunities, especially in the tradable sector, and restoring the competitiveness of the U.S. economy. African Americans would benefit disproportionately from such measures since African Americans are disproportionately represented in the ranks of low-wage workers.

Which strategies then might be effective in restoring rewarding employment opportunities for a full spectrum of Americans? For one, many economists agree, both the federal and state governments should invest in infrastructure, "which would create jobs in the short term and raise the return on private-sector investment in the medium to long term."[43] Commenting on the poor state of the U.S. infrastructure, George Packer notes with an ironic twist that "we can upgrade our iphones but we can't fix our roads and bridges."[44]

Of course, investment in technologies is also needed. Yet, a new focus on technologies that would "expand employment opportunities in the tradable sector of the U.S. economy at income levels other than the very top" should be adopted, Spence remarks.[45]

With regards to multinational companies, that move the production of goods and services around the world in response to supply-chain and market opportunities, various economists suggest attempting an alignment between private interests in profit and the public's interest in employment. While this is an ambitious goal, it is realistic with the involvement of labor, business, and government, as countries such as Germany have successfully demonstrated.[46] Thus, the U.S. could aim at regaining and retaining some of its advanced manufacturing activities in order to increase its job growth. Spence notes that

given the enormous size of the global labor force, the dial would not have to be moved very much to restore employment growth in the tradable sector of the U.S. economy. Specifically the right combination of productivity-enhancing technology and competitive wage levels could keep some manufacturing indus-

---

42   Spence, "Impact," 29.
43   Spence, "Impact," 39.
44   Packer, "Contract," 22.
45   Spence, "Impact," 39.
46   Spence, "Impact," 40.

tries, or at least some value-added pieces of their production chains, in the United States.[47]
Restoring job opportunities on the U.S. labor market, therefore, constitutes a vital aspect in meeting the challenges of the new global economic order, which has redefined the competition for employment and income in the United States. The efforts to expand employment opportunities will need to go hand in hand with an improved educational system. The U.S. will remain competitive only if progressive educational and training possibilities prepare employees for occupations relevant to the highly technological economy of the 21st century. In the context of the global economic order, where knowledge determines an employee's worth in the labor market, education needs to be made more accessible. Within the black community, the severity of unemployment and underemployment is directly linked to the relatively low proportion of African Americans with higher education. Wilson reports that the disparity in the earnings of black and non-black men is much less among high school graduates than among dropouts and almost vanishes among college graduates.[48] Thus, education plays a key role—all the more in the current structural changes—in enabling African Americans to secure employment.

Further measures proposed by analysts to increase the life quality of those who have lost out in the turmoil of global structural changes, include raising the minimum wage, offering health care to unemployed and low-skilled workers, transforming the tax structure, and ameliorating the Earned Income Tax Credit. All of these policies, while race-neutral in nature, would not be race-neutral in impact, since they would disproportionately benefit impoverished African American communities, who have borne the brunt of the structural changes in the global market economy.

6. Conclusion

Much is at stake, analysts agree, and the challenge the country faces in adjusting to the global marketplace is of utmost concern to all Americans. If the country does not adjust well, economic disparity, political instability, and the democratic

---

47   Spence, "Impact," 36.
48   William Julius Wilson, *More than Just Race: Being Black and Poor in the Inner City* (New York: Norton, 2009), 58.

malaise will increase. If the United States adjusts well, however, the structural economic changes will improve the living standards for all Americans, including – and especially for – impoverished urban African American communities.

The Impact of Globalization
on Iranian Middle Class Consumption Attitudes

Sina Ansari Eshlaghi

Globalization is a multi-aspect phenomenon, which influences economic, cultural and political resources. Hence, we can find a variety of definitions in different branches of social sciences, but mostly, it refers to economical changes and is defined as the distribution of the tariffs, export fees, and import quotes[1]. The focus on economical consequences of globalization has resulted in a lack of studies about the cultural effects of globalization; especially in developing countries. Globalization changes not only economic structure but also cultural values and the living styles of a society. Therefore, in this chapter, we try to study the impact of globalization on the needs and consumption pattern of the middle class in Iran.

Regarding cultural value changes, the middle class in developing countries will tend to assimilate its consumption patterns to western consumption patterns. These consumption attitudes are reflected in advertisements. Hence, we try to find out what kinds of advertisements are more common in Iranian middle class magazines and which advertisements are allocated to non-Iranian products. With a quantitative and qualitative content analysis of these advertisements, as a representation of consumption attitude, we can understand the impact of globalization on the Iranian middle class.

1. The Process of Globalization

For economical studies, globalization is a matter of the last centuries and began with capitalism. For social movements, the key issue is neoliberalism, which is the dominant paradigm of the last two decades. Hence, it is necessary to analyze the process of globalization historically. Globalization as a phenomenon has a history behind it and although it entered newly to the literature of social sciences, it has been mentioned by classical sociologists and economists.

Economic globalization is at times referred to as "corporate globalism"[2], globalization in politics is viewed as "postinternational politics", or the entry of non-state actors into international politics[3], also globalization from above differs

---

1 Jagdish N. Bhagwati, In Defense of Globalization (New York: New York University Press, 2004).
2 M. Gurtov, Global Politics in the Human Interest (Boulder: Lynne Rienner, 1988), 34.
3 James Rosenau, Turbulence in World Politics (Brighton: Harvester, 1990).

from globalization from below[4], but recently, Roland Robertson did analyze the process of globalization regarding historical facts.

For Robertson, the process of globalization began in the 15th century. He identifies five broad phases in the temporal historical path to the present, in which we experience a very high degree of global density and complexity. They are: (1) Phase I, the germinal phase, lasting in Europe from the early fifteenth until the mid-eighteenth century. (2) Phase II, the incipient phase, lasting from the mid-eighteenth century until the 1870s and issuing in the thematisation of nationalism-internationalism; especially and mainly in Europe. (3) Phase III, the take-off phase, lasting from the 1870s until the mid-1920s, which sees increasingly global conceptions of the correct outline of acceptable national society; the thematisation of ideas about national and personal identities; the inclusion of some non-European societies in international society; and the international formalization and attempted implementation of ideas about humanity. (4) Phase IV, the struggle for hegemony phase, lasting from the early 1920s until the mid-1960s. (5) Phase V, the uncertainty phase, beginning in the 1960s and displaying crisis tendencies in the early 1990s, including the inclusion of the Third World and heightening of global consciousness in the late 1960s[5]. Hence, globalization is a process which has begun about 500 years ago and in second half of the 20th century it became conspicuous for us. Especially, in the last decades of the 20th century, the impacts of globalization can be seen on non-Western countries. As globalization has many dimensions, its effects on developing countries can be categorized regarding different definitions and dimensions.

It is important to mention that each cultural and political context generates its own discourse on globalization. Globalization is construed by Ulrich Beck as a continuing project initiated by European Enlightenment[6]. He considers this project as liberating individual reason from authority of the Christian community and its tradition. For Beck 'Globalization' and 'Individualization' constitute the latest stage in the liberation process initiated by the first Enlightenment. Beck believes a new sociological paradigm is needed to overcome methodological nationalism and to build a frame of reference to analyze the new social con-

---

4   Richard Falk, On Human Governance: Towards a New Global Politics (Cambridge: polity, 1994), 53.
5   Ronald Robertson, "Mapping the Global Condition: Globalization as the central Concept," in Global Culture: Nationalism, Globalization and Modernity, M. Featherstone (London: Sage Publication, 1990), 26-27.
6   Ulrich Beck, "The Cosmopolitan Society and its Enemies," Theory, Culture and Society 19 (2002): 23.

flicts, dynamics and structures of the second modernity[7]. The Enlightenment project had begun as a campaign to deny the rational basis of religious divisions; the evils of World War II demonstrated the need for denial of the rational basis of national divisions. Globalization, Beck argues, is a non-linear, dialectic process in which the global and local do not exist as cultural polarities but as combined and mutually implicating principles[8].

With this point of view, globalization can be seen as the process through which the world is uniformed and standardized regarding technological, commercial and cultural synchronization emanating from the West. We can conclude that globalization is tied up to modernity. Albrow defines globalization as "all those processes by which the peoples of the world are incorporated into a single world society, global society"[9]. Indeed, we have a new society, whose borders are global and national borders of countries have nothing to do with events around us.

In contrast to most theorists who focus on economic and global capitals as drivers of globalization, Giddens notes that globalization also involves changes to the role of nation-states, a reconfiguration of the world's military order and international division of labor[10]. Giddens' theory can be categorized under political and philosophical aspects of globalization, but a political view on globalization is mainly known by Huntington.

In 1993, Samuel Huntington, as president of the institute for strategic Studies at Harvard University, published a controversial paper in which he argued that "a crucial, indeed a central, aspect of what global politics is likely to be in coming years … will be the clash of civilizations … With the end of cold war, international politics moves out of its Western phase, and its centerpiece becomes the interaction   between the West and non-Western civilizations and among non-Western civilizations". The imagery is that of civilization spheres at tectonic plates at whose fault lines conflict, no longer subsumed under ideology, is increasingly likely. The argument centers on Islam: the "centuries-old military interaction between the West and Islam is unlikely to decline"[11].

---

7   Beck, "Cosmopolitan Society," 18.
8   Hans Löfgren and Prakash Sarangi, The Politics and Culture of Globalization; India and Australia (New Delhi: Social Science Press, 2009), 22.
9   Martin Albrow and Elizabeth King, Globalization, Knowledge and Society: Readings from International Sociology (London: Sage Publications, 1990), 9.
10 Anthony Giddens, The Consequences of Modernity labor (Cambridge: Polity Press, 1990), 22.
11 Samuel Huntington, "The Clash of Civilizations," Foreign Affairs 72 (1993): 31-32.

The idea of dividing the world into civilizations goes back to medieval era, which mostly based on religion. Anyway, Huntington constructs 'West' as a "universal civilization", "directly at odds with the particularism of most Asian societies and their emphasis on what distinguishes on people from another"[12.] Clash of Civilizations was criticized by other scholars[13]: they agree that globalization has an impact on role of nation-states, but it involves reconfiguration of states, not erosion of states. Earlier analysis believed that globalization leads to the retreat and erosion of states[14], but despite this forecast, some scholars like Giddens believe that not only the state will not erode, we have a new order worldwide and its role changes[15].

In the sociological level, we can study the McDonaldization Theory of Ritzer which is a version of worldwide homogenization of societies through the impact of international corporations. George Ritzer defines Mcdonaldization as "the process whereby the principles of the fast-food restaurant are coming to dominate more and more sectors of American Society as well as the rest of the world"[16]. McDonaldization is somehow a variation to the classical theme of universalism and its modern forms of modernization in a world, in which capitalist relations spread.

Modernization and Americanization are the latest versions of westernization. If colonialism delivered Europeanization, neocolonialism under US hegemony results in Americanization. Marx and Weber both believed in some kind of evolutionism. Marx' thesis was the worldwide spread of capitalism and Weber considered rationalization as final aim. Both perspectives fall within the general framework of evolutionism, a single track universal process of evolution through which all societies, some faster than others progressing[17]. However, Shannon Peters examines the McDonaldization thesis through ethnography of McDonald's in Moscow and finds the argument inaccurate on every score. The McDonald's in Moscow does not represent cultural homogenization but should rather be understood along as global localization. Rather than cultural homogenization McDonald's and other western Fast-Food restaurants usher in difference and variety, giving rise to and reflecting new, mixed social forms. They are

---

12　Huntington, "Clash of Civilizations," 41.
13　see Jan Nederveen Pieterse, Globalization and Culture, 56.
14　Susan Strange, The Retreat of the State (Cambridge: Cambridge University Press, 1996).
15　Giddens, Consequences of Modernity, 22.
16　George Ritzer, The McDonaldization of Society (Thousand Oaks, Calif.: Pine Forge Press, 2004), 19.
17　Jan Nederveen Pieterse, Globalization and Culture (Maryland: Rowman & Littlefield, 2004), 49.

adapted to culture and environment of the local conditions. There are now oriental fast food restaurants all over the world[18].

David Held provided a useful categorization of different schools regarding
globalization. Due to this categorization, there are three main schools: Hyperglobalists, the skeptics, and transformaionalists[19]. Hyperglobalists hold to a view
of globalization that generally privileges emergence of a single global market
and the principle of global competition as harbingers of global congress. Hence,
hyperglobalists believe in neo-liberal doctrine. The hyperglobalist version of
neo-liberalism claims that we are experiencing a new period of history and human progress, characterized by new empirical tendencies, particularly the expansion of global markets. The two key assumptions are that globalization is
historically inevitable and economically necessary.

Another recurrent theme is suggesting a link between globalization and local
identity politics and a combination of integration and fragmentation. Does globalization mean erosion of local identities? Do we have after completion of process of globalization a single global identity, which produces similar culture all
over the world? In fact, to answer these questions, we have to consider the consequences of globalization on nation-states and cultural changes regarding globalization.

---

18 Shannon Peters Talbott, "Analysis of Corporate Culture in the Global Market-Place:
    Case Study of McDonald's in Moscow" (Paper presented at International Institute of So-
    ciology Conference, Trieste, 1995).
19 David Held, Global Transformations: Politics, Economics and Culture (Cambridge: Pol-
    ity Press, 1999), 2.

As we can see, there are many different ideas in interpreting and defining globalization, but there are also many similarities among them. Nederveen Pieterse did summarize consensus and controversy of globalization by different discourses. Table 1 shows these similarities and differences.

Consensus
- Globalization is being shaped by technological change - Involves the reconfiguration of states - Goes together with regionalization - Is uneven
Controversy
- Is globalization essentially economic or multi-dimensional? - What is globalization? - Is globalization a recent or long-term historical process? - Does globalization exist, or is it rhetoric, "globaloney"? - Is globalization neoliberal capitalism? - Is globalization manageable?

Table 1 - Consensus and Controversy in relation to Globalization[20]

The facts which Nederveen Pieterse mentions are the most important points of globalization. New technologies and especially ICT (Information and Communication Technologies) play the main role in connecting different cultures. Together the globalization of finance, demand, supply and competition form a series of interlocking currents circulation of information, which is wired in turn to make production more flexible. Regarding new changes of technologies, people all over the world are familiar with consumption patterns of Western countries, which impacts the way of consumption in developing countries.

Beside technologies, role of states has been changed through the process of globalization. Governments have to reconsider their relation to other governments; especially if they want to be an important actor after globalization. One measure for weaker states has been regionalization which makes it possible for countries to have enough power to take part in negotiation. Therefore, changes in the role of states and regionalization are two trends which are obvious.

Globalization is uneven. Income and wealth are unequally distributed. In the period of 1980-1991, 14 percent of the world's population accounted for 80 percent of investment flows and in 1992, for the 70 percent of the world's trade[21].

---

20   Nederveen Pieterse, Globalization and Culture, 8.
21   Nederveen Pieterse, Globalization and Culture, 13.

The ratio of income of the top 20 percent of the population to the income of the bottom 20 percent has jumped from 30:1 in 1960 to 78:1 in 1994[22].

In contrast to consensuses about globalization, on which different scientists have more or less the same opinions, controversies about globalization include variety of problematic. For example, the definition of globalization depends on weltanschauung. As we have seen, there are many different definitions of globalization and also different aspects of globalization, which have been considered by theorists. One aspect of globalization is its cultural consequences, if we consider globalization a multidimensional phenomenon; and not only an economical process. Hence, we have to review theories of cultural globalization with more consideration.

2. Cultural Globalization

As globalization, modernity and cultural capitalism coincide together in the last decades; it has been discussed to explain links of them. Although globalization has been considered as an economic phenomenon, globalization and culture is also a well established theme. It has first come up with the theories of Roland Robertson and his major book in 1992.

Robertson makes reference to the deep history of globality, particularly in relation to spread of religions, but contemporary globalization refers to cultural and subjective matters and involves awareness of the global human condition, a global consciousness that carries reflexive connotations[23]. Nederveen Pieterse refers to globalization, modernity and culture as a package which con not be separated. Hence, he criticizes ideas like clash between Islam and modernity; because it is not really a clash. Besides, he believes that modernity is a sociological way of saying capitalism[24]. As we can see, for Robertson and Nederveen Pieterse, globalization and cultural capitalism have too many similarities. Hence, any definition of globalization includes similarities of consumption of cultural goods. "Cultural globalization refers to transmission or diffusion across national borders of various forms of media and arts"[25].

Globalization regarding cultural changes is not emergence of homogenized global culture corresponding McLuhan's global village anymore, it is recog-

---

22 UNDP 1999.
23 Ronald Robertson, Globalization: Social Theory and Global Culture (London: Sage, 1992), 183.
24 Nederveen Pieterse, Globalization and Culture, 113.
25 Crane Diana, "Culture and Globalization; Theoretical Models and Emerging Trends," in Global Culture: media, arts, and globalization, ed. Diana Crane (New York: Routledge, 2002), 1.

nized as a complex and diverse phenomenon consisting of global cultures from many different nations and regions. Models of globalization regarding culture can be categorized as follow:

- *Cultural imperialism.* In this model, there are central actors (like Western countries) who define the global cultural values and peripheries are just some consumers. The main actors of this field are global media and at the end, we have a homogenized culture. A good example of these kinds of tries is film production in Hollywood. The produced films represent a type of homogenous, uniform culture permeated by Western capitalistic values. Beside Hollywood distribution system, there is also United States' TV, which represents 50 percent of the programs in some countries and about one-third in Europe[26]. It must be mentioned that in countries like Iran, in which production and availability of media has been severely limited or restricted, the arrival of foreign programming may greatly increase the range of cultural choices. In the cases, which purchasing this kind of films is not legal, black market plays an important role. A common thesis in media and cultural studies is global cultural homogenization.

- *Cultural flows and networks.* In this model, process of cultural transmission is a two-way flow. All cultures take part in making the final product. At the end, we have a hybridized culture. An example of this model is popular music industry. The American share of the global music market has changed in the last decades. The ways in which new music is created, make it possible for new music to develop in many different countries. Especially with development of technological instruments, it is possible to produce pop and hip-hop music at private studios and low-budget; which means the dependency on market and state support is not necessary anymore. The international music has an impact on domestic production; but in a process which empowers minorities and increase international dialogue and building progressive solidarity.

- *Reception theory.* This model has been used to explain responses to cultural globalizations by publics in different countries. The public acts actively confronting mass-mediated news and entertainment and different national, ethnic and racial groups interpret the same materials differently. Reception theory looks at people's response to specific to specific cultural products. It theorizes the long-term effects of cultural products on national and cultural identity. A number of factors play role regarding dominance

---

26 Curran, "Crisis of public communication: a reappraisal," in Media, Ritual and Identity, ed. T. Liebes and J. Curran (London: Routledge, 1998), 41.

of Western cultural products, which identifies audience taste toward cultural goods. Audiences generally prefer local programs, because they find it easier to identify with the style, values, attitudes, and behaviors expressed[27]. In some countries, studies showed that preference for national material is related to social class. Lower-middle class and working class prefer national and local culture. Upper-middle and Upper class prefer Western culture[28]. Generally, audience response to global programming are highly differentiated, depending in part on levels of exposure to national, regional, and global fare and in part on social characteristics of specific publics. Availability of foreign programs does not necessarily imply that its values and ideological content are widely consumed.

- *Cultural policy strategies*. This model considers national strategies regarding global changes. The main actors in this field are governments, which can introduce new cultural values and consumption patterns.

Most critics of globalization have denounced it as a form of cultural imperialism. However, while this takes into consideration the external aspects of globalization and its expansionary tendencies, it fails to account for the internal processes crucial to its formation. Imperialism is defined as territorial expansion of a nation and its domination over other countries. Regarding the meaning of culture, Raguramaraju distinguishes between cultural imperialism and globalization. Cultural imperialism "refers to process which one culture, or even a culturally embedded nation, tries either through persuasion or coercion, or mixture of both, either stealthily or openly, to impose itself on another culture. Unlike this mode of transformation, what seems to lie behind globalization is a worldview which first seeks to de-culture itself from my regional cultural context or moorings, emptying of cultural elements[29].

At this point, two main phenomena should be considered regarding cultural globalization. Firstly, the usage of technology in developing countries is an inevitable tendency and can be neither neglected nor interpreted as imperialism. Wallerstein mentions this change, "The West has emerged into modernity; the others had not. Inevitably, therefore, if one wanted to be modern one had in some way to be Western culturally. If not Western religion, one had to adapt to

---

27 Chadha and Kavoori, "Media imperialism revisited: some findings from the Asian case," Media, Culture and Society 15 (2000): 48.

28 Straubhaar, "Beyond media imperialism: asymmetrical interdependence and cultural proximity," Critical Studies in Mass Communication 8 (1991): 48.

29 A. Raghuramaraju, "Ontology of Permanence and Change: A Critique of Globalization," in The Politics and Culture of Globalization; India and Australia, ed. Hans Löfgren et al. (New Delhi: Social Science Press, 2009), 43.

Western languages. And if not Western languages, one had at the very minimum to accept Western technology, which has said to be based on the universal principles of science"[30]. Therefore, technology and globalized usage of new technologies is not only an effect of imperialism but also a need for change in contemporary world.

Secondly, globalization produces a "proliferation of hyphenated, cosmopolitan identities. Nationalism connects identities to imaginations of place, home, boundary, territry and roots; cosmopolitanism catches something of our need to ground our sense of mutuality in conditions of mutability, and to learn to live tenaciously in terrains of historic and cultural transition"[31]. Therefore, role of globalization in forming new identities is not an imperialistic effect on developing countries and partly produces a new cosmopolitan identity which can be seen as a global culture.

This is a meta-theoretical reflection on cultural difference that argues there are three perspectives on cultural difference: cultural differentialism or lasting difference, cultural convergence or growing sameness, and cultural hybridization or ongoing mixing. The first view, according to which cultural difference is immutable, may be the oldest perspective on cultural difference. The second, the thesis of cultural convergence, is as old as the earliest forms of universalism, as in world religions. The third perspective, hybridization refers to a postmodern sensibility of traveling culture[32]. Of course, we can talk about "Post-hybridity" now. For example, Ariane Mnouchkine's use of Kabuki style to stage a Shakespeare play leads to the question of which Shakespeare play. It can be considered as a level after post-hybridity.

Hybridization is a mixing of the two other ideas about globalization. With the respect to cultural forms, hybridization is defined as "the ways in which forms become separated from existing practices and recombine with new forms in new practices"[33]. The most obvious form of hybridization was shown in the famous motto of "think globally, act locally", which shows the tendency of bringing a global way of thinking to a local way of acting. Another interesting

---

30 Immanuel Wallerstein, "Culture as the Ideological Battleground of the Modern World-System," in Global Culture: Nationalism, Globalization and Modernity, M. Featherstone (London: Sage Publication, 1990), 45.

31 Glenn D'Cruz, "The Good Australians; Anglo-Indians, Multiculturalism and Cosmopolitanism," in The Politics and Culture of Globalization; India and Australia, ed. Hans Löfgren and Prakash Sarangi (New Delhi: Social Science Press, 2009), 201.

32 Nederveen Pieterse, Globalization and Culture, 42.

33 William Rowe and Vivian Schelling, Memory and Modernity: Popular Culture in Latin America (London: Verso, 1991), 231.

observation about hybridization is the role of immigrants in developing countries. A common observation is a mix culture and language of home and destination, which is mentioned by Feddema as "Muslim in the daytime and disco in the evening"[34].

We can also identify a wide range of hybrid formations. The articulation of modes of production follows a principle of hybridization. The dual economy argument saw neatly divided economic sectors. With hybridization, globalization is not a dualism of "imperialism" and "multi-culture". There are some other dispositions between these two. Interestingly, we have found a theory that enables us to analyze the process of globalization in developing countries. Globalization has an impact on values and attitudes in developing countries. The globalized values and attitudes seem to be universal and unique, but they would change due to culture and background history of the destination country. The result is a hybrid culture.

The role of middle class in this situation is very important, because it carries the dominant factors of culture in the country in one side, and on the other side, it represents the global consumption pattern. The middle class in developing countries participates in the global circuits of advertising, brand name consumerism and high tech services, which, at another end of circuitry, exclude the lower class in advanced economies. The term exclusion ignores the many ways in which developing countries are included in global processes: they are subject to global financial discipline (as in structural adjustment and interest payments, resulting in net capital outflows) and part of global markets (resource flows, distribution networks, diaspora and niche markets), global ecology, international politics, global communications, science and technology, international development cooperation, transnational civil society, international migration, travel and network crimes[35].

In sum, globalization, regarding improvements in ICT, makes it possible for people all over the world to get informed about lifestyle in other countries. It results in new needs in middle class of developing countries, who prefer to follow lifestyle of middle class in Western countries. Regarding the culture in developing countries, the lifestyle would change itself to a new kind of consumption pattern, which is called a hybrid culture of consumption in this paper. It has elements of a global (especially Western) culture, which is adapted for the destination culture. The role of middle class in this process is very important, hence,

---

34 Robertson, Globalization, 37.
35 Jan Nederveen Pieterse, "Globalization and Emancipation: From local empowerment to global reform," New Political Economy 2 (1997): 80.

we have to consider development of Iranian middle class to get a view of all process.

3. Iranian Middle Class

Iran is a typical example of non-Western countries, in which middle class came to existence with international relations and not due to change of way of production. Originally, the way of production before capitalism in Iran was totally different in comparison to feudalism in Europe. The mode of production in the Iranian agrarian system was similar to Serfdom, but the relation of Master and Slave can not be understood as Serfdom. By international trade, the Iranian Tradesmen could accumulate money for expanding their trade. This Process of accumulation resulted in the establishment of a middle class, which is identified regarding its economical capital and not its position in production system. The tradesmen who became middle class can be called traditional middle class because of their connection to religion and non-modern beliefs.

Abrahamian mentions that second group of Iranian middle class was established after the time which Iranian high-status families decided to send their children to European countries for studying at the end of 19th century[36]. These students learned about changes in the new world and then brought back their experiences to Iran. Besides, they came back with a new lifestyle, which was developed during their stay in European countries. They had new needs and demands. Hence, at the beginning of the 20th century Iranian Bourgeoisie was consisted of two groups: traditional and modern middle class.

The Iranian traditional middle class consisted of tradesmen who could accumulate gold and money after the possibility of expanding their trade beyond Iranian borders. Hence, this money came from trade and commerce and had nothing to do with production. This capital was not invested in production. After that time, export and import of goods to other countries was the main activity of this group. Especially after exploration of oil in Iran, the Iranian state became the most important and richest trade organization. Due to statistics of Central Bank of Iran, over 75 percent of Iranian export has been oil and oil products during years from 1930 to 2009[37]. As we can see, economy of Iran is fully dependent on international Trade and naturally the traditional middle class is dependent on international relations.

---

36 Ervand Abrahamian, Iran between two Revolutions (Tehran: Ney, 2000), 65.
37 Hadi Salehi Esfahani and Hashem Pesaran, "The Iranian Economy in the Twentieth Century: A Global Perspective," Iranian Studies 42 (2011): 188.

The Iranian modern middle class came to existence after cultural relations of Iran and Western countries. In the 19th century, the need for exploring the new world and using new technologies forced Iranian Shahs (kings in Iran are called Shah) to invite Western experts in order to benefit from their knowledge and skills. At the beginning of 20th century, this ply became a two way street. The need for expanding bilateral relations resulted in sending some Iranian students to European countries. At first, just the noble families had the opportunity to send their children to Europe with state support. After some time, children from high and middle class families could study at European universities. That was a new opportunity for these students to take a job in government and to make a fortune. It should be mentioned that due to international relations and bureaucratic reforms in Iran, variety of new jobs were required by the government. Regarding illiteracy rate of 5% at the beginning of 20th century, graduates who had studied abroad could help the government to do reforms in different statecrafts. Beside their contribution to reform the governmental organization, these students did have an impact on spreading new philosophical thoughts. Scholars like Abrahamian, Katouzian and Moaddel mention the role of these students on the constitutional revolution of 1905[38]. Regarding their role in state, the bureaucratic and civic servants could accumulate money and due to their lifestyle, they could consume Western goods. That is why Abrahamian considered them as modern middle class. The important thing is that the modern class is defined with its consumption model and not production position. Interestingly, both Iranian middle class – traditional and modern – are related to Western countries and culture. The former came to existence after expanding trade to Western countries and the latter came to existence after the time which Iranian government and some rich families sent their children to European countries.

Iranian middle class is defined regarding to its position and relation to Western culture; hence, it is not surprising, if consumption pattern of middle class in Iran is a copy of Western way of consuming. In the era of globalization, two important effects had impact on the way Iranian middle class consume. Firstly, Globalization made world a global village, hence; Iranian middle class get informed about consumption pattern in Western countries through internet and satellite. Secondly, Globalization was a measure of capitalism to overcome its new crisis, because new markets help capitalism to get over its overproduction crisis.

---

38   see Ervand Abrahamian, A history of Modern Iran, 2010; Ervand Abrahamian, Articles on Iranian Political Sociology, 1997; Ervand Abrahamian, Iran between two Revolutions, 2000; Mansoor Moaddel, Class, Politics and Ideology in the Iranian Revolution, 2003.

4. Iranian Middle Class and Globalization

Globalization has made it possible for people all over the world to get familiar with consumption on other countries. Satellite, Internet, magazines and travels are the main ways of this uprising consciousness. These technological changes are one of the fields, which can be seen as a consensus between different theorists. The impact of this globalized observation is the tendency toward a new consumption pattern in developing countries and in our case Iran.

Political issues like sanctions or Iranian political propaganda did not play any affecting role in not consuming and flow of information made it possible for Iranians to know about consumption opportunities in Western countries, especially in the United States. Many Iranians know about famous international brands. In contrast to Huntington's clash of civilization theory which supposes that there is always "a military interaction between West and Islam", nothing stops the people in Islamic countries to consume Western products and follow Western lifestyle. There is a combat in political field, but cultural field acts with its own logic. Iranians would like to go to Fast-Food restaurants. It can not be McDonalds, because of the pressure and bans of Islamic Republic, but it is Fast-Food. That's why, we can observe the growing quantity of Iranian Fast-Food restaurants, especially in Tehran. Statistics show that going to Fast-Food restaurants is one of the most popular leisure time activities of Iranians (Statistical Centre of Iran – database of income-expenditure – analyzed by author). Hence, it is not exactly McDonaldization, but it is a kind of similar change in Iran.

Fast-Food is not the only field, in which we can observe the impact of globalization in Iran. Dressing style is another important figure of consumption in Iran. Some famous brands (e.g. Zara, Armani, Geox and Gap) opened their branches in Tehran and some other cities. In this case, there is a connection between globalization and lifestyle. The preferences of some people in Iran are to use foreign goods. The same story is visible about appearance. One of the most popular operations in Iran is beauty operations. Many Iranian like to have a face just like Western people. That is why many advertisements in magazines are about successful nose, chin, and cheek operations or blonde hair colors. Hence, we can observe a complicated impact of globalization on Iranian middle class. It is not a unidirectional effect of global cultural values on Iranian middle class. There is an interpretation of these values due to Iranian culture.

In sum, globalization generates new needs of consumption in Iranian middle class and the opportunities of consumption grow due to different facilities of the modern world. The consumption pattern is not just the same as Western culture and it is a new interpretation of this culture. The kind of consumption in Iran, which is noticeable in advertisements, guides us to the interpretation of consumption tendencies in Iran; the tendencies which are complicated combinations of globalized values and local culture.

5. Content Analysis of Magazines

One way to get an overview of Iranian middle class consumption is to analyze advertisement of Iranian magazines; especially magazines which are popular among middle class. The advertisement shows, what kind of goods are more popular, and the sellers hope to sell which commodities more. Of course we have to consider that there are some hindrances in Iranian laws for advertisers. For example, it is not possible to use photos of Iranian actresses and artists without scarf, which is an important advertisement resource in Western magazines.

I chose two of Iranian most popular middle class magazines, which are best-sellers. To define popularity I used two sources: firstly, Namayeh. Namaye is an enterprise which gathers information on all publications (including newspapers, magazines, papers, and articles) in Iran and has the most complete database of Iranian magazines. Among 2000 published magazines, I chose 20 magazines whose contents were about social life and lifestyle and chose these two magazines because they were most popular due to information of Namaye Co. My second source to choose popular magazines were magazine sales booths and newspaper boys, who admitted that 'Zendegi Ideal' and 'Movafaghiat' are very popular and many people buy them. *'Zendegi Ideal'* means *'Ideal Life'* and *'Movafaghiat'* means *'Success'*. Both of them are published every two weeks. 'Ideal Life' is a more luxury magazine with a better quality and costs 20000 Rials (about 1 Euro), and the advertisement goes on furniture, beauty operations, culinary and especially cloths. The latter has more advertisement on university entrance exam preparation courses and beauty operations. It costs 12000 Rials (about 0.6 Euro[39]) and has low-quality papers. For the analysis, six volumes from the last year were chosen accidently.

The main articles in *Ideal Life* are about superstars; especially from cinema and pop music. In all analyzed magazines, there is at least one long interview with an actor or a director. There is also news about the life of these superstars (e.g. the film they take role and future plans). Other articles are about beauty operations, design and reports about touristic travels. The magazine *Success* has

---

39   The old price was 10000 Rials and since 6 months it has been changed to 12000 Rials.
Persian magazines
Zendegi ide'al (Ideal Life) – Volume 87, 89, 94, 97, 105,110
Movaffaghiat (Success) – Volume 199, 202, 203, 208, 211

information about themes which are supposed to make someone successful. These kinds of information include beauty operations, practical psychological tricks (e.g. how to overcome shyness or how to increase our self-esteem), and university entrance exam. Other fields of interest are entertainment and Astrology.

The main difference between two magazines (beside appearance and quality of papers) is that the articles of *Ideal Life* are more analytical and written for a higher educated people. As told before, the quality of paper and photos of *Ideal Life* has obviously a better quality. Due to quality and content, it seems that *Ideal Life* is a magazine for upper middle-class, in comparison to *Success*, which is a periodical for middle and lower middle-class. Six volume of every periodical from the last year have been chosen probabilistic for content analysis.

6. Advertisements in Iran

Branch of Advertisement	Magazine			
	Ideal Life		Success	
	Quantity of Ad. (percent in all)	Quantity of Ads. with Western content (percent in branch)	Quantity of Ad. (percent in all)	Quantity of Ads. with Western content (percent in branch)
Crocker and Kitchenware	23 (11,4)	15 (65,2)	3 (2,4)	1 (33,3)
Clothing, Bags and Shoes	18 (8,9)	13 (72,2)	0 (0)	0
Beauty Crèmes	29 (14,4)	26 (89,6)	0 (0)	0
Culinary	20 (9,9)	8 (40)	1 (0,8)	0 (0)
Jewelry	8 (4)	5 (62,5)	0 (0)	0
Internal Design	17 (8,4)	3 (17,6)	0 (0)	0
Make-up and Hygiene	15 (7,5)	13 (86,6)	11 (8,8)	8 (72,7)
Hairstyle and Beauty Institutes	13 (6,5)	4 (30,7)	22 (17,6)	0 (0)
Atrophy	8 (4)	5 (62,5)	3 (2,4)	3 (100)
Beauty Operations	20 (9,9)	3 (15)	38 (30,4)	0 (0)
Electrical devices, Cameras and etc.	7 (3,5)	6 (85,7)	3 (2,4)	3 (100)
Toys	5 (2,5)	5 (100)	0 (0)	0
Medical specialists	0 (0)	0	7 (5,6)	0 (0)
Entrepreneurship Institutes	1 (0,5)	1 (100)	9 (7,2)	0 (0)
University Entrance Exam Preparation	0 (0)	0	16 (12,8)	0 (0)
Bank	3 (1,5)	0 (0)	5 (4)	0 (0)
Misc	14 (7)	3 (21,4)	7 (5,6)	0 (0)
Sum	201 (100)	110 (55)	125 (100)	15 (12)

Table 2 - Quantitative content analysis of advertisements in Ideal Life / Success

Firstly, all advertisements in both magazines were quantitatively analyzed to notice which areas are more common in Iranian magazines' ads. Table 2 shows the result of this analysis. The first column includes branches of advertisement.

Between two magazines, the rate of foreign advertisement is much more in *Ideal Life* and is about 55 percent. *Ideal Life* is a journal of upper middle-class; hence, it means that this upper-middle class is the main target of foreign goods and commodities advertisements. In table, we can see that most popular advertisements are beauty-related ads. Beauty operations are the most common advertisements in these two magazines. About 30% of advertisements in *Success* are about beauty operations. They are naturally domestic, because the specialists are mostly Iranians; the ratio in Ideal Life is 10%. In comparison, there are a lot of advertisements for beauty crèmes, which are mostly produced abroad. The percentage in all advertisements is about 15% and about 90% of these crèmes are imported. Atrophy (crèmes, instruments, and operations) is another beauty-related branch which is commonly advertised in Iranian media. In sum, more than 40% of advertisements in the analyzed magazines are related to beauty operations and institutes and in cases that usage of non-Iranian products are possible, more than 75 percent of products are non-Iranian.

Ideal Life advertisement analysis shows that 20% of its content is about shoes and cloths. More than 70 percent of ads are for foreign products. Interestingly, *Success* has no related advertisement. It seems that *Ideal Life*, which is an upper middle class magazine, is more concentrated on fashion and mode, in contrast to *Success*, which has too many ads on preparation courses of university entrance examination and commercial success. Graphic 2 and 3 show ads on Pierre Cardin and Puma. Interestingly, we can see Maradona in ads of Puma.

| Graphic 1 – Two ads for beauty operation with photos of two non-Iranian women Source: *Success*, Jan. 2012 | Graphic 2 – Advertisement for bags and shoes of Pierre Cardin Source: *Ideal Life*, Vol. 106 | Graphic 3 – Advertisement for Puma with picture of Maradona Source: *Ideal Life*, Vol. 110 |

Toys, electrical devices and jewelry are other products which are advertised in middle class magazines. Interestingly, most of these products are non-Iranian (100% for toys, 85% for electrical devices, and 62,5% for jewelry), which means Iranian middle class consumers are more interested in nondomestic products. Graphic 4 is an example of toys advertisement. Hello kitty is a very famous brand of toys and there is an ad on that.

Another point of interest in these magazines is the photos in advertisements. In some advertisements, it is not necessary to use photos of non-Iranian (e.g. in an article about success in Iran, a photo of Jim Carrey was used or in another advertisement about beauty operation, a typical photo of a man with blonde hair and blue eyes was used), but interestingly, we can see that advertisers preferred to publish photo of non-related non-Iranian in their ads. Graphic 5 shows two examples.

Graphic 4 – Advertisement for Hello Kitty toys
Source: Success, Apr. 2012

Graphic 5 – Two articles with photos of non-Iranians. The first one recommends useful therapies, if somebody catches cold and second one is about marriage. None of them are related to photos of two non-Iranian are selected with no reason.
Source: Success, Feb-Mar. 2012, Ideal Life, Vol. 89

7. Conclusion

There is a coincidence between globalization, modernity and cultural capitalism in the last decades. Hence, a study of the impact of globalization on developing countries needs to analyze cultural changes. One of the fields which cultural capitalism affects is lifestyle. The middle class in developing countries prefer to follow lifestyle of middle class in Western countries. Therefore, there is a tendency in these countries to consume the same goods and commodities as in Western countries. The lifestyle of middle class, especially the modern middle class, would change due to needs and cultural elements of destination culture. In this case we have a hybrid culture and lifestyle. It has elements of a global (indeed Western) culture, which is adapted for the destination culture.

The new lifestyle reflects itself in advertisements. Advertisements can show attitudes and demands of the society for consumption. Advertisers hope to sell their commodities by introducing in ads. This paper was a try to open a window to consumption of Iranian middle class. The results of our content analysis of popular middle class journals indicate that upper middle-class is more demanding toward lifestyle of Western middle class. More than half of the ads in upper middle-class magazines are allocated to non-Iranian goods. Interestingly, in cases that domestic products have no advantage (like cloths) the ratio is more than 75%, which means foreign commodities are preferred. For middle class, success is a very important factor and due to magazines the factors which show success are studying at universities, having an appearance like Western people and gathering money. For this reason, many ads in middle and lower middle-class journals are about beauty operations, university entrance exam preparation, and entrepreneur institutes and enterprises.

We confront a hybrid cultural globalization, which is a new form of Western culture adapted for a new country. There are many similarities, which are visible in the first view (e.g. ads on cloths and crèmes) and there are some differences, which should be interpreted regarding destination culture. For example, entering university is not a success factor per se, but in the historical development of Iranian middle class, it became an advantage, because an academic degree makes it possible to get a decent job and earn more money. The necessity of capital comes from global culture of capitalism and it is adapted for Iran. That is why we can call it the *new global hybrid culture*.

Creative Portfolio of Viennese-Turkishness
Globalisation and Design Anthropology

Özge Subasi

This article seeks to trace the local and global roots to material objects of migration from Turkey to Europe, specifically to Vienna. The study is set between disciplines of design anthropology, material culture and cultural history of migration. Creative design potentials of the Viennese Turkishness are sought, by following *collective memories*, the governmental and non-governmental *narrative on history* and the *visual milestones of mass-migration*. As a result examples from a material portfolio from early years of turkish mass migration is introduced. The objects of the portfolio are situated in their relations to broader practices of mobility, scarcity and creativity. They are therefore framed as the embodiment of collective creative practices and interwoven transnational relations in a global context.

1. Image design of the guest-worker: Urban suit made in Turkey

Our village is near Kars [...] My father lived together with two brothers and two younger sisters [...] We were about 20 people in a house. We had many animals, sheep, and cows, everything that belongs to a farm [...] Only one tractor was missing for my father to this farm. And this tractor he wanted to earn in Germany. Maybe he also went to buy a few good steers and to make life a bit easier[1] During the years of early mass migration from Turkey to Europe, the high incomes and hope of saving money in a short time were given as the main motivations for coming to Europe[2]. The materialistic motivations of a migrant might have been a tractor, a house for the whole family or any other thing to make life easier in the future (as seen in the biographical example above). We also know that, in this period, from host country perspective "rights, interests and life goals initially played almost no role"[3] during recruitment process of guest workers. Looking back into those young men (and later women) in the historical docu-

---

1 Sefa I. Suvak, and Justus Herrmann, In Deutschland angekommen...: Einwanderer erzählen ihre Geschichte. (München: Wissen Media Verlag, 2008), 195.

2 Nermin Abadan-Unat, Bitmeyen goc: konuk isicilikten ulus-ötesi yurttasliga. (Istanbul: Istanbul Bilgi Universitesi Yayinlari. 2002), 114.

3 Heinz Fassmann and Rainer Münz. Einwanderungsland Österreich? Historische Migrationsmuster, aktuelle Trends und politische Maßnahmen. (Wien: Jugend und Volk, 1995), 46.

ments, in museums collections, documentaries, films, we see a stereotype image
of a Turkish guest-worker. It is a man with moustache, a tailor-made suit, "a traditional German hat and a radio on his shoulder"[4], a so-called *almanci* [Ger-
manling]. The term *almanci* [Germanling] is produced from *Almanya* [Ger-
many] to describe Turkish guest workers in Germany but is used to refer Turkish guest workers in all foreign countries[5,6,7].

The Germanling image has been one of the powerful material forms from
history of mass-migration from Turkey. Germanling was the material form of
new hybrid identities, objectified on their possessions and practices, such as tailor made new urban suits in early years. In 60s, in rural Turkey, tailor made suit
was an object of middle and upper class, as professional tailors were not available and accessible for everyman. Guest workers travelled home in their summer
holidays, where rural materiality such as traditional regional clothing was set as
the norm against the new urban suit. This setting was the "constitutive of our
understanding of ourselves and others"[8]. The new urban suit of guest-worker
than, was interpreted as reflection of a European modernity against to a rural
everyday. In this case normative image of a rural person was used against the
image of the returning guest-worker to create the other[9]. In parallel with this
practice, the new suit and other early mass migration possessions can be discussed as being the material possession and demonstration of social honour[10].
They can be perceived as the material form of a desire of bringing the urban
modernity to the rural areas, similar to the beautiful dress of Thai workers[11]. Together with any other possession, such as gifts, electronic devices, the urban-suit
can be seen as accumulation and presentation of economic capital in form of

---

4   Ozlem Savas, "Taste community: The aesthetic and material practice of belonging."
     PhD diss., (University of Applied Arts Vienna, 2008), 70.
5   Ayse Caglar, "Go Go dog and German Turks' demand for pet dogs." Journal of Material
     Culture 2, no. 1 (1997): 77–94.
6   Seyhan Ateş, Der Multikulti-Irrtum: Wie wir in Deutschland besser zusammenleben kön-
     nen. (Berlin: Ullstein, 2007).
7   Savas, "Taste community".
8   Daniel Miller, Material culture and mass consumption. (Oxford, Cambridge: Blackwell,
     1987), 215.
9   Lila Abu-Lughod, "Writing against culture." In Anthropology in Theory: Issues in Epis-
     temology, edited by Henrietta L. Moore, and Todd Sanders, (Malden: Blackwell, 2006),
     466–479.
10   Thorstein Veblen, The theory of leisure class. (New York: Mentor Books, 1957).
11   Mary Beth Mills, "Contesting the margins of modernity: Women, migration and
     consumption in Thailand." American Ethnologist 24, no. 1 (1997): 42.

goods, that than replaced the lack of cultural capital[12]. Further, as Caglar pointed, those posessions aimed to contribute to social struggle to belong to middle class of this group[13].

Figure 1 Sketch visualisation of a typical Almanci [Germanling]

From a design anthropological perspective however, there is another point to make. I have followed the production and consumption channels of particular objects, such as tailor-made suit. Here, oral and biographical records pointed to a transnational process in the making of this image. According to the biographical notes[14], and a document from Domid archive[15] in Germany, there existed a requirement of having a proper outfit for the journey prior to arrival in Europe.

Get a clean suit, a shirt, a tie, a hat for departure. Those who are badly dressed are not going to be sent to Germany[16.]

And oral history and biographies indicate that, those suits were bought prior to leaving Turkey. In Aysegül's memories:

I saw my father, a handsome urban young man, with black hair and moustache, with an old suitcase in hand the climbing the steps. He had bought his new suit, hat and tie from his last money. … [17]

12   Bourdieu, Distinction. Pierre Bourdieu, Distinction: A social critique of the judgement of the taste. (Cambridge: Harvard Univ. Press, 1984).
13   Caglar, "Go Go dog".
14   Hilke Gerdes, Türken in Berlin. (Berlin: Be-bra Verlag, 2009).
15   DOMiD - Archiv. Accessed December 29, 2010.
      http://www.domid.org/seiten/archiv/archiv-de.html
16   Gerdes, Türken in Berlin, 81.
17   Aysegul Acevit and Bingul Birand, Was lebst Du? Jung, deutsch, türkisch - Geschichten aus Almanya. (München: Knaur Verlag, 2005),11.

Stallybrass[18] in his article *Marx's Coat* identifies how Karl Marx needed his coat as a key materiality for being counted as a gentleman and to have access to the library. Similarly, tailor made suit was a key object of mass-migration, a necessity for getting into the host country. Tailor-made suits were among the earliest transnational products of migration of guest-workers. They were required by host-countries. They were purchased and consumed prior to guest worker's arrival to host country. As both the production and consumption of the new suit took place in Turkey, the suit was the first material form of shifting class from rural authenticity to an urban modernity. The new suit was the first transnational material form, representing Istanbul modernity rather than European modernity in mass-migration context. Lastly, an urban modernity of turkishness was a prerequisite for the acceptance of guest workers to Europe.

2. Corporate Identity: Yearly vacations to home

"Almancilar Geldi"- "The Deutschländer have arrived". His Ford 17 M has seen better days: the paint is peeling off, fender and bumper are dented. But the car has survived. Three days and three nights did the trip at least take... Tax collectors looked grredily to completely overloaded vehicles with suitcases, blue rubbish bags and baby seats on the roof and tape recorders, transistor radios, cameras, nylon shirts, ties and women's stockings in the trunk[19].

The image of Germanling is constructed thorough their summer vacations to Turkey. A car was a symbol of materialized investments of early years of scarcity, either it be a Mercedes[20] or an old Ford 17 M[21]. Wealth was accumulated and stored not as money in banks but as things'[22]. When packing the car with the objects, the person seemed to be poor, it was the same person who seem wealthy and successful after 1000 km of travel[23]. The car was fully packed with gifts and objects for the future home and the family members. It was also the connections

---

18   Peter Stallybrass, "Marx's Coat." In Border Fetishisms: Material Objects in Unstable Places, edited by Patricia Spyer, (London: Routledge, 1998), 183–207.

19   DOMiD. 40 Jahre Fremde Heimat - Einwanderung aus der Türkei in Köln: 40 Yıl Almanya - Yaban, Sılan olur. (Köln: DOMiD, 2001), 50.

20   Savas, "Taste community".

21   DOMiD, 40 Jahre Fremde Heimat.

22   Stallybrass, "Marx's Coat", 202.

23   Wolfgang Kos, "Winken Zum Abschied. Winken Zum Aufbruch." In Gastarbajteri: 40Jahre Arbeitsmigration, edited by Hakan Gürses, Cornelia Kogoj, and Sylvia Mattl, (Wien: Mandelbaum Verlag, 2004), 12.

to past and future that were carried in form of gifts[24]. The gifts included "electronic devices, chocolate, German tea"[25] whiskies, dolls, velvet fabrics, Burda magazines, shop catalogues[26], home appliances that easens the food making process[27], specific devices that helps to prepare traditional food like *kiyma/ meat mincer* (alfa 10 meat mincer) and *eriste/pasta mincer* preparation tools [28],[29]. All these objects can again be perceived as the material form of a desire of bringing the urban modernity to the rural areas[30].

Among these objects, communication technologies can be analyzed differently, as they had a second role of combining temporal present to the pasts and futures of dislocated people. *Transistor radios, television and satellite dish* carried news from Turkey to rooms in Europe. *Photo machines* were bought to take and share photos of both countries, *audio-recorders, video recorders and players* replaced writing and sending letters. Lastly *television* and satellite dish have been added to the list. On two specific examples, radio and audio recording, we can follow their further potentials of creating space and new creative practices.

During mass-migration and settlement, communities were maintained and redefined with mass communication media in Turkish language, such as radio, newspaper and TV. This was "a media landscape, which is not visible to the majority of Austria"[31] and a "cultural holding device"[32]. Communication technologies helped for the construction of a home, as they provide the household to travel somewhere else and imagine themselves as members of wider transnational cultural communities[33]. First the *transistor radios* were bought to receive

24 Eugene Rochberg-Halton, Meaning and modernity: Social theory in the pragmatic attitude. (Chicago: University of Chicago Press, 1986).
25 Bernardino Di Croce and Manfred Budzinski. (Nicht) Auf Augenhöhe? Erfahrungen und Lebensgeschichten zum Thema Migration und Zweiter Generationen in Deutschland. (Karlsruhe: Loeper Literaturverlag, 2009), 103.
26 Savas, "Taste community".
27 Abadan-Unat , Bitmeyen Göc.
28 DOMiD – Archiv.
29 DOMiD, 40 Jahre Fremde Heimat .
30 Mills, "Contesting the margins of modernity", 42.
31 Cornelia Kogoj, „Geschichten Zur Migrationsgeschichte." In Gastarbajteri: 40Jahre Arbeitsmigration, edited by Hakan Gürses, Cornelia Kogoj, and Sylvia Mattl, (Wien: Mandelbaum Verlag, 2004), 81–86.
32 Asu Aksoy, "The possibilities of transnational Turkish Television." Accessed October 10, 2010. http://www.photoinsight.org.uk/text/aksoy/aksoy.pdf., 11.
33 Shaun Moores, Interpreting audiences: Ethnography of media consumption. (London: SAGE, 1993).

news from Turkey, e.g: Grundig concert boy[34]. Transistor radio became one of the earliest personal items in shared spaces. Eighty percentage of guest workers possessed a transistor radio just after their arrival[35]. Clearly the main function of the radio was to bring in news from home. But isn't it interesting that almost every guest worker possessed a personal radio, although they listened to the same Turkish radio channel? Why not sharing –expensive- radios, as they shared many other things? From a material point of view, in the early years of scarcity, radio sound might have acted "to create an environment for domestic living"[36], a way of creating a familiar environments defined by sound. In my fieldwork in today's modern Turkish café houses in Vienna, sound and the placement of sound system were used as a material strategy for creating a backstage, a sound texture that materializes the division, if a material backstage was not available. The placement of sound systems between two stages faced to the audience allowed the owners and workers to chat around freely on the other side of the bar in turkish. This was also the case of today's collective Turkish homes in Vienna, where the younger generations defined their spaces through the created soundscapes from their own tape or pc. Pink[37] also found that her participants associated different sounds with different rooms in the home. Clearly radio carried messages and news from home, but these radios might also have helped people to define and defend their space by using the sound. Radio sound was also an important materiality that creates a texture and identity. It might have been a material strategy to defend space for early guest workers in their dormitories. It was sure like this among second generation in their family homes and even today in Turkish café houses.

In early years of migration, recording audio cassettes became a popular alternative to writing letters. Guest workers were the active users of these objects, who recorded cassettes to transport memories from Europe and Turkey and vice versa.

Instead of speaking with my parents, I could only have written letters. My parents had no telephone and we kept contact over cassettes. We recorded cassettes

---

34   DOMiD, 40 Jahre Fremde Heimat .
35   Abadan-Unat , Bitmeyen Göc,125.
36   Jo Tacchi, "Radio texture: Between self and other." In Material cultures: Why some things matter, edited by Daniel Miller, (London: UCL Press Limited, 1998), 25.
37   Sarah Pink, Doing visual ethnography: Images, media and representation in research. (Thousand Oaks, CA: Sage Publications, 2001), 71.

with stories from everyday life, and sent greetings back and forth. The cassettes, I still have them today. The voices heard is a beautiful memory[38]
Letters and telegraphy were not easy to use as it needed some foreign language knowledge and literacy in writing. Telephone communication was not affordable. The new technology was just appropriate for exchanging memories and experiences. Richman and Rey studied transnational Haitian communities, specially illiterate Haitians and found how the audiocassette recorder „became so normal that for many Haitians the verb 'to write (a letter)'(ekri) means recording a cassette rather than putting pen to paper or typing a mail[39]. Similarly guest workers used audio recording for transferring different things:
...Who cannot write, needs help. Some dictates to a literate, what they have to say. Other invents a visual language from stick figures one better use cassettes, to sing and recite poems. Blessing wish, condolences, calls for help, advice - these are strategies of present absents, to participate in distant life[40].
The technology available has always enabled new ways of experimenting with creativity, for example usage of new cameras in the film industry. Via having the audio recording in hand and recording cassettes e.g. by singing for the family members, guest workers were empowered with this technology. Later they started to use it for producing new ethnic music cassettes in Germany. Selling and distributing traditional Turkish music through own networks or letting them play in café houses etc were some practices that were noted in archival documents[41], which can be seen as the early milestones of creative production on rap and hip-hop, a transnational production of Euro-turkishness[42],[43].

3. Product Design: The material footprint of early image in railway stations

For the migrant workers, the railway station were the "central" meeting place. The trains arrived with the newcomers, bringing packages and messages from home ... There were newspapers in their native language to buy. They read it

38   Michael Richter, Gekommen und geblieben: Deutsch-türkische Lebensgeschichten. 8 Hamburg: Körber Stiftung, 2004), 232.
39   Richman and Rey, "Congregating by cassette", 151-152. Karen Richman and Terry Rey, "Congregating by cassette: Recording and participation in transnational Haitian religious rituals." International Journal of Cultural Studies 12 (2009): 149–166.
40   Suvak and Herrmann, In Deutschland angekommen..., 176.
41   DOMiD, 40 Jahre Fremde Heimat .
42   Ayhan Kaya, "German-Turkish transnational space: a separate space of their own." German Studies Review 30, no. 3 (2007): 483–502.
43   Caglar, "Go Go dog".

standing somewhere, leaned on the wall, without having to pay for the stay in cafe next door.[44]
Südbahnhof [South railway station of Vienna] was the destination of trains departing from Istanbul to Austria, transporting the guest workers. Railway stations were therefore the first acknowledged *"mass*-migration" spaces in Austria, hosting large groups of guest workers, and later larger Turkish families, who joined to the guest workers starting from 70's. Railway stations served as main community spaces until means of transport has changed. The most obvious material objectification of Turkish community in railway stations in Europe was their visibility in crowd. The imagination of the Turkish community "as a homogeneous and distinct entity, always fixed in terms of meaning and significance"[45], is materialised in newcomer photos and on newspaper articles. These photos and articles are available in every migration archive. There are even some products that can be discussed as material footprint of this visibility, for example Preiser human figures of a Turkish family.

Preiser is a company that sells realistic model making materials for hobbyists since 1949. *Passanten no 10343*[46] is a set of human figures for model railways that is produced in Europe and sold by this company. The set includes three children, three veiled women and two men, one of which with a younger look and black moustache. This set is categorized as exclusive in the catalogues. Online user forums, stores are full of comments from model makers, naming it as "Muslim family, Turkish family, Turkish guest workers". The production and consumption of such a set can be discussed in relation to its materiality and politics. In a study on beer can design, Shanks and Tilley[47] found that the beer can designs are "relating to meaning of consumption of alcohol" and therefore they are political. Similarly, the Passanten no 10343 is a product that is sold to people who realistically create railway models. *Passanten no 10343* set is frequently named as "guest-worker family", and sold as an exclusiv set. It is a product consumed in Europe and it is related to the meaning of guest workers in railway stations' everyday.

---

44   Suvak and Herrmann, In Deutschland angekommen..., 97.
45   Aksoy, The possibilities of transnational Turkish, 5.
46   Paul M. Preiser GmbH. "Passanten 10343." Accessed February 2, 2011. http://www.preiserfiguren.de/download.php?file=PK%2025%20Seite%20002-021.pdf
47   Michael Shanks and Christopher Tilley, Re-Constructing archaeology: Theory and practice. (Cambridge: Cambridge University Press, 1987), 186.

Figure 2 Sketch visualisation of Preiser Small Figures in Exclusive Serie:
Passanten/Passanger 10343

4. Service Design: Ethno-services and ethno-businesses

Starting from early years of mass-migration, demands and routines of guest workers created innovative transnational service solutions. For example, the demand of cheap-summer-travel-back-home was the pushing force for many start-up companies as Reisebüros [travel agency] owned by guest worker communities. In the beginning, these places were offering bus-tickets between two countries[48] but later, this service turned out to be a new ethnic business, that defined Turkey as a touristic country.

The human networks and know-how on both countries allowed ethnic business owners to develop a sustainable business plan even without a large capital investment. Special offers that focus on the needs of guest workers such as specific flight seasons, guest worker discounts, family discounts helped them preserve their core customers even in hard times. Öger Tourism, a big tourism agency with ethnic roots in Turkey, for instance, has long been producing solutions for specific needs of crowded Turkish families with specific travel dates and unusual travel destinations. As an example they offer extraordinary luggage allowances tat attracts many people from the community. They have 30kg luggage allowance per person, additional 20kg for a child and even another 10kg for babies whereas standard flights from Europe to Turkey neither have luggage allowance for children nor for babies. Such ethnic companies use local community's media channels in Turkish to advertise in European countries. Even today,

---

48 Initiative Minderheiten. „Gastarbajteri Virtuelle Ausstellung." Accessed December 29, 2010. http://www.gastarbajteri.at

such offers are the main motivators for preferring a Turkish ethnic company for travel.

If we did not have 3 children, I would have preferred to fly with Austrian Airlines as they have direct flights to Ankara. But you know, with so many packages and the baby strollers, they [Austrian Airlines] are too strict with all these things but we are crowded and we need to carry all the stuff with us. So better a connected flight with known people (Field Notes 2007_22, 2007 August, Hale 31).

Tourism agencies based in Vienna with close connections to local life in Turkey have been perceived as material visibilities of migrant-enterpreneurship in several corners of Vienna with their repetitive aesthetic style, flyers, advertisement strategies. Inside the community, the sensitive approach on the special needs, support and sponsorship in community events have a return on investment in multiple forms. Most importantly these community-centred approaches build a prestigious businessman image with ethnic background for many of the ethnic-business owners in Austria, which further open doors in the business world of Turkey. Additionally, they have given rise to Turkey being a touristic country. Last but not least, they have created worldwide known business figures in global tourism area.

5. User Innovation: Yearly Vacations and Transnational Materialities

In the1970s guest workers started to possess cars. In parallel a new geographical term was born, *guest-worker route*, a trans-European route, that connects host countries of guest workers to their home countries[49]. During summer holidays, the fully packed cars, accidents and constant traffic have been the symbols of those routes of migration[50]. Although flights are cheaper and covering many cities nowadays, this route and practices around it are perceived rather as a ritual. This ritual has also been a practice that binds community members. For example, in social media, the phenomenon of *"sila yolu" [homeway]* takes huge attention of new generations [born in Europe] as a means of planning and sharing of this ritual with other community members. Many online platforms give information on comparison of services, hotels e.g. on their friendliness, dirtiness, offers. *"Sila yolu"* [homeway] videos on YouTube document current experi-

---

49   Peter Payer, „1972 Gastarbeiterroute." In Gastarbajteri: 40Jahre Arbeitsmigration, edited by Hakan Gürses, Cornelia Kogoj, and Sylvia Mattl, (Wien: Mandelbaum Verlag, 2004), 125–127.

50   Kos, "Winken Zum Abschied."

ences. The comments part of the videos are also used to exchange knowledge, good wishes to others and arrange car-share activities during summer. The materiality of the route, individualised services and products, governmental welcome activities on the board are all given as cherishing activities that adds value to car-travel experience.

In a closer look, those routes created their own material blueprints in years, such as service points, restaurants that serve Turkish food, recreation areas with *"helal"*, Muslim proper, food and Turkish newspaper, hotels and prayer rooms, that are seasonally opened between June and September for the travellers[51] where they can relax, practice their religion and so on[52]. There are multiple services that are specific to this route. Single indviduals, small and large companies even the government set diverse preperations for the season, especially on the northern borders of Turkey. As an example Sekerbank, a bank in Turkey, started the following advertisement campaign[53]. Human billboards (real people wearing advertisement boards) were placed on the road. They weaved and invited „Turks living in Europe", to bring in their investments to Sekerbank. The advertisement design included the licence plates of both Turkey and Germany, probably indicating their sensitivity to the issue of dual citizenship, which usually cause bureaucracy in case of transferring investments. *"Memleketim"* [my country] word was written, in the Turkish licence plate and *"hesabi"* [its account] in the German one, where an emotional vs. financial belonging can be further discussed. Most of my participants mentioned that, this type of activities give a sense of belonging and relaxation as they are welcoming and warm. For example, those advertisements being real humans and waiting there for hours, evoke feelings of self-worth, feeling oneself important and valued, even if people who have those feelings do not see any practical connection to this country any more.

---

51   Di Croce and Budzinski, (Nicht) Auf Augenhöhe?.
52   Initiative Minderheiten, "Gastarbajteri Virtuelle Ausstellung."
53   Haber7. "Ayaklı reklam panoları Kapıkule'de." Accessed July 28, 2012.
    http://www.haber7.com/guncel/haber/567915-ayakli-reklam-panolari-kapikulede

Figure 3 Sketch Visualisation of Human Billboards with Licence Labels

Another example is about food experience. During summer, close to the Turkish border in Edirne, local sellers bring food, home made specialities along the motorway. In contrary to the of-the-shelf products, here one can find bigger portions of cheese (10kg.), pickle, and similar that is packed specifically for the community of guest-workers, who didn't find time to buy them during vacation or didn't have relatives who can prepare the homemade food for their return way to Europe.

On the way back, the cars were then loaded with barrels cucumber, feta cheese in cans, olives and other edibles.[54]

By the consumption of food, people stay linked to their country of origin, to their past and their culture as Sengün pointed[55]. On the border of Turkey, "Familiar tastes, smells, tunes and gestures" that "provide pleasure and comfort, reducing the anxiety of separation"[56] are bought. The food from home was also about a larger network of associations such as values, practices, "cooking, cleanliness, family, sociability, care, all subsumed within the idea and ideal of home" [57].

To sum up, besides the negative image of guest worker route from governmental perspectives, inside the community, these routes have created their own

54 Necla Kelek, Die fremde Braut: Ein Bericht aus dem Inneren des türkischen Lebens in Deutschland. (München: Willhelm Goldmann Verlag, 2006), 145.

55 Asu Aksoy, and Kevin Robins. "Banal transnationalism: The difference that television makes." Transnational Communities Program WPTC-02-08. Accessed October 10, 2010. http://www.transcomm.ox.ac.uk/working%20papers/WPTC-02-08%20Robins.pdf, 5.

56 Ibid.

57 Elia Petridou, "The taste of home." In Home possessions: material culture behind closed doors, edited by Daniel Miller, (Oxford: Berg, 2001), 101.

material supply chains and experience designs. Those were shaped for the specific consumption habits of the year time for guest-worker communities and added value to the yearly vacation experiences. Starting from the 1980s, it was not anymore people who moved to Europe as a part of mass-migration, but the practices and objects of Turkish everyday life. The objects of daily practices (incl. food) were first carried to service stations on the guest-routes, which were out of the borders of Turkey. Further the new package and service designs that were created during those years are transformed to food consumption practices of specific Viennese-Turkish shops after the 1980s. Today, it is possible to find any object in those shops that are related to practices of Turkey and cannot be found in Viennese shops, such as brooms, Turkish tea glasses, daily dusting devices, small teaspoons.

6. A materialistic approach to migration culture and the creative potentials

...I have an idea for the car manufacturer from Stuttgart, every fifth of Turks drive a car with a star [a mercedes], but only every 17th of Germans. So, how about the following advertisement? Leaving the exciting landscape of the wedding behind, a Turkish couple takes off in their decorated Mercedes with flowers. A pleasant male voice promises: "It is not only the marriage that lasts until death, but also the car[58].

The text above is a suggestion from a second-generation member for a Mercedes advertisement. Mercedes cars were (and still partly are) important images from early years of mass-migration. Mercedes is one of the important brands, that is shaping today's global car market. This simple idea for an advertisement is only one way of using the important creative potential of the specific transnational experiences to *brighten our lives.*

In this article I have introduced some of the visual blueprints from the early years of guest workers, where an emphasis was given to *objects, their introduced context in migration history, their cultural embeddedness in transnational practices, and transformations in their biographies.* In my ethnographic work, in analysis of correlations among official documents, oral history and contemporary experiences, it is clear that objects, services and spaces did not only carry or create meanings through dislocations in context and space. They gained their own agencies, their transnational new meanings and they have given rise to new innovative designs.

---

58   Acevit and Bingul, Was lebst Du?, 45.

The objects introduced here did not only contribute to a visual history that is fixed in time. These objects were constructors of some of today's experiences. Specifically to name, it has long been discussed how a guest worker is materialized through his/her belongings as a Germanling in Turkey. This article tried to show how the host country's regulations and urban made in Turkey products contributed to the Europeannes/Turkishness of the Germanling.

The new geographic term of guest-worker routes was presented here not to point car crashes and complaints as in majority of history books. It was not only about how people and objects were transported between two countries. Examples given in this work discusses how the practices, infrastructure and objects gave birth to new business models that are sensitive to cultural experiences and specific needs of transportation. This is also about the interrelations between global and local, how transnational success was reflected through social networks and spherical connections among different classes both in Turkey and in Europe.

The communication objects of mass migration years (e.g: tape-recorders, videos, photograph machines) did not only create new communication channels. They also produced material textures (e.g: spaces filled with sound) for empowering people having their own space. The practice of using these objects in multiple ways and in transnational contexts resulted in new businesses and creative potentials (e.g., music business, call shops and satellite TV).

The materiality of mass-migration is a multi disciplinary debate. This article looked into some of the objects and practices to uncover this multi-facetted rich materiality for their creative potentials. A deeper understanding of relations was achieved by using design anthropology lens. The major result here is the pinning down of the creative processes that were embodied in single objects. The creative potentials of these spaces, objects and experiences belong to neither Turkey nor Europe. They are a result of the transnational setting and practices of mass migration.

International Economic Law as the Answer to Globalization

Kristina Anđelić

The process of economic globalization has brought multiple changes, and impressed them into all aspects of economic life. The state and its attributes of sovereignty have not remained immune to this effect, but had to adapt to the changing times. The modern world is faced with the growing complexity of international relations and multi-dimensional problems. In the international arena, globalization affects the field of trade relations in two ways: by reducing the potential of the nation-states to control international relations, and therefore the possibility to regulate them and by deconstructing the dominant process of creating the law - by increasing the number of entities that can create the law and by increasing the challenges when deciding which specific areas to regulate and what to be the content of the regulations in question.

This paper explores how the openness of national economies affects the normative activity of the state and tries to explain why International Economic Law is the best response to the changes and challenges that economic globalization brought.

1. Challenges of Globalization

Economic globalization is a process in which we witnessed the opening of national economies, the destruction of boundaries in business and releasing flows of business operations. Movement of goods, services and capital gradually became driven in the direction of competitiveness in international markets and the ability to increase their value becomes a measure of success. Development of technology, reduction of transport costs and innovations in the means of communication, result in increasing the volume of trade flows across borders. Also, there is an expansion of networks of transnational linkages and growing interdependence between national markets and business entities operating in different countries. Self-sufficiency and protectionism in the closure of the state is only a rudimentary form of economic activity. The process of economic globalization sets the principle of free trade as the imperative behavior in the international market.

Protectionist walls that surrounded the economic entities of nation-states have opened and these subjects became participants in the international economic competition. Globalization is a process that leads to the "mobile economy", "internet economy" and linked capital markets. The state is no longer able to independently control all these processes within its own borders – but has to face the emergence of a global economic system which stretches beyond the control of a single state (even of dominant states)[1] . In addition, the assets that a single state has are not sufficient to bear the risks of world economic trends. Therefore the nation-states, in compliance with companies that are carrying out their economic activity on those states' territories, have to respond to the changes occurring in the economic environment and adapt to them. As one of the subjects of International Economic Law the state must keep pace with these changes by showing its functionality and the further necessity of carrying the prerogative of sovereignty.

Although the performance of business operations is determined by rules of the market, it is necessary that all market participants are familiar with the rules of conduct governing the relations between them in performance of these tasks. These rules must be known in advance, before market participants perform any kind of business operation, in order to create a business environment that is characterized by consistency, security and stability. Creating such an environment implies the existence of a legal framework to regulate relations arising among the participants of the international market.

Bearing in mind this new era of openness to the international market, and that there are economic entities that operate in multiple countries, and that sometimes it can be difficult to determine their nationality (multinational companies), the state is no longer able to regulate their activities by using national legislation solely. Their activities rise beyond its control. To be able to set the framework for the operation of businesses, the state must coordinate its normative work with other countries, because regulatory boundaries no longer coincide with national boundaries. The state's function is no longer reflected in the attributes of power that can be demonstrated in its own territory, but in the ability of good governance of processes that result from economic globalization.

Economic globalization has proved not only to be a process that has changed the business undertakings by orienting them to a broader market and introducing the use of specialization and economies of scale, but also the process that has set specific requirements for the states. The nation state is faced with the task to actively participate in creating an international consensus on the needs of the global economy. In fact, its role becomes twofold: first, it is still accountable to the domestic actors with a task to channel their interests towards the international market and second, the state must participate in creating international business environment that would meet those interests in the best possi-

---

1   Leo Panitch, „Globalistaion and The State," The Socialist Register (1994): 62.

ble way. The state is faced with redefining the role it plays in business undertakings on its territory as well as injecting new content to the concept of sovereignty. The sovereignty of the state becomes "a policy-weighing process"[2] in which the state should find itself as an active participant in the global economy and should be able to reconcile the way it appears before foreign partners and the way it responds to the needs of local social forces. Along with these trends, it faces new demands placed upon its normative activities.

On the one hand - it is no longer able to independently control all the processes taking place in the world economic scene, and on the other hand - there is still awareness of the need to create and sustain a stable business climate, which should structure the market and allow it to function normally. The attempt to regulate business operations that local companies undertake in cooperation with international partners, exclusively by national regulations would lead to the self-isolation of the state. Unilaterally managing interests solely of its own business entities, not taking into account the rules that exist in other jurisdictions or rules of conduct imposed by international markets - lead to the closure of the national economy for foreign partners and the restriction of trade with the region.

In order to foster the principle of freer trade, the state must seek to create a business environment that is built on partnerships and respect for the reciprocity in mutual rights and obligations. The creation of common rules requires a high level of cooperation and coordination of activities among different countries, as well as reconciliation of their individual interests. The common starting point for all of them must be the maintenance of the system of the international market as a whole and not its individual members, with constant efforts that these two co-exist and overlap rather than stand opposite to each other.

The state is faced with a new challenge: it is no longer the only entity that provides the rules of conduct nor has appropriate instruments at its disposal which are supposed to ensure effective implementation of these rules (shift from a system in which the state, as the sole legislator, on a limited territory, under the threat of sanction for non-compliance with its rules, ensures their effective implementation). The role of rule-making is shared with other entities which results in constant efforts of the state to improve its ability to negotiate and maintain influence in shaping those policies.

Legislative actions have to deal with the need to implement reforms in the legal system that will take into account the spread of economic activities across national boundaries and limits of the national law. On the other hand, there must

---

2   John H. Jackson, „Global Economics and International Economic Law," Journal of International Economic Law 1 (1998): 20.

be awareness that too large and too rapid reform could undermine the basic principles of safety. The tension between these two requirements could lead to ad hoc approach to reform, which creates not a legal system but "oasis of regulations" in the broad field of misrule.[3]

Faced with competitive actors in the normative sphere, different participants in the international arena have varying bargaining power. In such conditions, negotiating rules of conduct can be a form of power oriented system, although the manner of the occurrence of these rules meets the formal requirements of cooperation and coordination. Behind the reached agreement on the content of the rules, often can be a failure to resist the external pressure due to the lack of economic or political power that guide as well as determine the outcome of the negotiations.

The existence of different interest groups, which have great economic power can influence the creation of rules in two ways: their economic power can channel political efforts to create consensus to regulate only those relations that are in their best interest. This leads to fragmented regulation, subordinate only to a specific orientation to the small part of market participants, which creates inconsistent and incomplete regulatory systems. Such a method of regulating not only tends to ignore to regulate all the areas in which the appropriate legal framework is needed, but also neglects to identify new areas where the conditions for imposing new regulations have been met. That way some areas have multiple regulations that bring insecurity on the content of rights and obligations, and other areas are not regulated even though there is objective need for that and the time is right to "sit down" and negotiate what kind of regulations those should be. The second mode of action of these groups is reflected in their impact on the content of the rules that are made: they are designed specifically to meet their interests, and as such favor unfair competition, directly inhibit the achievement of the equality of all market participants, and also they are arbitrarily variable. All of this contributes to creating an unstable atmosphere to perform, with the imposition of business conditions operating from a position of economic strength of individual participants.

In the assessment of these types of challenges brought by economic globalization, we should keep in mind particularly the multinational companies, whose economic power justifies consideration of their impact on the creation of legislation, not only at the national level but also internationally. Multinational companies create their own rules of conduct. Their extremely strong market position enables them to impose their general business conditions and business

---

3   Edward F. Greene and Omer S. Oztan, "The attack on national regulation," Capital Markets Law Journal, Vol. 4, No. 1 (2008): 9.

enables them to impose their general business conditions and business practices as mandatory requirements in all business relations they have with other companies. Willingly or unwillingly, although formally non-binding, they are imposed as such, and are eventually accepted as obligatory. This kind of impact multinational companies have on the creation of rules and regulations is described as the "new feudalism".[4] It appears as if they have their own territories with "subordinates" that gravitate towards their "legal gravitation field". This "field" attracts lack of sound economic choices, lack of freedom of business will determined by the need of smaller companies to survive the competition and become the part of business network that multinational companies create. Their compliance with strict and rigid conditions which are made to benefit solely the multinational companies is orchestrated by the necessity of doing business, even if it needs to be done this way. What is written in the statutes and legal documents of multinational companies becomes generally accepted as long as they have more and more partners who do more and more business with them. The longer these rules are in use, the longer there is awareness of their applicability in a wide range of cases, so one tends to use them by inertia in any other similar case. And of course, there is always helplessness – even if you know you don't have to behave according to these rules, you know there is not much you can do to change them (insignificant bargaining power). But that kind of system, if we may call it that way, brings us to this: there are as many rules of conduct as there are multinational companies.

Another of the unique challenges brought by economic globalization is the survival of the rules in the time of crisis. Namely, when the normal flow of international trade is affected, and when its volume decreases, the world economy falls into recession and threatens the collapse of many national economies, the gap between the efforts for trade liberalization and its regulation at the global level and efforts to introduce national protectionism intensifies. Awareness on the need for common rules is reduced due to the need of self-preservation, and each seeks those solutions that lead to the simplest of outputs. To be able to maintain the ideal of trade liberalization and the creation of a freer market precisely in such times of crisis it is necessary to achieve greater discipline of the participants of international business operations and continuity in their relationships. But there always remains the question how to preserve consensus among all those actors on how international market should be regulated in the crisis.

---

4   Darko Polšek, „Kamo ideš striče Sam? Izazovi globalizacije,“ Politička misao, VOL. XLV br. 1 (2008): 95.

2. International Economic Law as the answer

International Economic Law should answer the question of how to most effectively and in the most functional way respond to the challenges brought by economic globalization.

International Economic Law can be viewed as a response to the needs imposed by the globalized market and as a tool that structures it and allows its smooth functioning.

International Economic Law is based on the fundamental principles that give equal opportunities to the participants in the international market in terms of fair business: the principle of fair treatment, the principle of freer trade, most favored nation principle, the principle of reciprocity, national treatment and others. International Economic Law further elaborates on these principles, giving them a more concrete content and brings them into the economic life of the international market.

International Economic Law identifies the interests and needs of different social forces and the different areas that need to be managed. It recognizes entities that make the rules and takes into account their different activities in the regulation of relations related to the performance of international business operations. Through its mechanisms of making rules, International Economic Law allows the channeling of their different interests in the common rules. Compromise is not only reflected in the reconciliation of economic forces behind the various negotiating factors, but also in reconciling the various existing rules and legal systems, as well as legal traditions that were once regulating these relations. International Economic Law thus aims to be widely accepted and universally applied.

When thinking about important instruments in creating the appropriate legal environment for doing international business, it is important to consider the role of economic international organizations[5], and especially the World Trade Organization. These organizations should pave the path to permanent trade liberalization and the creation of a legal superstructure that would allow it. They provide developed mechanisms for creation of legislature that can incorporate all of the diversified ideas that emerge from legal ground of all participants in that process. Even though we have to be realistic and recognize the fact that these mechanisms are not perfect, and that there is a chance that regulations that are created by using them can too be interest driven and power dictated, international organizations have more chances to create neutral ground for negotiations.

---

5   John H. Jackson, "Global Economics and International Economic Law," Journal of International Economic Law 1 (1998): 4.

These organizations symbolize participation in making rules. This way they become the vehicle through which the sovereignty of the state is realized[6]. Armed with the rule of transparency, they are good indicators for states' future behavior, so the states become burdened by the necessity of gaining good reputation in order to survive among other international actors. More importantly, these organizations do not have importance only in the creation of rules, but also in providing mechanisms for their interpretation and application. The General Agreement on Tariffs and Trade (GATT) and the rounds of negotiations that resulted (among other accomplishments) in the creation of the World Trade Organization (WTO), recognized the need for gradual and permanent trade liberalization in the way that responds effectively to the process of globalization. Negotiations that occurred under the GATT rules and within WTO indicate the period of intense regulation of international trade that paved the way for reconciling the different intentions of all the member states. Also, WTO's Dispute Settlement Understanding meant a crucial change in resolving trade quarrels because it shifted the power oriented application and implementation of rights and duties to the rule oriented system.

However, when discussing the role of international economic organizations we should bare in mind that international trade can not be viewed in isolation, but in interaction with many other activities that directly or indirectly may affect it. For example, adoption of appropriate legislation that regulates the fishing industry, without taking into account the law of the sea, would be impossible.[7] So, for more comprehensive consideration of all the problems and needs of international trade, it is necessary that different international organizations that deal with specific areas, work together, share experiences, point out problems and cooperate in the creation of International Economic Law, each contributing in its own specific fields. On the other hand, regulating solely international trade is not enough to have a complete system, and there are other areas that should not be neglected, such as labor rights, environmental issues, international financial flows, banking system, monetary system as well as the definition of global economic policy.

Also, we must not forget the activities of regional organizations. Although opinions are divided on the importance and role of regionalization, and some see it as a threat to the economic integration of countries at the global level, and some see it as an accelerated path to it, there is no doubt that in the framework

---

6   Kal Raustiala, "Rethinking the Sovereignty Debate in International Economic Law," Journal of International Economic Law 6 (4, 2003): 856.
7   Thomas Cottier, "Challenges ahead in International Economic Law," Journal of International Economic Law 12(1, 2009): 13.

set by regional organizations interests of the states are coming closer and reaching a consensus on rules that should be adopted becomes easier.

Regulations that are created should not only reflect what we have learned so far and demonstrate our ability to convert those experiences into legal rules, but our awareness of their importance should grow and direct us to the new roles they should take. For example, the global economic crisis has taught us that the regulation of the banking system and international financial flows was not sufficient, and that the right regulations should not only bring order and disciplined behavior in specific areas, but should also provide mechanisms that may act preventively.

Of course, International Economic Law should be viewed in the spirit of criticism. It is not a perfect system, but is one that provides us with a framework which globally coordinates efforts[8] aimed at consistency in the regulation of international trade relations. It reflects the growing role of rules that regulate mutual relations of the participants in the international market and it secures that the base on which rests the rule of law is not violated even in the international arena. International Economic Law is a response to the needs of economic globalization: consensus on the needs of the world economy can not replace legal obligation, thereby providing a stable foundation and structure of the market. Its shortcomings remind us that it needs to be constantly improved and upgraded. But while debating about these problems, we should not be too strict, because even on national level we can never completely free laws from the impact of different interests. After all, the law is supposed to reflect the movements brought by different social gropups, or the state of the art in society as a whole. We can only rely on the fact that International Economic Law can help us overcome the difficulties that arise from trying to reconcile needs of those groups in question.

3. Conclusion

The process of economic globalization and networking of national economies have created the need for a legal superstructure that could regulate the behavior of businesses worldwide. In this process the nation-state loses its role as an exclusive creator of law. Rapidity in performance of business operations caused by globalization has influenced the creation of appropriate forms of legal sources, which can properly adapt to those requirements.

---

8   Edward F. Greene and Omer S. Oztan, "The attack on national regulation," Capital Markets Law Journal, Vol. 4, No. 1 (2008): 28.

Although efforts to create the legal superstructure of economic globalization have given results in terms of creating rules that would allow trade liberalization, there are numerous challenges that must be answered. International economic organizations play a great role in structuring the rules of the market, by acting as a forum for negotiating the content of regulations in the international economic arena, and by equipping them with a strong sense of legitimacy. Still, we have to be aware that it is impossible or very difficult to control the process of globalization. International Economic Law is one step forward to this high set goal. It provides a global framework in which there is enough space to plan, develop strategy and create the best possible legal system which is based on the cooperation of different international entities and takes into account specific factors in international economic relations.

So, once we have learned that there is an answer to "what to do with all the changes globalization brought to economic life on business entities from all over the world", it is easier to guide ourselves toward further developing it and to take the next step on the way to overcome its shortcomings. One can only hope that this will be the thing we choose to do.

The Globalization of International Human Rights Norms through Transitional Justice and Its Critics

Christian Wlaschütz

When in 1948 the recently established United Nations approved the Universal Declaration of Human Rights, it did so remembering the atrocities committed by totalitarian regimes such as National Socialism and Stalinism. Millions of killed people and a war that was caused by Hitler´s megalomania cried for a universal agreement on fundamental rights.

Since then the human rights norms gained efficiency and recognition. The Cold War, however, split them into several generations that confronted each other ideologically. Political and civil rights on the one hand and social, economic and cultural rights on the other hand were the banners of the West and the East respectively. In 1989, when the Berlin wall came down, the human rights norms recovered their inseparable character, although the political rights were still in the focus. I will argue that this undermines the credibility of human rights particularly in the countries of the south.

This article shows the globalization of human rights norms by the application of transitional justice that deals with past violations in transitional periods. I hereby follow Kathryn Sikking´s justice cascade-approach that focuses on individual criminal responsibility. In the second part of the article I will, however, confront this view with its critics. My own experience with the Colombian transitional justice policies will help me to illustrate shortcomings of the focus on the legal dimension of transitional justice and the political and civil rights at the expense of economic and social rights. These should be overcome in order to strengthen the achievements of the past decades.

1. The Justice Cascade

In her book *The Justice Cascade*, Kathryn Sikking presents the idea that the trend to hold individual state officials, including heads of states, accountable for their human rights violations is on the rise. The term cascade indicates that all started with a small stream of thought that favored criminal accountability such as illustrated by the Nuremberg and Tokyo trials, but gained momentum in the 1970s, when the democratic government of Greece decided to put former state officials on trial.[1]

---

1 Kathryn Sikking, The Justice Cascade: How Human Rights Prosecutions are changing World Politics (New York: W.W. Norton & Company, 2011), 5

In the meantime, three sitting presidents have been indicted for mayor crimes: Slobodan Milosevic, who died before being convicted by the International Criminal Tribunal for the Former Yugoslavia (ICTY); Charles Taylor, who fled to Nigeria after the defeat of his troops in Liberia, and was extradited to the Special Court for Sierra Leone in 2006; and Omar al-Bashir of Sudan, who has been indicted for crimes against humanity in Darfur.

Finnemore/Sikking analyze the emergence of the cascade by applying an actor-centered approach in order to highlight the committed work by "norm entrepreneurs". These are international lawyers, human rights activists, victims and others, who have fought tirelessly for the respect and enforcement of their rights and those of the relatives. The authors describe a norm "life cycle" as a three-stage-process, where the norm first emerges, then through a "tipping point" converts itself into a "norm cascade" and finally is internalized. In international relations this tipping point consists of sufficient state actors that adopt this new norm.[2]

The ideational base for the cascade consists of three apparently obvious convictions: First, that violations of human rights such as torture, mass executions or disappearance cannot be justifiable acts by state officials; second, that the perpetrators must be brought to justice; and third, that the accused also have the right to due process. It is this last point that distinguishes human rights trials from political trials that are traditionally applied to strengthen regimes against former leaders or internal enemies.[3]

2. Transitional Justice

The development of transitional justice is closely related to the before analyzed justice cascade of human rights. The term refers to the concrete tools to apply human rights norms in transitional periods in order to prevent a recurrence of atrocities and fortify the rule of law. These times present an extraordinary opportunity to put human rights on the agenda.

Although transitional justice has had many manifestations throughout history[4], the theoretical elaboration is still deficient. So it is hard to speak of a new concept; it is rather a set of instruments used to achieve certain political goals according to specific interests and judicial frames. They emerge as "an answer

---

2   Martha Finnemore and Kathryn Sikking, "International Norm Dynamics and Political Change," International Organization, 52/4 (1998): 893ff.

3   Sikking, Justice Cascade, 13

4   For an exhaustive analysis of how transitional justice instrumente have been applied from the old Greeks onwards, compare: Jon Elster, Closing the Books: Transitional Justice in historical perspective (Cambridge: Cambridge University Press, 2004).

to demands and interests of political and social actors"[5]. This means that the construction of theories follows a posteriori its empirical manifestations.

The term includes the concept of justice that refers to an abstract value that has generally positive connotations despite the diverse interpretations it raises; but it also means the concrete judicial reaction to actions that are socially rejected. In this regard the term suggests accountability and in the end punishment. This is why transitional justice is often considered as the field for international and national lawyers and judges, who are the experts with regard to criminal law. Justice has certainly other meanings, too. In addition to this retributive dimension, there are the distributive justice that emphasizes the need to better distribute resources and the restorative justice that is more focused on the improvement of social relationships. Despite the prevalence of the retributive aspect by means of trials, the other levels of justice are significant parts of what is called transitional justice, although unfortunately underestimated as will be discussed later.

UN Secretary General Kofi Annan, in his 2004 report *The Rule of Law and Transitional Justice in Conflict and Post-Conflict Countries. Report of the Secretary General* (S/2004/616), defined transitional justice as follows: "Transitional Justice comprises the full range of processes and mechanisms associated with a society's attempts to come to terms with a legacy of large-scale past abuses, in order to ensure accountability, serve justice and achieve reconciliation. These may include both judicial and non-judicial mechanisms with differing levels of international involvement (or none at all) and individual prosecutions, reparations, truth-seeking, institutional reform, vetting and dismissals, or a combination thereof."

Thus, transitional justice is not only about analyzing and addressing past crimes and atrocities. It is of utmost importance that the main focus remains on the present and the future. It is clear that the goal is the transformation of a society that perpetuates violence into one that does not need it to resolve its conflicts.[6]

This balance between punishment and forgiveness requires of a society in transition, but particularly of the victims, the abandonment of vengeance and of

---

5   Delphine Lecombe, "Una paz conflictiva: luchas epistémicas en torno a la definición de la justicia transicional en Colombia," in Transiciones en Contienda: Dilemas de la justicia transicional en Colombia y en la experiencia comparada, ed. International Center for Transitional Justice (Bogotá: ICTJ, 2010), 213

6   Amanda Lyons, "Colombia: hacia una transición justa," in Transiciones en Contienda: Dilemas de la justicia transicional en Colombia y en la experiencia comparada, ed. International Center for Transitional Justice (Bogotá: ICTJ, 2010), 27

the perpetrators the best possible reparation.[7] Reconciliation, furthermore, implies that society as a whole has to ask itself what structural elements led to violence and what transformations are necessary to prevent it. In this effort no social sector can be spared.[8]

In the following chapter, I am elaborating more on the most notable and controversial element of transitional justice – trials as the manifestation of individual criminal responsibility that opposes impunity that used to be the by far most recurrent way to deal with past crimes.

3. The Individualization of Criminal Responsibility

The impunity-approach is deeply rooted in history. Before World War II both the state and its officials were exempt from justice for various reasons. On the one hand, it was felt that the monarch could not do any wrong, on the other hand, immunity was meant to provide the necessary space to administer the state´s affairs. This model came to an end due to the effects of the holocaust. It became obvious what atrocities an unrestrained state is able to commit. The victorious allies initiated the Nuremberg and Tokyo trials as a first step to hold individuals accountable. The human rights declaration of 1948 and the more specific human rights treaties of 1966 ended the state´s immunity by providing important instruments to hold the state as such accountable – but not yet individual state officials.

The increase in severe human rights violations demonstrated that there was the need for further instruments. Human rights defenders increasingly argued for individual prosecutions as a means for deterring human rights violations. A basic term in this context is accountability understood as "practices where some actors hold other actors to a set of standards and impose sanctions if these standards are not met."

Despite the continued existence of both impunity and state-responsibility, the spread of the idea of individual responsibility is obvious when we look on the available data. From the beginning of the 1990s onwards, the number of prosecutions multiplied with a regional emphasis in Europe and Latin America. The so-called "contagion-effect" that explains this diffusion of the norm can be characterized by the imitation of state behavior by other regional neighbors, but also

---

7   Compare: Martha Minow, Between Vengeance and Forgiveness: Facing History after Genocide and Mass Violence (Boston: Beacon Press, 1998)

8   Compare: David Bloomfield, On Good Terms: Clarifying Reconciliation (Berlin: Berghof Report No. 14, October 2006)

by the new human rights movement through a concerted effort by concrete human beings such as lawyers and activists in a wide range of countries.[9]

But how did it start? Kathryn Sikking traces the development back to two different "streams" and a solid "streambed" that initially were separated from each other. The first stream consisted in the tradition of the Nuremberg and Tokyo trials that led to the international tribunals on Yugoslavia and Rwanda. The second stream and practically independent of the first consisted in the domestic trials that took place in Greece, Portugal and particularly Argentina in the 1970s and 1980s respectively. In the course of these two streams a new international legal framework was built to fortify the human rights related instruments, the streambed. When in 1998, the delegates approved the Statute of Rome that established the ICC, there was already a firm legal and practical base to further develop individual penal prosecution. Nevertheless, at every stage concrete human agency was necessary to evolve the cascade.

A central step in the creation of a streambed was the individualization of international law, thus the emphasis on individual responsibility for human rights violations, but also the care for individual victims. It was the Convention Against Torture (CAT) that first shifted the focus from state to individual responsibility. Prominent legal experts such as the Egyptian Cherif Bassiouni had an important impact on the inclusion of progressive clauses such as the need to domestically prosecute individual perpetrators of torture or to extradite them to another country willing to do that; the universal jurisdiction that stipulated that torturers may be prosecuted in any country that had signed the convention; and that all acts of torture are criminal offenses in domestic law. The convention was approved in December 1984 and came into effect in 1987.

The new legal contents of the CAT became reinforced by international legislation on forced disappearance such as the Inter-American Convention on Forced Disappearance of Persons of 1996. This Convention contains similar language to the CAT, particularly with regard to universal jurisdiction.

A major step towards the individualization of criminal law was the integration of humanitarian law ("War Law") into the human rights discourse. On the one hand it allowed human rights organizations to gain in neutrality criticizing both the governments and the guerrilla groups in internal armed conflicts, on the other hand it facilitated the eventual merging of these two branches in the international tribunals on Yugoslavia and the ICC. By 1993 the individual prosecutions on the domestic level increased rapidly; it seems that the end of the Cold War accelerated the diffusion of the justice norm. However, human rights or-

---

9   Sikking, Justice Cascade, 13-24

ganizations such as HRW were skeptical about the efficiency of domestic trials
(second stream); thus they kept pushing for international tribunals (first
stream).[10]

The idea of a Nuremberg-tribunal re-emerged in the early 1990s when it became clear that Saddam Hussein had committed genocide against the Kurds in
the Anfal campaign, in which around 100.000 Kurds were killed, partly by poi-
son. However, there was no venue available to try Hussein then. Furthermore,
the failure of domestic trials and the amnesty laws that blocked trials in Argentina and Chile led to the conclusion that it did not make sense to wait for internal
tribunals in Yugoslavia. The decisive factors for the creation of the tribunal were
the end of the Cold War, the documentation on genocide and widespread crimes
against humanity and the success of the international NGO´s campaign for such
a court. The ICTY had positive impacts on the creation of domestic courts, but
also of the International Criminal Tribunal for Rwanda (ICTR) in 1994. These
events helped to mobilize state support for the eventual creation of the ICC.

The work of the group of like-minded states supported by the Coalition for the
International Criminal Court, a network of around 2000 NGOs was decisive to
mobilize support for the idea. At the time of the Rome conference, the group
consisted of around 60 countries, although with a Western bias. The 1998 approved Rome Statute was firmly based on the individual criminal responsibility,
explicitly including head of states and state officials.

With the creation of the ICC the two streams converged into a court that would
prosecute perpetrators regardless their position. In 2002, much earlier than expected, the treaty entered into force. By 2010, 110 states have ratified the statute.[11]

4. The critics

While the creation of the ICC was probably the highlight for the movement that
defends universal jurisdiction, several critics raised their concerns about the
shortcomings of criminal prosecution. From the vast literature, I will select two
arguments represented by Jack Snyder/Leslie Vinjamuri and Rosmary Nagy.
The first doubts the beneficial effects of criminal prosecutions for peace and
democracy, the second points to important deficiencies of the human rights discourse in transitional periods.

Snyder/Vinjamuri published one of the most influential critical articles in
2004. They basically argue that the sequence of first claiming the implementa-

---

10   Sikking, Justice Cascade, 96-109
11   Sikking, Justice Cascade, 109-121

tion of universally accepted norms and then building the necessary institutions for the rule of law is flawed. Amnesties for past offenses may be necessary to curb future violations; international tribunals have proved to be unsuccessful in this respect. Thus the first steps are political bargaining and effective coalition-building to limit the impact of the spoilers.[12]

The authors believe that normative persuasion is not enough to change behaviors that are strengthened by a specific set of institutions and patterns of political power. Furthermore, the mere existence of international tribunals does not create a deterring effect. This is only achieved by the enforcement of norms. If the corresponding mechanisms are weak, "pragmatic bargaining" is in place to remove the perpetrators from power. As a conclusion, the authors reject the mere legalism in the absence of institutional and social preconditions.

According to the authors, actors would rely on norms only if they are effective to achieve the objective to reduce the atrocities. This is guaranteed by strong institutions and political coalitions. Thus the sporadic punishment of past violations should be secondary to the improvement of effective legal institutions. Consequently the analysis should focus on the strength of potential spoilers. If they are too weak to derail a democratization process, they can be put to trial; if not, the institution-building must enjoy precedence. So the criterion to prosecute should be the strengthening of the rule of law. If amnesties are needed for this purpose, they should be applied.[13]

Kathryn Sikking undertook the task to empirically rebut Snyder/Vinjamuri´s arguments. Based on the U.S. State Department´s *Annual Country Reports of Human Rights Practices* that include information on judicial and human rights practices in 198 countries over 26 years, she and her team created a transitional database that included the criminal prosecutions for past human rights violations. Taking the Latin American experiences, she convincingly shows that prosecutions have not undermined the democratic transformations in the region. Quite on the contrary, Latin America is the region with most prosecutions and the most stable development towards democracy. She also rejects the notion that trials lead to further atrocities, although the data is not conclusive with regard to the expectation that prosecutions improve the human rights record. This finding is confirmed by another research-group headed by Leigh Payne. Although they differ on the importance of trials for the improvement of human rights standards,

---

12 Jack Snyder and Leslie Vinjamuri, "Trials and Errors. Principles and Pragmatism in Strategies of International Justice," International Security 28/3 (1994): 5-7
13 Snyder and Vinjamuri, Trials and Errors, 11-15

they both came to the conclusion that trials do not exacerbate the human rights record.[14]

In the following, I would like to focus on another set of critical arguments. Rosmary Nagy[15] suggests a review on transitional justice that has obtained widespread acceptance. There is a consensus that past atrocities must be addressed. However, Nagy points towards issues such as the transitional justice´s blindness towards gender or social injustice and its applicability in contexts outside its liberal, Western origin. It also focuses on legal considerations that are far away from life-realities.

The notion that transitional justice takes place in a well defined transitional moment from war to peace or authoritarianism to democracy that separates a "now" from a "then" may obscure continuities of violence and repression. One example is the tendency that violence against women increases in "post-conflict" situations, when for instance former combatants return home.

Transitional justice is also applied almost exclusively to non-Western countries. Consequently the same criticism that is raised against the universalism of human rights is raised with regard to transitional justice, namely that the West imposes its values on other contexts. This argument is aggravated by the definition of what is a transitional moment. In Iraq, for example, the transition refers to the fall of Saddam Hussein´s regime, but not to the illegal US-invasion or the ongoing violence. Transitional justice instruments, thus, convert themselves in educational tools for the Iraqi people, but not for the Western invaders, thus reinforcing the impression of a double standard.

The denial of the ICTY to investigate violations of the international humanitarian law by NATO bombing and that of the ICTR to look into allegations of war crimes committed by the ruling Rwandan Patriotic front confirmed suspicions of victor´s justice.

Thus, it appears that transitional justice serves other ends than justice; Western powers appear to only apply instruments of transitional justice notwithstanding their involvement in repressive systems or armed conflicts. This is particularly true for trials that are about individual responsibility; truth commissions would be more appropriate to investigate the larger picture, but usually they do not include "outsiders". The recent commissions in Sierra Leone and East Timor, however, have named the responsibilities of the international community.

---

14   Sikking, Justice Cascade, 148-151; 187f.
15   Rosmary Nagy, "Transitional Justice as Global Project: critical reflections," Third World Quarterly 29/2 (2008): 275-89

Due to its legalistic focus, transitional justice instruments address violations of political and civil rights and criminal offenses, but neglect structural violence and social injustice. Nagy mentions the experience of the Truth and Reconciliation Commission (TRC) in South Africa. Focusing on bodily harm, it did not emphasize the structural violence of the apartheid system, but of single acts of violence. Everyday racism and poverty remained outside the scope of the TRC. Quoting Louise Arbour, Nagy makes the point that many root causes of conflicts can be found in the second generation of human rights, the economic, social and cultural rights that are usually not addressed by transitional justice.

Women often appear only as secondary victims, as widows or mothers of killed men. "Truth" often neglects the violence women suffer from in post-conflict and conflict situations, including the economic harms. Although the recognition of sexual violence as a crime against humanity is highly significant, the reference to this violence does not capture the whole extent to which women and girls are vulnerable both in times of peace and war. Truth commissions may be better positioned to do that; the commission of Sierra Leone for example made recommendations regarding marriage age, discriminatory inheritance legislature and other aspects that harm women.

5. The Colombian experience

These arguments deserve very serious consideration. There is an ample literature[16] on these and similar issues, which I would like to use to approach the Colombian transitional justice experience that I have been working in for the last six years. Among others, Nagy refers to two major concerns that have the potential to derail a transitional process. The first is the almost exclusive association of transitional justice with international legal norms; the second is the focus on political rights ignoring the so-called "root causes" of conflicts that usually consist in inequality, widespread corruption and cleptocratic states.

Colombia offers several insights in these regards, particularly because this country is the most recent case, where national and international actors have been working on transitional justice designs for several years. It started with the so-called "Justice and Peace"-Law that served as a legal base for the demobilization of the paramilitaries. It included legal and economic benefits for the ex-combatants and was severely criticized, because it virtually ignored the victims.

---

16 Compare among others: Rosalind Shaw and Lars Waldorf, eds., Localizing Transitional Justice: Interventions and Priorities after Mass Violence (Stanford: Stanford University Press, 2010); Kieran McEvoy and Lorna McGregor, eds., Transitional Justice from Below: Grassroots Activism and the Struggle for Change (Portland: Hart Publishing, 2008)

The "Victim´s Law" of 2011, signed in the presence of UN-Secretary General Ban Ki-moon, on the contrary, includes stipulations on reparation, truth and in its accompanying law even land restitution thus addressing the issue that according to most authors lays at the root of the Colombian conflict.

However, truth and reparation are still largely confined to the direct effects of the armed conflict; they do not include the systemic corruption that deprives millions of young people of professional opportunities or the disastrous health system that causes thousands of deaths every year. Thus, one can conclude that the pursuit of truth remains on the surface in the sense that it concentrates on people who visibly violated first generation human rights, which is important, but does not tackle the underlying systemic deficiencies that cause and perpetuate violence and simply replace the imprisoned perpetrators. It is obviously easier to sacrifice a few prominent figures for their crimes than to address a pattern of discrimination and exclusion due to gender, ethnic origin and class affiliation.[17]

With regard to the legal bias of transitional justice, Colombia confirms this view. The multitude of local initiatives with regard to truth-searching, reintegration of ex-combatants and reconciliation hardly find official recognition. The implementation of reparation-designs and related issues is centered on very young, inexperienced alumni from Bogota´s elite-universities, who through contacts perpetuate a very discriminatory hiring system based on personal contacts and not on experience. This disconnect between rural communities that have suffered from the conflict for decades and state-officials, who are mostly unable or unwilling to empathize with this situation, creates frustration and certainly does not contribute to the building of trust into the state´s institutions. Consequently, the implementation of the best laws will not take into consideration the needs and priorities of people, the state officials do not understand and often do not care about. In a country, where the state has virtually no civilian presence in vast territories, the focus on the legal dimension must fail, because there is no institutional framework that would be able to implement it. In this regard, Snyder/Vinjamuri have a point.

In these cases, where the disconnect between transitional justice discourse and practice and the realities on the ground are that huge, I would suggest a multi-level approach that values the multitude of need-oriented and particularly

---

17 Colombia´s cities are actually subdivided into "estratos" that officially range from "estrato 1" to "estrato 6". Each address belongs to a estrato, which on the one hand means that in a lower estrato one pays less for services such as water, on the other hand stigmatizes people, who live in a lower estrato. In the end the system serves to put people in class-related categories, from which it is very difficult to escape.

legitimate activities on the local level. This obviously does not exclude high-level activities such as land reform, security sector reform or judicial reforms that must be implemented at the top, but would open channels of communication that allow for a higher participation of those who suffered most from violence and its causes. This would actually strengthen the legitimacy of the state and in the end the transition towards an inclusive democracy.

6. Conclusions

This article showed the impressive increase of accountability of individuals for their decisions and actions that led to widespread human rights violations. Former and present dictators are not safe from prosecution anymore, which gives victims hope that one day their rights will be respected and, where possible, re-instated. The creation of the ICC on the basis of the vast knowledge gained by the temporary tribunals for Yugoslavia and Rwanda was a milestone for international jurisdiction for the most heinous crimes based on due process and the observation of the defendant´s rights.

However, the next step of this extraordinary achievement must be to make people understand the reasons of why it is so important for them. The discussion about the alleged Western bias of human rights, but particularly the absence of crimes that matter most for the daily life of the people on the ground (corruption, structural violence, exclusion, lack of basic goods such as clean water) must be addressed urgently in order not to lose legitimacy for human rights. If human rights in general and transitional justice in particular are seen as the business of wealthy, well educated experts only, the emotional connection to them will be minimal. This would certainly undermine the justice cascade, at the core of which is human dignity and the conviction that there are inalienable rights that are part of human nature.

Westernization and Malaysian Television

Sabariah Mohamed Salleh

Malaysia is a country populated by various races and ethnicities which include Malays, Chinese and Indians. A society rich with traditional beliefs and culture, Malaysia, according to Shamsul (2005) can be considered a plural society, as it comprises different communities living together while not necessarily having close or meaningful bonds with each other, thus "stimulating a sense of ethnic identity and separateness" (Milner, 2008: 121)[1]. In essence, Malaysia seems like a trouble free country where its' plural society live peacefully amongst each other. However, it must be pointed out that there were several tragedies, like the 13 May 1969 and the Kampung Medan racial riot in 2001, which were greatly influenced by racial disparities. How did this come about? For decades before gaining its independence from the British colonization, Malaysians have been living separately in distinct locations and occupy different positions in the society, according to their respective races. This divide and conquer technique utilised by the British saw Malays living in rural areas and working as farmers, Chinese in the cities as business entrepreneurs and Indians as labourers and estate workers. The different social positions divided these various races socially, economically and politically. As noted by Syed Hussin (2008: 171)[2], there is a social distance between the various races and "most Malays do not know Chinese values very well and most Chinese are quite ignorant of Malay values, despite the fact that they have been living side by side for so long."

Given the circumstances, it does seem like a daunting task to promote unity especially given that the society which was inherited after being colonialized were racially segregated and categorized, which has undoubtedly left a huge impact. After gaining its Independence from the British in 1957, the new government had a difficult time to create a unified society. The racial segregation by British has somewhat increased disparity and created a feeling of insolence among people of different races. So, what can be done in order to foster a better understanding between these races? Not only that, the Malaysian society are also divided according to social class (Shamsul, 2005; Syed Hussin Ali, 2008) and tensions are easily generated based on these number of differences.

---

1   Milner, The Malays (Oxford: Wiley Blackwell, 2008), 121
2   Syed Husin Ali, The Malays: Their Problems and Future (Kuala Lumpur: The Other Press, 2008), 171

This is where mass media, according to Syed Hussin (2008: 171)[3], especially television, can play a big role. Syed Hussin (2008) commented that mass communication have not been used to its full effect to promote a better understanding of people of different cultures and values. But, how effective is television as a tool to promote racial unity?

The debate on westernization, cultural imperialism and Americanization, especially in relations to the media, therefore, is a tremendous cause of concern for the Malaysian government. On top of the government's apprehension in promoting unity and understanding between each races within the Malaysian society, there is also now the concern of locals imitating and practicing cultures which are deemed foreign and as threatening the society's traditions. However, it must be pointed out that there is a lack of empirical evidence with regards to the claim or westernization through the media.

The media industry in Malaysia is flourishing and the country now boasts six free-to-air television channels and also a satellite broadcasting service. This means that audiences are exposed to a variety of content in the media. Thanks to rebranding of several free-to-air television stations, the six channels are packaged according to cater to specific races, for example TV1, TV3, TV9 for Malays and 8TV for Chinese. Astro also offers packages tailored for the needs of these different races as channels with Chinese, Malay and Indian dialects are often grouped together and offered in one exclusive package. My question is, how would this approach help foster unity amongst the society members? How is this going to help young Malaysian understand the cultures of those in different race? Can a Malay better understand a Chinese with this specially tailored television channels to suit a specific race? Will it affect the process of socialization among the youth of different ethnicities? Will it create bias and stereotypes about people of different culture backgrounds? As it is, in a finding by TV 3 on top television programs on free-to-air-television watched by Malay and Chinese adults, the top 9 programs are programs in their native dialects, respectively. So, would this approach help them to understand other culture better or increase racial disparity instead?

Not only that, satellite broadcasts by Astro exposes Malaysians to foreign culture as well, such as American and Japanese culture. So, on top of negotiating meanings from local television texts, they are also trying to decode meanings of the foreign contents. Already, Syed Husin Ali (2008: 185)[4] noted that in the process of modernization, "Western elements become stronger (and), the tradi-

---

3   Syed Husin Ali, The Malays: Their Problems and Future, 171

4   Syed Husin Ali, The Malays: Their Problems and Future, 185

tional elements (with relations to culture) tend to get correspondingly weaker." So, how do audiences negotiate the different values and beliefs showcased on television? Are they becoming more westernized or does it make them more aware of their cultural identity?

Hence, the core of this paper involves looking at the content of television programs in Malaysia, in order to unearth the truthfulness of the sweeping generalization made with regards to media globalization, and particularly media and cultural imperialism in Malaysia. Are the contents filled with Western or foreign values? In the first part of this paper, I will be explaining the methods which I used to answer my queries. Then, I will discuss at length on the contents of television programs with relation to the number of hours each free-to-air station allocates for both local and imported program. Next, I will elaborate on the results obtained from a content analysis conducted on the top locally produced television series, *Seram*. The reason I opted to do a content analysis on the top program watched on free-to-air television is because it could be accessed by all walks of life, unlike Astro which can only be watched by those who can afford the subscription fees. The content analysis will enable me to ascertain the forms of culture that are being represented in the program most watched by the Malaysian audience and if there are any traces or hints of foreign elements in it.

Having said that, the author acknowledges Tomlinson's (1991: 34-35)[5] opinion that the analysis of [television] text is not sufficient to address the issue of media imperialism. However, I see it as the first step to understand the extent to which local audiences are exposed to foreign cultures or elements of Westernization, especially through locally produced text and if the local texts are actually a form of imperialism. Simply said, I will look at locally produced texts and investigate if it showcases elements of westernization.

1. Methodology

The first phase of my research consists of an analysis of Malaysian free-to-air television program contents. I did a one week analysis of the Malaysian television guide in order to determine the number of hours allocated for local and imported programs.

Then, I proceeded with a detailed content analysis, which I would define as being qualitative in nature. It is to my believe that a qualitative content analysis is a good method to describe the content of television programs as opposed to merely counting frequencies of specific occurrences, as it will enable me to find

---

5   Tomlinson, John *Cultural Imperialism: A Critical Introduction* (London: Continuum International Publishing Group, 1991), 34-35

out and understand the televised contents that Malaysian are exposed to. As noted by Struppert (2006: 11)[6], a qualitative content analysis is advantageous because it is more in-depth and less standardized.

The content analysis will be looking at occurrences of representation of local and foreign culture in selected television programs. Among others, it addresses elements which are considered as Malaysian local culture and culture – practiced by the actor- which is considered foreign or Western. Although the content analysis I planned is qualitative in nature, I followed Berelson's (1952: 133)[7] suggestion to: "state as precisely as possible just what indicators are relevant in the particular categories [...]". Through this content analysis, I hope to find out the pattern of local Malaysian culture featured in a chosen television program as opposed to foreign cultures. Local Malaysian culture, in this case, refers to the culture practiced by the three main races in Malaysia which comprises of Malays, Chinese and Indians. In light of this matter, I prepared a coding sheet which will serve as a guide for the coders in order for them to be aware of elements to look out for while doing the detailed analysis and to ensure that the method of analysation is uniformed in order to avoid discrepancies.

The program which I plan to analyze is currently rated as number two among Malay viewers on Malaysian free to air television. It is a 60 minutes horror drama aired during prime time (between 9.30pm and 10.30pm every Thursday in a slot aptly titled *Seram* (Horror). The slot usually features 13 episode dramas that revolve around black magic, sorcery, ghosts and the supernatural. The title of the drama which I choose to analyze is *Roh Kembali* (Return of the Spirit). Three random episodes were chosen for the purpose of this paper.

2. Malaysian Television Program Contents

The re-branding of local TV stations in Malaysia during the late 90s has seen an increase in the creation of new TV stations with specific target audience. These new stations also offer a lot of programs which cater to specific races like Chinese through 8TV and Malay through RTM1, TV3 and Channel9. However, program in languages other than Bahasa Malaysia are usually supplied with subtitles and consequently gained popularity among the Malay viewers.

---

6 Struppert, Anika. "Images of Turks, Italians and Indians in Germany's Most Famous Ethnic Comedy Show" Paper presented at the annual meeting of the International Communication Association, Dresden International Congress Centre, Dresden, Germany, Jun 16, 2006.

7 Berelson, B, Content Analysis in Communication Research (Illinois: The Free Press, 1956), 133

Those subscribing to Astro (Malaysia's very own satellite television channel) have access to special channels which are broadcast in Chinese, Malay and Indian dialects. Subscribers can also watch the programs broadcast on channels with English medium in local dialects (especially in the cartoon channels) by merely pressing the remote control as Astro also provides a dubbed version of English language programs to local Chinese, Malay and Indian dialects.

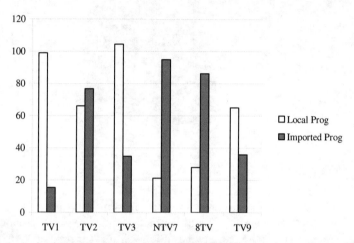

Figure 1: A six day analysis of local vs. imported program (according to hours) on free-to-air television

In a six day analysis of contents of free-to-air television (according to hours), it could be seen that TV2, NTV7 and 8TV allocated more time to broadcast imported program than local programs while TV1, TV3 and TV9 allocated more hours to broadcast local programs. TV3 broadcasted the most hours for local programs while NTV7 broadcasted the least hours for local programs. As for imported programs, NTV7 topped the list while TV1 broadcasted the least hours for imported programs.

Sabariah Mohamed Salleh

Percentage of Local versus Imported Program

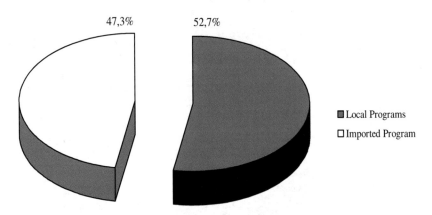

Figure 2: Local vs Imported program

Overall, based on the analysis, it can be concluded that the percentage of hours allocated for local programs is not that much different than that for imported programs. Local programs still topped the broadcasting hours but only by a mere 5.4 per cent lead. This may be due to the fact that the broadcasting industry in Malaysia has trouble finding program to fill the airtime (Shanti 2000: 162)[8]. The trend of importing foreign program started since television was first introduced in Malaysia. According to Tai Suet Yee (1997) there was initially an equal time ratio of local and foreign program. However, foreign program soon make up the majority of program content. This became especially obvious when the broadcasting industry opened its doors to private television stations. Tai Suet Yee (1997: 479)[9] noted that "when TV3 was first established, it was permitted to broadcast 30 per cent local and 70 per cent imported program on the basis of its position as a private television station and its dependence on advertising revenue."

Currently, there are no laws or legislation which control the ratio of foreign content to local content. The government hopes for a 60 per cent local content

---

8   Shanti Balraj – Ambigapathy "An Assesment of Children's Television Programs in Malaysia" in Hogan, G. (ed.) Growing up with Television: Asian Children's Experience (Singapore: AMIC, 2000), 162

9   Tai Suet Yee "Protecting our culture: a comparative study of broadcasting content regulation in Malaysia and Canada," Singapore Journal of International and Comparative Law (1997): 479

and 40 per cent foreign content ratio, but this desire, as could be seen from the pie chart above, has yet to be unattainable as the numbers of production houses in Malaysia that are able to produce local programs are still inadequate. Moreover, importing foreign programs are less costly than producing a local program. According to Awang Rosli (in Shanti, 2000) the cost of producing a local drama ranges between RM200,000 and RM350,000 as compared to the cost of a syndicated movie of about RM100,000.

However, the effort to increase local content intensified because foreign program are said to "threaten the traditions and cultures of Asian society" (Yao in Tai Suet Yee, 1997: 487)[10]. Not only that, the influx of foreign television program is said to be able to introduce and innovate culture. As noted by Silverstone (1999: 59)[11], media globalization has form and reformed culture and he argued that the topics discussed in the media may be global, but it remains as the resource for culture and establishment of one's identity. Karthigesu (1998) argued that foreign programs broadcasted in Malaysia did not enrich the local culture. These programs, which are mostly imported for the United States and Britain, are deemed as Western and are believed to be 'immoral' (Yao in Tai Suet Yee, 1997: 487)[12].

What intrigued me was that, according to a report by TV3, the top television series on Malaysia's free-to-air television remains to be a locally produced drama. Granted, that this could be due to the fact that Malays make up the majority of population in Malaysia's society but all the talk about the influence of Western culture seems to indirectly indicate that there may be hints of western or foreign influence in locally produced programs as well.

Hence, the content analysis on *Seram* which follows will be analysing the program to determine if there is indeed foreign influence and if there is any cause for the Malaysian government to worry about the notion of 'westernization' and 'cultural imperialism'.

3. Findings from Content Analysis

As mentioned in the methodology section, the title of the drama from the *Seram* slot which I choose to analyze is *Roh Kembali*. It tells a story of Zaidi, who is involved in a successful business and lives luxuriously. His wife, Zahirah is a homemaker and together, they have a son named Ehsan, who is very clever.

---

10   Tai Suet Yee "Protecting our culture: a comparative study of broadcasting content regulation in Malaysia and Canada", 487
11   Silverstone, R. Why Study the Media? (London: Sage, 1999), 59
12   Tai Suet Yee "Protecting our culture: a comparative study of broadcasting content regulation in Malaysia and Canada", 487

They are the model family; happy, kind and well-liked by friends and neighbours. However, secretly, Zaidi's life is not peaceful. Unknown to others, Zaidi's success is partly due to his involvement in an organised crime with Taukeh Boon. Under Taukeh Boon's order, Zaidi killed an innocent woman, Lillian Chan. Now, Lillian's spirit is haunting Zaidi but Zaidi kept mum about it, too afraid that his secret involvement with the organised crime would be exposed.

The main character in this drama is Zaidi, a thriving Malay businessman who is often depicted in formal suits, shirts, ties and slacks. At home, he is often dressed in *kain pelikat* -- a piece of chequered cloth worn wrapped around the waist, very much like a pareo, usually worn by Malay men at home – and t-shirt. His character is very caring and is shown through scenes in which he could be seen joking around with his family, bringing his wife medication when she was sick and comforting his child when he had a nightmare in the middle of the night. Overall, he is pictured as someone very humble, nice and kind and one would never be able to associate him with an organised crime from how he has been portrayed. Is it possible that he be considered as someone deceitful and conniving since he seem to portray himself as someone kind and nice but in actual fact is quite ruthless and would do anything to get what he aimed for?

Another obvious aspect in the drama is that men are always the leaders. This not only applies to Zaidi but also to other characters. For instance, there are scenes in which man were seen giving orders or asking their wives to do a chore and their wife always instantly obeys. Whatever men say are not to be questioned and are to be followed. Men are also the breadwinner and support the wife financially as there are scenes in which men gave women pocket money and pay her meals. What does this say about Malay men? Does it in any way reflect those living in the West?

If we look at it through Hofstede's dimension of culture (1980: 176)[13], the examples above clearly point out that Malays are more masculine than feminine. This is parallel with Hofstede's findings in which Malaysia had a score of 50. It is said that members of cultures which are high in masculinity, value performance, ambition, things, power and assertiveness (Hofstede, 1980: 176pp)[14]. That means, the society places importance on material things and strives for power. This can be seen from the drama in which Zaidi obviously finds material wealth and power important to the extent that he got himself involved with organised crime and murder in order to achieve it.

---

13 Hofstede, G. Culture's Consequences: International Differences in Work-Related Values, (Beverly Hills CA: Sage, 1980), 176
14 Hofstede, Culture's Consequences: International Differences in Work-Related Values,176pp

However, on the other hand, the drama shows that family plays an important role in their lives. This could be seen from the way Zaidi treats his son and wife and how the relationship is portrayed. Zaidi is seen as caring and loving. Thus, it could be derived that the community is very collectivistic in nature. This is because the drama seems to show a lot of scenes featuring families for instance family having meals and conversations together and also joking among themselves. Not only that, the characters were shown to be friendly towards their neighbours and people around them to the extent that they often go out of their way to help these people out. This co-relates to the score which Malaysia obtained in Hofstede's dimension of culture (2001: 70)[15], a low score of 26. A relatively low score in individualism – collectivism means Malaysia practices a collectivistic culture. As opposed to and individualistic culture in which one places priorities on themselves and immediate family only, a collectivistic culture see its people look after each other within a bigger group.

What intrigued me about the drama is how they equate being successful with one who is able to obtain material wealth especially by being involved in business ventures. All male characters are involved in business and the drama is constantly peppered with still shots of big houses and expensive cars. Is this to show that being involved in business is a sure way for one to be rich? Also, the relationship between Zaidi and Taukeh Boon somehow portrays that Chinese are still the ones who dominates and are in control of businesses.

These racially stereotypical roles date back from the colonial times when the British ruled Malaya and employed the divide and conquer tactic (Mahathir Mohamad, 2010: 15-16)[16]. They had indeed, in the olden times, segregated jobs, in which Malays were peasants and merely followers which were deemed as lazy folks by the British, Chinese encouraged to be involved in business and the Indians worked in the estate or do hard labour. These portrayals seem to still be dominating in the televised shows, as interpreted through the content analysis. However, what I find a bit different is the fact that Malays are also shown to be involved in business in the drama. Could this be an indirect way in encouraging Malays to be involved in business in order to be as successful as the Chinese? Interestingly, in the drama, Chinese is shown to be more successful than Malays and ordering Malays around as in the situation in which Taukeh Boon ordered Zaidi to kill Lillian.

---

15 Hofstede, Geert Culture's Consequences, Comparing Values, Behaviors, Institutions, and Organizations Across Nations (Thousand Oaks CA: Sage Publications, 2001), 70.
16 Mahathir Mohamad The Malay Dilemma (with a new preface) (Singapore: Marshall Cavendish, 2010), 15-16

As for religion, the only religion showcased was Islam and this was proven with montage of Verses from the Al-Quran, Muslim's Holy Book, in the beginning and ending of the drama, shots of Zaidi and his wife praying, scenes at Muslim burial grounds, characters reading the Quran and several still shots of mosques. Indirectly, it depicts that Malays in Malaysia are Muslims and does not practice other religion. Interestingly, even Article 160 of the Malaysian Constitution states that a Malay is defined as someone who is born to a Malaysian citizen, professes to be a Muslim, habitually speaks the Malay language and adheres to Malay customs.

Can how the Malays are portrayed in the drama be considered as part of their cultural identity? If we look at the drama, the characters would be considered typical Malay because they profess to be a Muslim, speaks the Malay language and adheres to Malay customs. Would it be essentialist for one to attempt to specifically define or categorize a specific race or ethnicity? Scholars argue that an attempt to specifically describe or categorize a race or ethnicity - which I consider as part of one's cultural identity - according to their way of life, values and beliefs may be seen as quite essentialist and be misconstrued as homogenizing a group of people without considering their differences and uniqueness. Kahn (1998: 20-21)[17] opined that establishing a set of signifiers for a specific racial category can be seen as a simulacrum as it romanticises the idea of race being referred to a limited set of signifiers such as cuisine and dresses. Furthermore, Hall (1996: 51)[18] argues that identities are dynamic and are constantly undergoing transformation so it may be quite nonsensical to specifically describe an ethnicity or race according to categories.

However, according to Shamsul A. B (1996: 480)[19], in Malaysia's case, the definitions of ethnicities and race actually accommodate changes brought with time and are not limited to a set of signifiers. "What seemed to be an analytical convenience, in fact "orientalist" in spirit, has developed into a scientific approach thus 'Malay' or 'Malayness' as a social category has been problematised or perceived as something constructed, invented, artificial despite the fact that "what it means" and "what it is" have always been altered, redefined, reconstituted and the boundaries expended according to social-historical circumstances, especially after the introduction of colonial racism and racial category into the

---

17 Kahn, J. Southeast Asian Identities: Culture and Politics of Representation in Indonesia, Malaysia, Singapore and Thailand London: I.B Tauris & Co, 1998), 20-21

18 Hall, Stuart "Introduction: Who needs Identity" in Hall, S. And du Gay, P. (eds.) Questions of Cultural Identity (London: Sage, 1996), 51

19 Shamsul A. B. "Debating about identity in Malaysia: A Discourse Analysis" in Southeast Asian Studies (1996): 480

realm of authority defined and everyday defined social reality in British Malaya." (Shamsul A. B, 1996: 480)[20] Hence, the term Malays, Chinese and Indian is not static and make room for changes but it still maintains its fundamental roots in values and beliefs (Mee, 1998: 229)[21].

Other ways in which Malays have been categorized or to some extent stereotyped are as speaking and only fluent in the Malay language, ladies wear the *hijab* and *baju kurung* – a traditional Malay dress-- while male wear the *songkok* – a traditional headgear worn by Malay men-- and all this was depicted in the drama I analyzed.

4. Americanization, Cultural Imperialism or simply nonsensical concern?

According to Jeremy Turnstall (1979) globalisation is not an equal process as it champions the United States, especially in spreading their ideologies and beliefs. In the 1970s, the media landscape was indeed dominated by the United States because it was here that media forms were first industrialised. With the United States' domination in the media industry, people became more agitated and concern about the cultural impact of the so-called one way flow of cultural product (from United States to other countries) and how this would spread their ideologies and create hegemony. Malaysia is not spared from this fear but with recent development, the fear may be unfounded.

Looking at the one week analysis of television programs, it was identified that local programs still topped the broadcasting hours, but, with merely a 5.4 per cent lead. However, it should be noted that not all imported programs are from the United States but are mostly Indonesian and Chinese serials imported from Indonesia, Taiwan, Hong Kong and China. This is in line with what Hesmondhalgh (2007: 220pp)[22] termed the geo-cultural markets in which programs from other countries (aside from United States) are well received because people share the same cultural affiliations. In this case, Indonesian and Chinese serials are imported, not only because of the similar language[23], but also due to the similar cultural beliefs and values.

---

20   Shamsul A. B., Debating about identity in Malaysia: A Discourse Analysis, 480

21   Mee, Wendy "National Difference and Global Citizenship" in Joel Kahn (ed.) Southeast Asian Identities: Culture and Politics of Representation in Indonesia, Malaysia, Singapore and Thailand London: I.B Tauris& Co, 1998), 229

22   Hesmondhalgh, David The Cultural Industries (London: SAGE Publications, 2007), 220pp

23   Indonesian language is very similar to the Malay language. Chinese in Malaysia also speak Mandarin and Hokkien, language used in Chinese serials.

Furthermore, Hafez (2007) said that satellite television may be able to offer
a lot of foreign or specifically American programs but the number of people
who actually watch it is still uncertain. As aptly said by Hafez (2007: 62)[24]:
"The world market for satellite television has been growing, since the 1990s and
has often been interpreted as a sign of globalization of the media. In many countries in Asia, Africa and Latin America, however, people tend to want satellite
dishes not in order to receive Western programs but to watch new satellite channels based in their own country or the extended language area. Regular consumption of European and US programs remains limited to small elites in most
countries." Hence, the concern that satellite television in Malaysia would bring
in more 'Western' programs with beliefs and values which are detached from
local values can be put to rest because it is quite impossible to determine who
watches what on television. Also, it should be noted that if audiences do indeed
watch the 'Western' programs, they may not be that easily influenced as messages are polysemic and can be read in multiple ways.(Hall, 1980: 169)[25]

Aside from that, most prime time program on Malaysian television is still
dominated by local programs and the most popular program still remains a Malaysian produced program. As argued by Uwe Hasebrink and Anja Herzog (in
Hafez, 2007: 59)[26], satellite television is still not met with much response which
means that people still prefer to watch local programs on local television channels. Hence, when looking at program imports per se, it is nonsensical to say
that Malaysians are subject to Americanization or Westernization and victims of
cultural imperialism because the most watched programs are produced by Malaysians and programs are not only imported from America but from other
neighbouring countries like Indonesia, China, Phillipines and Thailand as well.

What about the content of the programs itself? The content analysis which I
conducted on *Seram* shows no signs of an attempt to emulate Western or American values and in fact seem to reiterate Hofstede's scores in his research on Malaysia's culture dimension and also stereotypes on local cultural identities. The
only thing that is a little 'Western' is the usage of corporate suits and ties. But,
logically this cannot be pinpointed as an effect of cultural or media imperialism
because the characters in the drama still wear traditional suits like *baju kurung*
and *baju melayu* and they still speak in Malay language. No presence of what
would be considered as foreign culture or anything which might be considered

---

24 Hafez, Kai The Myth of Media Globalization (Polity: Cambridge, 2007), 62
25 Hall, Stuart 'Encoding/decoding'. In Centre for Contemporary Cultural Studies
    (Ed.): Culture, Media, Language: Working Papers in Cultural Studies, 1972-79 (London:
    Hutchinson, 1980), 169
26 Hafez, The Myth of Media Globalization, 59

as Western or American could be detected in the drama. In fact, it can be said that the drama is very Malay in nature because of the presence of black magic and *bomoh* (witch doctors) which is very synonym with Malay culture.

Thus, it could be said that the drama was not at all affected by the influx of foreign programs in the Malaysian broadcasting scene. It did not try to emulate or mimic foreign drama but instead showcased a typical Malay story. As said by Hafez (2007: 84)[27] the influx of cultural products from United States or the West does not necessarily mean that it automatically suppresses indigenous cultures and that people are easily influenced and readily accept what they watch without questioning it. In this case, a reinforcement of own cultural values, instead of following foreign cultures, could be detected. For instance, the drama showcases a lot of Islamic values which are synonym to Malays.

5. Conclusion

Cultural imperialism is a cause of concern for third world countries like Malaysia as the government not only has to work on creating unity within the people of different races and ethnicities but also try to preserve local traditions which are viewed as being threatened by the influx of American and Western elements through the media. But is the fear reasonable? Fred Fejes (in Tomlinson, 1991: 35-36)[28] aptly said: "While a great deal of the concern over media imperialism is motivated by the fear of the cultural consequences of the transnational media – of the threat that such media poses to the integrity and the development of viable national cultures in Third World societies – it is the one area where, [...], little progress has been achieved in understanding specifically the cultural impact of transnational media on Third World societies." The apprehension on effects of media globalisation and the need to understand cultural impact of transnational media on Third World societies has prompted me to conduct a small study on program contents on Malaysian free-to-air television.

It was found that the difference of hours allocated between local and imported programs was only 5.4 per cent. The difference may look alarming and be a cause of concern especially on the effect of cultural imperialism through globalisation of the media but rest assured, that the bulk of imported programs are from other Asian countries which have similar language, culture and beliefs.

As for the content analysis which was conducted on a local drama, no evidence of Western culture could be traced. Instead, the drama portrays a typical Malay life and seems to reiterate Hofstede's findings in his research on Malay-

---

27   Hafez, The Myth of Media Globalization, 84
28   Tomlinson, Cultural imperialism: a critical introduction, 35-36

sia's cultural dimension. Hence, the concern on the society emulating 'Western' culture which is considered as threatening the local traditions may be unfounded because the content of one of the most watched drama does not contain Western or American elements. Not only that, even the imported programs are brought in from Asian countries with similar culture and beliefs.

Cultural imperialism is probably best thought as a much broader process of cultural change which involves a lot of other contributing factors, aside from the media. One must remember that being exposed to the media text does not mean that the audience read the text as it is meant to be read. Messages are after all polysemic and could be decoded in numerous different ways (Hall, 1980: 169)[29]. Hence, I would suggest a future research on audience reception of the media messages showcased on Malaysian television to further understand and make sense of the effect of media globalisation on Malaysian society.

---

29   Hall, 'Encoding/decoding',169

Jewish Immigration into the Land of Israel/Palestine during the 19th Century

Shaped by Ideology or by Globalization?

Friederike Ruth Winkler

The way how Jewish immigration into the land of Israel/Palestine (in Hebrew: *Eretz Israel*, referring to the biblical Land of Israel) is described, often is connected to ideological or political approaches of the authors, and two threads can be distinguished: The Jewish-religious approach, especially among the Religious-Zionist camp, but also among Israel-friendly Christians, usually stresses that Jewish immigration took place nearly all the time from the middle ages up to modern history. This approach does take into account that there were serious crises, when Jewish life in the land was severely restricted or even nearly destroyed (like the destruction of the ancient Jewish communities by the Crusaders). However, whenever the economic and political circumstances permitted, such loss of Jewish presence in the land was compensated by a new wave of immigration. Arie Morgenstern has pointed out that a certain level of organized immigration typically appeared before the turn of centuries (according to the Jewish calendar), when messianic expectations would increase.[1]

The second thread, which I would call the secular (often socialist) approach, defines the beginning of Political Zionism with Theodor Herzl and his act of founding the Zionist Congress. This approach tends to exclude from the picture all or most of the waves of Jewish immigration which took place before Herzl's activities. This may be historically less correct, but can be defended on the ground that the immigration-movements before the Zionist Congress were much smaller.

In both cases the high impact new technology (railways, steamships, international post offices...) had on Jewish immigration into the Land of Israel/Palestine is rarely considered. This paper aims to discuss two examples, showing how external conditions shaped the results of a movement beyond its ideology. Our first example will be the movement of the "Disciples of the Vilna Gaon" during the early decades of the 19th century. The second example will be the Bukharian Immigration to Jerusalem around the 1880s. Whereas the immigration of the "Disciples of the Vilna Gaon" was shaped by an ambitious hope

---

1 Arie Morgenstern, "Dispersion and the Longing for Zion, 1240-1840." In New Essays on Zionism, ed. David Hazony et al. (Jerusalem: Shalem Press, 2006), 304-356.

for a large-scale revival of Jewish life in the Land of Israel and by messianic expectation, the Bucharian immigration was motivated by a simple traditional
longing for living in the "Holy City" of Jerusalem. One might expect that the
more ambitious movement would also leave the greater impact on the ground.
But we will see that this was not the case.

1. Messianic hopes connected to the year 5600 of the Jewish Calendar

Two sources, one from the Babylonian Talmud and the other one from the Zo-
har, the main-work of Jewish *Kabbalah*, attribute a special role of the year 5600
according to the Jewish calendar (corresponding to 1839/40 in the Gregorian
calendar):

> - The Babylonian Talmud brings in tractate *Sanhedrin* (99a) an opinion,
> that "the days of the Messiah" will be 400 years. In the same tractate (97a)
> it is said, that the world will last for six-thousand years. From the combi-
> nation of both it follows, that the 400 "years of the Messiah" will start in
> the year 5600.

> - In the *Zohar* (*Wayera* 117a) it is said, that after 600 years of the sixth
> millennium the gates of "the upper wisdom" and the springs of the "lower
> wisdom" [= the earthly wisdom] will open, and the Lord will remember
> the community of Israel.

This raised a multitude of messianic expectations in the decades before 5600
(1839/40). Sources mention not only European Jewry, but also the Persian-
Kurdish region and Morocco.[2] Connected to the messianic hopes around 1830 a
stronger wave of immigration into the Land of Israel can be identified.[3]

A *post facto* rather amusing source, confirming an increase of migration
from Bohemia and Galicia towards the Holy Land from approximately 1811 on,
are documents from the Austrian imperial intelligence service: Austrian offices
took note of the emigration of Jewish families, and were concerned that those
people took money with them. The concern of the Austrian authorities was not
the emigration of Jewish subjects, but the transfer of property towards a foreign
country: In 1826 a decree made clear that not the emigration itself was to be limited, but the unauthorized transfer of money.[4] Also from Russia and Poland Jew-

---

2   Arie Morgenstern, Hastening Redemption: Messianism and the resettlement of the land
     of Israel (Oxford: Oxford University Press, 2006), 25-36.
3   Morgenstern, Hastening Redemption, 52.
4   N. M. Gelber, „Aliyat Yehudim miBohemia we-Galitzia le-Eretz Yisrael 1811-1869", in
     Yerushalayim ed. M[ichael] Ish-Shalom et al. (Jerusalem: Mosad ha-Rav Kook, 1953)
     243-249.

ish migration towards *Eretz Yisrael* is testified from inner-Jewish tradition as well as from external sources during the years from 1811 up to the 1820s. And even Christian missionaries noticed the Jewish expectations and concluded that now time has come to establish Christian missionary activities in the Holy Land. An interruption was caused through the Greek war of independence – which blocked the travel routes from Europe to the Ottoman Empire.[5]

2. The movement of the Disciples of the Vilna Gaon (Talmidei haGra)

Among the general messianic movement towards 5600, there was one group with a more elaborated program and a higher degree of organization: The "Disciples of the Vilna Gaon", known under the Hebrew term *"Talmidei haGra"*.

The "Gaon" ("genius") Rabbi Eliyahu from Vilna (1720-1797) – also known under the acronym of his name as the *GRA* – is counted among the greatest rabbis of Jewish history. It is known, that the Gaon himself intended to immigrate to the Land of Israel. Letters, which he wrote to his family on the way, testify that he actually had started the trip. But for unknown reasons he was hindered on the way to continue.[6] A tradition among his students tells that, after several attempts, he had concluded that he had not received permission from Heaven to go. His students saw this as a sign that his soul was related to the soul of Moses, who also had not received permission to enter the land.[7] From such an interpretation it follows that the students themselves were not hindered to go, on the contrary: Like Moses hat prepared the people of Israel in biblical times to enter the land, maybe the role of the Gaon had also been to prepare his followers to enter the land.

Soon after the Gaon's death attempts for immigration took shape. One of the leading families involved was the Rivlin family, who could trace their family tree back to a number of Jewish scholars and were related to the Gaon. According to their own family tradition, the plans had developed already during the Gaon's live-time. The implementation started in 1805 with the founding of the society *„Hazon Tzion"* („Seers of Zion") in Shklov (Belarus). A leading figure of the movement, Rabbi Hillel Rivlin, arrived with a group of 70 *"Talmidei ha-Gra"* in Safed in 1809.[8]

---

5   Morgenstern, Hastening Redemption, 58-60.
6   Morgenstern, Hastening Redemption, 80.
7   Re'uven Rivlin, Yosef Rivlin, and Goni Rivlin-Tzur, U-va'u Tzion be-Rinah (Jerusalem: Rivlin, 5769/ 2009), 8; Haim H. Rivlin, and Yosef Rivlin, Hazon Tzion: Shklov wi-Yrushalayim (Jerusalem: 5762) 31.
8   Rivlin, Rivlin, and Rivlin-Tzur: U-va'u Tzion be-Rinah, 8.

There is also evidence of immigrants who came to Tiberias already in 1808, and another source claims that the whole initiative had been started already in 1800 by Rabbi Haim of Volozhin, who is known in Jewish history as the founder of the famous *Yeshivah* of Volozhin. Whereas he himself stayed in Volozhin as the head of his *Yeshivah*, he also eagerly supported migration to the land of Israel.[9] The question why he did not attempt to go has been discussed by Raphael Shuchat in his work on the Gaon's theory of redemption: First, after the Gaon's passing Rabbi Haim was seen as the leading figure of Lithuanian and Belarus' Jewry, which was a reason to stay there. Second he saw his *Yeshiva*, propagating new methods of studying, as an utmost important project. Third, the ideology of the *Talmidei haGra* was two-fold: Aside the worldly task of immigrating and building the land, there was also the spiritual task of improving religious observance and the spiritual level of the Jewish people. It may well be that Rabbi Haim saw his place in the spiritual part of the project, while at the same time supporting the worldly activities to the best of his means.[10]

The groups of immigrants would start their way in spring and arrive in the late summer. Every group was lead by a personality of some importance – a Rabbi or one of the more prominent members of the community. The outbreak of an epidemic in the Galilee in 1813 caused a severe backlash, but the stream continued: A bigger group is known to have immigrated in 1826, lead by a prominent Rabbi from Pinsk, Haim ben Peretz. Distinguished donors from Vilna supported the project, but as far as possible the *Talmidei haGra* hoped to be able to support themselves in their new settlements. So we find that a certain Gershon Harkavy, a very rich member of the group, bought vineyards after his arrival in Safed. The income from the vineyards was to support the *Yeshivah*.[11]

The *Talmidei haGra* were not only part of the messianic expectation anticipating the year 5600, but they based their activities on a more developed set of ideas:

They were sure that the Jewish people had to do something for the redemption not only by religious piety and observance of the commandments, but also in the worldly realm. This is based on a verse in the book of the Prophet Malachi (3.7): „Return to me, and I will return to you". The verse was understood as a call to "return" not only spiritually but also literally in preparation for the re-

---

9   Morgenstern, Hastening Redemption, 81f.

10 Raphael B. Shuchat, A World Hidden in the Dimensions of Time: The Theory of Redemption in the Writings of the Vilna Gaon, Its Sources and Influences on Later Generations (Ramat Gan: Bar-Ilan University Press, 2008), 90ff.

11 Morgenstern, Hastening Redemption, 53ff.

demption, by "returning" to the Land of Israel. With the year 5600 approaching in a near future the *Talmidei haGra* concluded that now it was time to start. Specific goals of the movement were:

- To increase the number of Jewish population in the land. This is based on a passage from the Babylonian Talmud (Brachot 58a), claiming that only a number of at least 600,000 people can be called a mass of people. Therefore at least 600,000 Jewish people have to live in the land to ensure that the presence of God can „rest" upon them.

- To erect a center of Jewish scholarship in Jerusalem
(It shall be noted that in course of time two branches within the group reached different conclusions, whether first Jerusalem or first Safed should be „built". There was a theological reason not to start with Jerusalem, since in the daily prayer, among the requests for redemption, the building of Jerusalem comes after the general return of the Jewish people.)

- To establish a leadership, consisting of upright „men of faith", who would be able to lead the process.

- To build academies for studying and houses for living in those places of Israel where once they had been destroyed.[12]

In spite of the continuing immigration the number of the Jewish population did NOT increase in a lasting way until the 1840s. Among the reasons were epidemics, like cholera, which spread in Syria and the Galilee, and also the earthquake which shattered the Galilee in 1837.[13] The Egyptian conquest from 1831 to 1840 brought a regional war. And we may not forget that the groups of immigrants were small to begin with. Around the 1810s or 1820s travel from Europe was still a costly and long enterprise. We have mentioned that the travels lasted from spring to the late summer! Obviously not everyone who might have been interested could afford this.

3. The Bukharian immigration to Jerusalem

A very different example is the Bukharian immigration to Jerusalem. Before we speak about the immigration itself, we want to take a short look on the Bukharian Judaism of earlier times.

The term Bukharian Jewry describes the Jewish communities (and later their descendants), which were to be found until the 20th century in the Central Asian region north of Afghanistan – in modern terms Uzbekistan, Kyrgizstan and Tadjikistan. Aside the city of Bukhara herself especially Samarkand and Tashkent

---

12   Rivlin and Rivlin, Hazon Tzion. 37ff.
13   Morgenstern, Hastening Redemption, 66.

have to be counted to the realm of "Bukharian" Judaism. Until the 16th century they were culturally connected to Persian Judaism. Then the border between Shiite Persia and Sunni led dominions in Central Asia and Afghanistan cut Bukharian Jewry off from other parts of the Jewish world. The isolation caused a decline in Jewish scholarship and observance.[14] For the 18th century it is documented that Bukharian Judaism was even on the verge of disappearing. Ongoing regional wars of local Emirs against each other often led in the name of a fanatic Islamization brought with them suppression of the Jewish communities.[15] The rediscovery of Bukharian Judaism towards the end of the 18th century is attributed to Rabbi Maman, a scholar originally from Morocco, who had settled in Safed. He had learned about the existence of Jewish communities in Central Asia during a fund raising trip through Persia. Seeing the need, he decided in 1793 to stay in Bukhara as a teacher and Rabbi. From now on Bukharian communities would donate money to the congregations in *Eretz Israel*, and Rabbis from *Eretz Israel* would go to Bukhara to take care of the spiritual needs of Bukharian Jewry.[16] But in spite of the new contacts, migration from Bukhara to the Land of Israel remained rare up to the 1860s, due to the extreme difficulties of the long, expensive and dangerous journey.

The conditions for Bukharian Jewry changed radically after the 1860s brought the Russian conquest of a large part of the region. (In the south a formally autonomous Emirate of Bukhara, *de facto* dependent from Russia, remained, whereas the northern parts of the region became "Russian-Turkestan".) Although Russian politics in the European parts of the empire was seriously anti-Jewish, the Russian government granted relatively better civil rights to the Jewish population of the newly conquered Central Asian province – the only group of non-Muslims was considered as a factor of stability for the new rulers. In connection with the improved security after the Russian conquest, Bukharian Jewry was now able to reach an economic growth. In the late 1880s the railway connection from the Central Asian Russian territories to Orenburg (then the Russian Gate from the southern Ural to Central Asia) was erected, and now it was possible to travel from the Turkestan region via Russian railways on a rather safe and relatively fast connection to Odessa – and from there via Istanbul

---

14 Dror Warman, Ha-Bucharim u-Shchunatam bi-Yrushalayim (Jerusalem: Yad Yitzchak ben Zwi, 5772/ 1991), 10.

15 Giora Pozailov, From Bukhara to Jerusalem: The Immigration and Settlement of Bukharan Jews in Eretz Israel (1868-1948) (Jerusalem: Misgav Yerushalayim, 5755/ 1995), 31f.

16 Pozailov, From Bukhara to Jerusalem, 31f; Warman, Ha-Bucharim, 10.

to the Holy Land. The trip to Israel now took two up to three weeks.[17] The ancient travel routes from Bukhara to *Eretz Israel* by camel or donkey had taken months and had sometimes led through dangerous areas. Some versions of ancient routes are known: The land way via Persia and Baghdad, or via what is today Pakistan and by sea from the Arabian sea to the Persian Golf, then continuing via Baghdad. A route known from the early 19th century led via Central Russia to Vienna and from there via Italy. An inner-Russian route before the building of the railways was to cross the Caspean Sea and the Black Sea towards Istanbul.[18] In comparison, the option of reaching Jerusalem within two to three weeks by train and steamship was a huge revolution regarding safety, speed and costs!

The new possibilities were not only used by actual immigrants but also by pilgrims. Often pilgrimages by well-to-do Bukharian merchants, led to the establishment of second homes of Bukharian families in Jerusalem.[19] The fact that also the delegates from Jewish communities in *Eretz Israel* to the Bukharian communities could now travel much faster, further helped to motivate immigration, since information could be gained much easier.[20]

In 1889 a society of „Hovevei Zion of the Bukharian Communities" was founded in Jerusalem. This society arranged for the purchase of land in the (then already developing) suburbs of Jerusalem outside the Old City walls – the Bukharian quarter of Jerusalem was born.[21] The name „Hovevei Zion of the Bukharian communities" obviously refers to the European group of Russian Zionists who named themselves „Hovevei Zion". But in spite of this borrowing of the name, we do not see a political ambition among the Bukharian immigrants.

In the course of time a religious school (*Talmud Torah*) was opened in the new Bukharian quarter. While in those days Jewish children used to study the Biblical books with a translation (Hebrew-Yiddish, Hebrew-Ladino, Hebrew-Arabic,...) and acquire their knowledge of Hebrew by these bilingual readings, the Bukharian *Talmud Torah* would teach „Hebrew in Hebrew" (like it is largely done in Jewish schools of today). But no connection to any political Zionist program can be seen, which could have been the reason for choosing this teaching

---

17 Warman, Ha-Bucharim, 12-13; Giora Pozailov, Ha-Aliyot ha-gedolot me-Artzot ha-Mizrach, Vol. 5, Bukhara (Jerusalem, Machon ben Zwi, 2000), 3.
18 Pozailov, From Bukhara to Jerusalem, map on the inner coverpages; Pozailov: haAliyot hagedolot, S. 6.
19 Pozailov, From Bukhara to Jerusalem, 105.
20 Pozailov, Ha-Aliyot ha-gedolot me-Artzot ha-Mizrach, 4.
21 Warman, Ha-Bucharim, 19; Pozailov, From Bukhara to Jerusalem, 87ff.

method.[22] If the „Hebrew in Hebrew" curriculum was not part of a political ideology, what was its reason then? I suggest that there was not too much of a choice. In the northern parts of Central Asia, which were under direct Russian rule, Bukharian Jewry started to speak Russian and drop the ancient Bukharian language. But unlike Yiddish, Ladino, or Judeo-Arabic, Russian lacked the image to be a "Jewish language". Furthermore, an availability of any Hebrew textbooks with Russian translations in Jerusalem around 1880 is hard to imagine (probably Jewish textbooks in Russian didn't exist yet at all), so what could the teacher do? The nearest choice was to teach "Hebrew in Hebrew".

In its earlier days the new Bukharian quarter was a wealthy and elegant neighbourhood. It represented Russian-European architecture of the late 19th century. But already before WW I, new immigration by poorer community members caused a decline of prosperity. The conditions in the land of emigration had changed. The Russian government did not see it necessary anymore to grant better rights to the Jewish subjects in Turkestan than in other parts of the Russian empire. Now also the Bukharian Jews started to be recruited to the Russian military service, which was extremely feared among Russian Jewry (the 25 year long service was connected with a severe Russification and in many cases with a more or less forced Christianization). So flight from the Tsarist repressions became a new motive for emigrating to Jerusalem in the early 20th century. In any case, with its various facets, the Bukharian settlement in Jerusalem is counted as part of the "Old Yishuv" (the "old settlement" of Jewish communities) in *Eretz Yisrael*, as opposed to the "New Yishuv" of modern political Zionism.[23]

In spite of its being counted to the "Old Yishuv", we should not underestimate that the Bukharian Quarter changed the structure of Jerusalem in a lasting way and influenced the socio-cultural composition of the town. True, the Bukharian Quarter was not alone, it was part of various neighbourhoods growing around the Old City from the 1880s on.[24] Still this was a big and highly visible step in the development of the town. Actually it is described as the most magnificent of the new city-quarters in its time.[25] Today it may give visitors a feeling of an old traditional neighbourhood, but when it was erected, it represented

---

22 Pozailov, From Bukhara to Jerusalem, 230f.

23 Warman, Ha-Bucharim, 16.

24 For a detailed description of the rapid building of new quarters in Jerusalem outside the Old City during the late 19th century see: Yehosua Ben-Arieh, A City Reflected in its Times: New Jerusalem – The Beginnings (Jerusalem: Yad Izhak Ben-Zvi, 1979), 209ff and 371ff.

25 Ben Arieh, A City Reflected in its Times, 248.

European zeitgeist of the 19th century and the wealth of merchants from Russia – an empire which more often than not had been a serious enemy to the Ottoman Empire. The style of the Bukharian Quarter does not differ so much from the architecture of the Christian settlements which were erected on the hills around Jerusalem's Old City in the same decades. In this way it may also have contributed to irritate the conservative Muslim elite in the Old City, no less than the many Christian-European enterprises which changed Jerusalem radically during the late 19th century, and no less than actual Political-Zionist activities which were about to appear soon.

4. Conclusion

When we ask what the Bukharian immigrants made better than the *Talmidei haGra*, we have to answer that it was not a theory or ideology or a better management which made the difference. The Bukharian Immigration just benefited from better conditions. Some of these conditions were regional, but not all of them.

The most obvious difference is the travel conditions. Actually we see the revolution caused by the travel conditions among the Bukharian activities themselves. The reason why Bukharian Jewry started to settle in Jerusalem just from the 1880s on was not any new idea, theory or book which might have appeared in Bukhara – but railways had been built and steamships had started to cross the seas.

Additionally we can conceive the improvement of security and safety in Jerusalem during the late 19th century as connected to the increasing European presence. The European interest in the "Holy Land" caused the Ottomans to take care of better security conditions in Palestine, hindering the outbreak of inter-religious violence (unlike in Lebanon or Syria).[26]

Russia had sparked the Bukharian immigration without any intentions to do so. The Russian intention was to control Central Asia – without being aware of the side effect of enabling a new Jewish presence in Jerusalem, which was maybe even against the Russian Christian ambitions in the Holy Land.

With these observations we may raise the question whether the impact of new technology may have been underestimated in research on Zionism by now. I do not want to deny the strong contribution of European social and political theories to the Zionist Congress. But it seems that another important factor was provided by the new opportunities of a globalized world. What would Herzls

---

26 Henry Laurens, La question de Palestine, Tome premier: 1799-1922 L'invention de la Terre Sainte (Paris: Librairie Arthème Fayard, 1999.) 69f.

Zionist Congress have achieved without railways, steamships and modern post offices? I would suggest that further research on Zionism should take into account the emergence of technology and the world „becoming smaller" in the late 19th century. Maybe the differences between the various Zionist or pre-Zionist activities should not only be seen in „socialist" or „national" or „religious" models, but also in the availability or lack of modern technology.

List of Authors

Lucía Alicia Aguerre was born in Buenos Aires, Argentina. She got her undergraduate degree in Philosophy from the Buenos Aires University, with a specialization in Practical Philosophy and a thesis about migration, globalization and citizenship changes. At the present she is a doctoral researcher at the University of Buenos Aires and fellow of the Argentinean National Council of Scientific and Technical Research (CONICET) and the German Academic Exchange Service (DAAD). Her doctoral research focuses on the ethical and political implications of the relation between power, culture and racism in the frame of (post)coloniality and globalization from a Latin-American perspective.

Kristina Anđelić has graduated from University of Niš, Faculty of Law in Niš in Serbia, and is currently working at University of Niš. She is a student at doctoral studies at University of Niš, Faculty of Law in Niš, and studies International Trade Law, International Economic and Financial Relations, Foreign Trade Investment Law and Transfer of Technology.

Sina Ansari Eshlaghi, born on 07.08.1978 in Tehran, is a PhD candidate at the University of Vienna. As an economic sociologist, his major field is welfare planning, consumption and middle class studies.

Jasna Cizler was born in 1984 in Serbia. She received a M.Arch. degree (2008) and a Specialist degree in Urban Regeneration (2011) from the Faculty of Architecture, University of Belgrade, where she is currently a PhD candidate in Urban Studies. She did academic research at School of Geography, University of Leeds (British Scholarship Trust grant, 2010), at Research Centre for Industrial Heritage, Czech Technical University in Prague (International Visegrad Fund grant, 2012) and at Karl-Franzens University in Graz (JoinEU-SEE grant, 2012/2013).

Andreas Exenberger is assistant professor of economic and social history at the school of economics and statistics of the University of Innsbruck, Austria. He earned his PhD in economics in Innsbruck in 2003. His major fields of interest are globalization history and hunger research.

Markus Gruber is doing his Doctoral Thesis at the University of Vienna. He was studying at the University of Antwerp and Vienna from where he holds an MPhil in Political Sciences and a Master in International Economics from the University Tor Vergata in Rome. His current work focuses on Organizational

Learning and Transformation in the context of Globalization and European Integration.

Manfred Kohler holds a PhD from the University of Innsbruck, Austria, in Political Science. His thesis was entitled "European Identity". His dissertation and research focused on European integration and identity, including matters of Economic and Monetary Union. He also holds a Master's degree in Translation Studies, including Spanish, English and German as working languages. He received the Nick Mueller Fellowship for outstanding academic performance from the State of Tyrol and the city of Innsbruck, also enabling him to conduct dissertation research at CenterAustria of the University of New Orleans in the United States.

Dawn Kremslehner-Haas's academic work on African American communities was inspired by the years she spent in Lawndale, a low-income African American neighborhood on Chicago's West Side. She received her PhD at the University of Vienna and currently teaches at the University of Applied Sciences in St.Pölten, Austria.

Christoph Mertl is specialized on global history (1995 master thesis on African development history, then continuously trainings about North-South issues. Since 2009 working on a doctor thesis about global history 1200 to 1350, based on a new scheme of global cultural analysis). Christoph Mertl works in the managing board of an inter-cultural NGO in Vienna.

Sarra Moneir Ahmed is an interdisciplinary academic who specializes in political sociology, studies of mass movements and behavior especially since the outbreak of the Egyptian Revolution of January 25, 2012. In addition to this, Moneir hold further specializations and research interests in areas related to political theory, political anthropology and Arab-Islamic philosophy. She earned her B.Sc. in Political Science from Cairo University in 2006 and her masters degree in Global History from the University of Vienna in 2010 on the topic of "Arab-Islamic Political Philosophy of the 18th and 19th Centuries: The Religious and the Political Problematic in Egypt". She is also currently a PhD candidate at the Institute for International Development Studies at the University of Vienna and is working on her PhD proposal on the topic "Masses and Politics Reborn since the 25 January Revolution in Egypt". In the meantime, Moneir was residing in Cairo- Egypt and works as an Assistant Lecturer of Political Science at the Future University of Egypt. At the moment Moneir is on a Scholarship by

the OeAD at the University of Vienna for the project of "The Democratisation Process in the Arab World with Focus on Egypt and Tunisia".

María G. Navarro holds a PhD in Philosophy and is currently a Juan de la Cierva postdoctoral fellow at the Spanish National Research Council. Prior, she was a postdoctoral fellow at the University of Amsterdam (The Netherlands). She is the author of *Interpretar y argumentar* (2009) and one of the editors of *Claves actuales de pensamiento* (2010). Her research interests include hermeneutics, argumentation theories, and epistemology. One of her latest articles is "On Fuzzines and Ordinary Reasoning" in *On Fuzziness. A Homage to Lotfi A. Zadeh* (2012), published by Springer.

Matthew Okeyim holds a BSC in Political Science, MSC in International Relations (University of Ibadan Nigeria), DEA in Welfare and Inequality (San Vicente Del RASPEIG) and PHD Jointly supervised European Doctorate by the Queen Mary University of London and the University of Alicante Spain in Social Welfare and Inequality. He is a Political Sociologist interested on Global issues, state theories, Human rights and Political theories.

Innocent Okoronye, holds LLM and PHD Degrees from Abia State University Uturu Nigeria and a BL From the Nigerian Law School. He is a Solicitor and Advocate of the supreme Court of Nigeria. He is Presently a Senior Lecturer at the Faculty of Law, Abia State University Uturu, Nigeria.

Makiko Ruike is currently a PhD student at the Institute of Contemporary History, University of Vienna. Her dissertation theme is representation of a city in city museums in the globalizing world. Her academic and professional background also covers education and gender studies.

Sabariah Mohamed Salleh is a PhD student at the Institute of Journalism and Communication Science, University of Vienna. Her area of interest are adolescents, audience reception and cultural identity. She looks forward to resume her work as a lecturer at Universiti Kebangsaan Malaysia in the near future.

Özge Subasi (PhD) is a senior research fellow at the Vienna University of Technology. Having both a design and design anthropology background, she has lead and been involved in various governmental, industrial, and private design projects with an emphasis on everyday design, design anthropology, extreme living situations and assistive environments. She is collaborating with leading universities, NGOs and various technology design companies across Europe.

Since 2011 she has also been the co-founder and co-chair of Institute for Design Anthropology, an independent research organisation in Vienna, Austria.

Philipp Strobl is a lecturer at the University of Economics in Bratislava and author of several books and articles about Economic- and Social History. He is also a PhD candidate at the University of Innsbruck. He holds a Master degree in Social- and Economic History from the University of Innsbruck and a Master degree in Contemporary History from the University of New Orleans.

Ana Tajder: After graduating with an MBA in 1997, Ana worked in diplomacy, international marketing, and one of the world's largest advertising agencies. Since 2008, she has been a freelance journalist and published two books. She is currently working on her third and writing her dissertation: "Singles as a Construct of Postmodern Capitalism – the Role of the Media in the Context of Social Change" at the University of Vienna, Department of Journalism and Communication Studies.

Bianca Winkler, Dr.phil., living and working as an independent scholar in Vienna. Specialized in the fields of history and philosophy of (human) sciences especially history, anthropology and sociology. Currently also working on a project about media, individuality and socialization.

Friederike Ruth Winkler, born in Vienna (Austria), holds a Master in Jewish Studies and is a doctoral candidate in Political Science at the University of Vienna. Among her research interests are Sephardic Jewish History and Jewish Political Thought. She is lecturing in educational institutes in Vienna on Judaism, Jewish History and Hebrew Language.

Christian Wlaschütz holds a MA in Political Science of the University of Vienna and a MA in International Relations of Syracuse University. He has worked for four years in peace programs in Colombia and is currently writing his PhD-thesis on the relation between peace building and transitional justice. He lives in Bogotá.